Published by
Ashgate Publishing Limited
Wey Court East
Union Road
Farnham
Surrey, GU9 7PT
England

Ashgate Publishing Company
Suite 420
101 Cherry Street
Burlington
VT 05401-4405
USA

www.ashgate.com

British Library Cataloguing in Publication Data
Gender and early modern constructions of childhood. – (Women and gender in the early modern world)
    1. Children in literature. 2. Parent and child in literature. 3. Sex differences in literature.
    4. English literature – Early modern, 1500–1700 – History and criticism. 5. Children in art. 6. Children – Europe – Social conditions – Early works to 1800.
    I. Series II. Miller, Naomi J., 1960– III. Yavneh, Naomi.
    809.9'33523–dc22

Library of Congress Cataloging-in-Publication Data
Miller, Naomi J., 1960–
   Gender and early modern constructions of childhood / Naomi J. Miller and Naomi Yavneh.
    p. cm. — (Women and gender in the early modern world)
   Includes bibliographical references and index.
   1. Gender identity—History. 2. Children—Family relationships—Europe—History.
3. Children's plays—Study and teaching. I. Yavneh, Naomi. II. Title.

HQ1075.M556 2011
305.23094'09031—dc23
                                       2011017702
ISBN 9781409429975 (hbk)

Reprinted 2012

Printed and bound in Great Britain by
the MPG Books Group, UK

For Erika Gaffney, our beloved editor and friend.
And, as always, for our children.

Contents

List of Figures

List of Contributors

Emilie Bergmann is Professor of Spanish at the University of California, Berkeley, specializing in sixteenth and seventeenth-century Hispanic literature and twentieth-century Castilian and Catalan women writers.

Caroline Bicks, Associate Professor of English at Boston College, specializes in women in early modern culture, Elizabethan and Jacobean drama, lyric and epic poetry, history of science, and seventeenth-century women writers. She is the author of *Midwiving Subjects in Shakespeare's England* (Ashgate, 2003) and, with Jennifer Summit, the co-editor of *The History of British Women's Writing, 1500–1610* (Palgrave).

Jane Couchman is Professor Emerita and Senior Scholar of French, Humanities and Women's Studies at Glendon College, York University (Toronto). Her research deals with the letters of late sixteenth- and early seventeenth-century Huguenot women. She has published articles and book chapters on Louise de Coligny, Catherine de Bourbon, Charlotte de Bourbon-Montpensier, Eléonore de Roye and Marguerite de Navarre. Her co-edited book (with Ann Crabb), *Women's Letters Across Europe 1400–1700: Form and Persuasion* (Ashgate) won the Award from the Society for the Study of Early Modern Women for the best Collaborative Project published in 2005. Her co-authored book (with Colette H. Winn) about Eleonore de Roye, princesse de Condé is forthcoming with Honoré Champion (Paris).

Carole Collier Frick is Professor and Chair of the Department of Historical Studies at Southern Illinois University. Her research focuses on the material culture of early modern Europe, Renaissance clothing and the semiotics of dress, and family and gender issues in fifteenth- and sixteenth-century art and images.

Katherine R. Larson is Assistant Professor of English at the University of Toronto. She is the author of *Early Modern Women in Conversation*, forthcoming in Palgrave Macmillan's Early Modern Literature in History series. Her work has also appeared in journals including *English Literary Renaissance*, the *Sidney Journal*, and *Early Modern Women: An Interdisciplinary Journal*.

Carole Levin is Willa Cather Professor of History and Director of the Medieval and Renaissance Studies Program at the University of Nebraska where she specializes in early modern English women's and cultural history. Her numerous books include *The Heart and Stomach of a King: Elizabeth I and the Politics of Sex and Power* (University of Pennsylvania Press, 1994), which was named one of the top ten academic books of the 1990s by the readers of Lingua Franca, September, 2000. She has worked on two major exhibits, "Elizabeth I: Ruler and Legend" at the Newberry Library in Chicago and "To Sleep Perchance to Dream" at the Folger Shakespeare Library in Washington, DC. She is the past president of the Society for the Study of Early Modern Women, the co-founder and president of the Queen Elizabeth I Society, and is Fellow of the Royal Historical Society.

Julia Marciari Alexander is Deputy Director for Curatorial Affairs at the San Diego Museum of Art.

Sara Mendelson is past president of the Society for the Study of Early Modern Women, current president of the Margaret Cavendish Society, and a fellow of the Royal Historical Society. Her books include *The Mental World of Stuart Women*, *Women in Early Modern England 1550–1720* (with Patricia Crawford), *Paper Bodies: A Margaret Cavendish Reader* (with Sylvia Bowerbank), and *Margaret Cavendish, Duchess of Newcastle*.

Naomi J. Miller is Professor of English and the Study of Women and Gender at Smith College, specializing in early modern women's studies, Shakespeare, and children's literature. Recent work includes a historical fiction novel about Lady Mary Wroth, as well as a young adult novel adaptation of Shakespeare's *The Tempest*, co-authored with Bruce Coville.

Kathryn M. Moncrief is Associate Professor and Chair of English at Washington College. She is co-editor, with Kathryn McPherson, of *Performing Maternity in Early Modern England* (Ashgate, 2008) and *Performing Pedagogy in Early Modern England: Gender, Instruction, and Performance* (Ashgate, 2011). She is also the author of *Competitive Figure Skating for Girls* (Rosen Publishing, 2001). She is currently at work on a book, *Unruly Bodies: Performing Femininity in Early Modern England*.

Patricia Phillippy is a Professor of English Literature at Kingston University, London. She recently edited Elizabeth Cooke Hoby Russell, *The Writings of an English Sappho* (CRRS/Iter, 2011) and is at work on a monograph on gender and early modern funeral monuments.

Diane Purkiss is Fellow and Tutor of English at Keble College, Oxford. She specializes in Renaissance and women's literature, witchcraft, and the English Civil War. In addition to numerous books on aspects of early modern English culture, she also publishes children's books with her son, Michael Dowling, under the pseudonym Tobias Druitt.

Marie Rutkowski is Assistant Professor of English at Brooklyn College. In addition to publishing on children and childhood in early modern England, she is the author of several novels for young adults.

Gregory M. Colón Semenza is Associate Professor of English at the University of Connecticut. In 2004, Semenza published his first book: *Sport, Politics, and Literature in the English Renaissance*. His other books include *Graduate Study for the 21st Century: How to Build an Academic Career in the Humanities* (2005; 2nd ed. 2010); *The English Renaissance in Popular Culture* (2010); and, with Laura L. Knoppers, *Milton in Popular Culture* (2006). He is currently at work on a monograph entitled *Fictional Milton*. Semenza has published numerous essays on such other topics as Comus for children, wrestling in *The Canterbury Tales*, Shakespeare and silent film, The Sex Pistols, and Milton's corpse.

Naomi Yavneh is Director of the University Honors Program and Professor of Language and Culture at Loyola University New Orleans, specializing in early modern women's studies, and gender and spirituality in Renaissance Italy. The former director of Undergraduate Research at the University of South Florida, she was the founding chair of the Council of Undergraduate Research's Arts and Humanities Division.

Acknowledgments

Not dissimilar to our joint experiences as parents, the experience of compiling this volume of essays on gender and constructions of childhood has taken far more time than we initially planned, including many interruptions for life itself. Consequently, our first debt and expression of gratitude goes to our assembled contributors, who stuck with us and maintained their patience even as the time frame for the volume kept extending like stretched and overchewed bubble gum! The outstanding quality of the essays in this volume bears witness to the extraordinary work of our contributors, who have been a pleasure to work with over the labor and delivery of this book.

Our biggest debt of gratitude goes to our Ashgate editor and longtime friend, Erika Gaffney, who kept the faith for us when we couldn't always see the next step ahead, until we were into the home stretch. Our formal dedication to the volume signals our deep appreciation for her gifts and patience as an editor.

Naomi Miller would also like to thank her faculty colleagues in the English Department and the Program in the Study of Women and Gender at Smith College for their support and encouragement, welcoming her return to her faculty identity. Most of all, she wants to attest to the joy of sharing her life with her four children—Fiona, Isaiah, Damaris, and Elias—whose presence in her life (as she noted in the dedication to her first academic book) puts everything in place, from book subjects to daily work.

Naomi Yavneh would also like to thank her friends and colleagues in the Honors College at the University of South Florida, especially Dean Stuart Silverman, Penny Carlton, Lauren Schumacher, and Alyssa Cobb, and her helpful and enthusiastic undergraduate research assistants Mariana Stavig, Aly Collins, Sarah Norris, and Natalie Wood. She is also extremely grateful for the love, kindness, and support of her friends and family, especially Adriana Novoa and Alex Levine, Julie Langford, Tenli Yavneh, and, of course, Naomi Miller. Finally, Naomi Y. wishes to thank her beloved children—Shoshana, Raphael, Isabella, and Lily Shattenkirk—who inform and inspire her work and life, and Stanley Klos, who has taught her much about children, childcare, and love.

Introduction:
Early Modern Children as Subjects:
Gender Matters

Naomi J. Miller and Naomi Yavneh

Although the umbrella term "child" was originally gendered female in early modern England, recent scholars such as Jennifer Higginbotham have observed that as "girl" and "boy" became the default terms for female and male children, the term "child" itself became increasingly gender-neutral, signaling the beginning of a shift away from cultural perceptions of childhood as a feminine stage into two separate worlds of boyhood and girlhood.[1] Indeed, Higginbotham points out that when Philippe Ariès declares that "boys were the first specialized children,"[2] he "misses the point that the special demarcation of boys did not mean that girls were excluded from the idea of childhood," especially given that the transformation of the vocabulary of childhood over the sixteenth and seventeenth centuries "reflected a growing sense of the need for language to mark more clearly the biological sex of female children."[3] Moreover, Will Fisher makes the instructive observation that "masculinity was not only constructed in contrast to femininity, but also in contrast to boyhood; as a result, we can say that men and boys were quite literally two distinct genders."[4]

Critical attention to childhood and its developmental relation to the construction of adult gender and sexual identities as a fundamental concern of feminist scholarship has framed the emergence of a number of recent books in the burgeoning field of childhood studies.[5] Some of these studies are more concerned

---

[1]   See Jennifer Higginbotham's excellent and comprehensive review of the terms for female child in her dissertation, *Fair Maids and Golden Girls: Early Modern Girlhood and the Production of Femininity* (University of Pennsylvania, 2007), esp. "Introduction: What is an Early Modern Girl?" (1–12), and "Chapter One: Vocabularies of Female Youth" (esp. 13–58; cited here from pp. 33 and 35).

[2]   Philippe Ariès, *Centuries of Childhood*, trans. Robert Baldick (New York: Knopf, 1962), 58.

[3]   Higginbotham, *Fair Maids and Golden Girls*, 34–5; see also Will Fisher, *Materializing Gender in Early Modern English Literature and Culture* (Cambridge: Cambridge University Press, 2006), on how "clothing materialized gender along with other, more corporeal features, and both were essential" (13).

[4]   *Materializing Gender*, 87.

[5]   See Robert Shaughnessy's introduction to *Shakespeare and Childhood*, Kate Chedgzoy, Susanne Greenhalgh, and Shaughnessy, eds (Cambridge: Cambridge University

with the perspectives of adults than of children,[6] and the relevance of gender to constructions of childhood does not always receive attention.[7] However, it is clear, as Kate Chedgzoy maintains, that "of fundamental importance for childhood studies are the closely connected questions of how childhood is to be defined and how children are to be known, perceived and enabled to articulate their own kinds of knowledge." The fact that "the evidence for early modern children's cultural presence and agency is richer and more extensive than has sometimes been thought"[8] offers an opportunity to engage not only with theories of childhood but historical evidence of children's voices and roles.[9] And as the essays in the present volume demonstrate, gender matters to early modern childhood, both explicitly and implicitly; thinking about gender advances work on early modern childhood, even as approaching gender within this historical frame offers an illuminating opportunity to contribute original material and perspectives to gender studies itself.

To identify a common starting point for scholarship in this area, perhaps the best-known fact regarding Renaissance children is that so many of them died. Although poor women who nursed their own children tended to deliver every 24 to 30 months, and wealthier women, able to afford wet nurses, gave birth as often as once a year, 20 to 50 percent of these babies did not survive childhood.[10]

Press, 2007), 1–11, and Kate Chedgzoy, "What, are they children?" in the same collection, 15–31. Other valuable recent collections of essays include *Childhood in Question: Children, Parents, and the State*, Anthony Fletcher and Stephen Hussey, eds (Manchester: Manchester University Press, 1999), and *Childhood and Children's Books in Early Modern Europe, 1550–1800*, Andrea Immel and Michael Witmore, eds (London: Routledge, 2006).

[6]   Keith Thomas points out the vital importance of not limiting research to "the history of adult attitudes *to* children" rather than the history *of* children, and argues that "differences of gender were even more fundamental" than differences of social class ("Children in Early Modern England," in *Children and Their Books*, Gillian Avery and Julia Briggs, eds (Oxford: Clarendon Press, 1989), 47, 50.

[7]   A notable exception, Kate Chedgzoy is particularly good at attending to gender liminality in Shakespeare's boy companies (see "Shakespeare in the company of boys," in *Shakespeare and Childhood*, Chedgzoy, Greenhalgh and Shaughnessy, eds, 184–200), and in unpacking the "meanings and experience of boyhood as qualitatively different from girlhood" (see "Playing with Cupid: Gender, Sexuality, and Adolescence," in *Alternative Shakespeares 3*, Diana E. Henderson, ed. [London: Routledge, 2008], 138–57).

[8]   Chedgzoy, "'What, are they children?'" in *Shakespeare and Childhood*, Chedgzoy, Greenhalgh, and Shaughnessy, eds, 17, 28.

[9]   Andrea Immel and Michael Witmore suggest that "perhaps it is only through comparative study, or at least the consultation of multiple national traditions, that we can piece together the culture of childhood in this period—a culture, that is, in every sense, co-extensive with early modern culture writ large" ("Little Differences: Children, Their Books, and Culture in the Study of Early Modern Europe," in *Childhood and Children's Books in Early Modern Europe, 1550–1800*, 15).

[10]   Children died not just from plague or childhood ailments such as measles or scarlet fever, but also dehydration brought on by diarrhea. Accidents were frequent as well: in an age of open fireplaces and no indoor plumbing, children might be burned, drowned in wells

At the same time, even though mortality rates were high for all children, wealthier ones were more likely to survive, while, in all socio-economic classes, boys fared better than girls, who were nursed for shorter periods of time and often farther from home than were their brothers, and who were more likely to be abandoned to foundling hospitals.

This extremely high mortality rate caused some scholars to question whether Renaissance parents loved their children, in studies more concerned to address parenthood than childhood per se. Philippe Ariès, for example, was highly influential in establishing the argument that medieval mothers and fathers deliberately sought to avoid affective ties, distancing themselves from their offspring both physically (by, for example, placing newborns in the home of a wet nurse and later in the care of a nanny) or psychologically, he suggests, through the use of nonspecific descriptors such as "it" or "creature." In such readings (drawn using evidence primarily from elite culture), "childhood" was not a privileged or even specified developmental period until the modern era.[11] Morover, British historian Lawrence Stone was particularly forceful in arguing for the "resigned acceptance of children" by both men and women, and, indeed, the lack of a "maternal instinct" during the Early Modern period itself, with research focused primarily on the middle and upper classes.[12] Stone maintained that affective intimacy was an outgrowth of the development of the middle class nuclear family in the late seventeenth and eighteenth centuries, and did not spread either to the aristocracy or the working classes before the nineteenth century.

---

or streams, or mortally injured while engaged in daily chores. Babies, swaddled and brought into bed with mothers or nurses, might inadvertently be smothered in a tragic circumstance known as "over-lying," although some scholars question whether such deaths were in fact a form of infanticide, on the one hand, or SIDS (Sudden Infant Death Syndrome, also known as "crib death") on the other. See, for example, Shulamith Shahar, *Childhood in the Middle Ages* (New York: Routledge, 1990); Alexandre Bidon and Didier Lett, *Children in the Middle Ages, 5th–15th Centuries*, trans. Jody Gladding (Notre Dame, Indiana: University of Notre Dame, 1999). Useful sources include Barbara Hanawalt, "Medievalists and the Study of Childhood," *Speculum* 77, no. 2 (2002): 440–60; Christiane Klapisch-Zuber, *Women, Family and Ritual in Renaissance Italy*, trans. Lydia Cochrane (Chicago: University of Chicago, 1985); Ilana Krausman Ben-Amos, *Adolescence and Youth in Early Modern England* (New Haven and London: Yale University Press, 1994).

[11] Ariès, *Centuries of Childhood*. Responding to the long-standing critical disagreements over Ariès's historical theories regarding childhood and the family, Patrick Hutton, Ch. 6, "Decades of Debate about *Centuries of Childhood*," in *Philippe Ariès and the Politics of French Cultural History* (Amherst: University of Massachusetts Press, 2004), offers a thoughtful consideration of the larger significance of *Centuries of Childhood* in terms of its readership as well as its authorship, observing that Ariès "put a long tradition of child-rearing, tacitly modeled and remodeled across the ages, into historical perspective," providing "not simply a contribution to scholarship, but a personalized portrait of the past" (p. 112).

[12] Lawrence Stone, *The Family, Sex and Marriage in England 1500–1800* (New York: Harper & Row, 1977).

After the work of Keith Wrightson, Linda Pollock, and Ralph Houlbrooke effectively corrected some of Stone's overdrawn conclusions,[13] scholars have examined a broader range of sources (record books and diaries, for example, and popular works such as saints' lives or advice manuals, as well as cultural artifacts such as monuments and birth salvers) in order to frame the consideration of family ties from within an examination of early modern gender and social constructions.[14] This research makes clear that, while the death of a child might not be uncommon, it was nevertheless an often devastating blow, greeted with violent grief, prolonged mourning, and, where possible, lasting monuments such as tombs, epitaphs, poems, or paintings.

Evidence of affection is not limited to grief for the dead. Indeed, the turn to naturalism in Italian Renaissance art is epitomized in the depiction of the beautiful young Madonna with an increasingly cherubic baby Jesus, the affective intimacy of the Mother and Child serving in part to help the viewer identify with the Incarnate God's humanity. Moreover, the very existence of a plethora of early modern books and popular advice manuals on upbringing and education suggests that a consuming interest in parenting is far from being exclusive to our own modern time period.

In fact, early modern correspondence and diaries suggest that children were a precious commodity, and that their arrival, especially in upper-class families, was usually celebrated as a "blessed event"; the mother (assuming that she survived the ordeal) would be presented with gifts such as fine cloth or clothing; silver forks, spoons, or cups.[15] Advice regarding childrearing practices commenced at birth, with virtually all childrearing manuals of the period advocating maternal breastfeeding as a means to safeguard the physical, mental, and moral health of the baby. Despite these recommendations, as well as descriptions of the dire consequences of providing a child with the wrong milk, the use of wet nurses – whether within or outside the home – was ubiquitous, with girls more likely to be sent out than boys.

---

[13]   See Keith Wrightson, *English Society, 1580–1680* (London: Hutchinson, 1982), Linda Pollock, *Forgotten Children: Parent-Child Relations from 1500–1900* (Cambridge: Cambridge University Press, 1983), and Ralph Houlbrooke, *The English Family, 1450–1700* (London: Longman, 1984).

[14]   See, for example, Jacqueline Marie Musacchio, *The Art and Ritual of Childbirth in Renaissance Italy*, New Haven: Yale, 1999, and David Cressy, *Birth, Marriage and Death: Ritual, Religion, and the Life-Cycle in Tudor and Stuart England* (Oxford: Oxford University Press, 1997). Useful discussions of the historiography of childhood include Hanawalt, "Medievalists and the Study of Childhood," and Lena Cowen Orlin's review article, "Rewriting Stone's Renaissance," *The Huntington Library Quarterly*, vol. 64, no. 1/2 [2001], 189–230. Although his equation of Florentine fathers with their participatory late twentieth-century counterparts is somewhat facile (and anachronistic), Louis Haas's *The Renaissance Man and his Children: Childbirth and Early Childhood in Florence, 1300–1600* (New York: Palgrave, 1998), compellingly argues for paternal attachment extending far beyond questions of economics or politics.

[15]   For Italy, see, for example, Jacqueline Musacchio, *The Art and Ritual of Childbirth*.

While the argument that childhood was unrecognized or children in general devalued has been greatly revised, not every child was wanted. There are widely ranging views regarding infanticide rates, with some scholars positing the ubiquity of the practice, and others, notably John Boswell, arguing that it was virtually replaced by the paradoxically loving abandonment of children, society's most valued resource following the demographic catastrophe of the Black Death. Whether abandonment was in fact a sign of love, foundling hospitals, where unwanted children could be left anonymously, were an established feature of the early modern city.[16]

Growing up was a matter not just of education and recreation, but of cultural imprinting, where early modern children were commonly expected to adopt adult customs as well as clothing at a defined stage of development, and often were expected to leave the world of childhood behind and be incorporated directly into the social, professional, and even political responsibilities of their family. Moreover, recent work on youth and adolescence as a category distinct from both childhood and adulthood has enabled further consideration of the transitional stages of growing up in the early modern world.[17] As Chedgzoy observes, "adolescence is a site where the gendering of childhood comes into particularly clear focus, revealing that not only the experience of childhood but the stages of life themselves may be different for boys and girls."[18] On the other side of growing up was the experience of growing old, where childhood customs and even traumas might resurface as grown children faced parenting responsibilities in a rapidly changing world, not to mention care of their own aging parents.

The evidence discussed above can tell us a great deal about how children were viewed and childhood conceptualized in the early modern period but, as Hugh Cunningham emphasizes in the introduction to his *Children and Childhood in Western Society*, it is important to distinguish between ideas of childhood and the actuality of adult–child relations. Cunningham observes that although "ideas about childhood in the past exist in plenitude," captured in sources ranging from

---

[16]   John Boswell, *The Kindness of Strangers: The Abandonment of Children in the West from Antiquity to the Renaissance*. New York: Pantheon, 1988. See also Nicholas Terpstra, *Abandoned Children of the Italian Renaissance: Orphan Care in Florence and Bologna* (Baltimore: Johns Hopkins University Press, 2005). Philip Gavitt, *Charity and Children in Renaissance Florence* (Ann Arbor: University of Michigan, 1990).

[17]   See esp. Ilana Krausman Ben-Amos, *Adolescence and Youth in Early Modern England*, on the importance of viewing "adolescence and youth in early modern English society … as a long and dynamic phase in the life cycle" (8), and Paul Griffiths, *Youth and Authority: Formative Experiences in England 1560–1640* (Oxford: Clarendon Press, 1996), on the documentation of "different rates of physical development for young men and women," as well as the imperative of regarding the "period of youth [as] a critical point in the social construction of gender when young men and women are introduced to particular functions and roles to crush any 'natural similarities'" (21, 28).

[18]   See Chedgzoy's introduction, "What, are they children?" in *Shakespeare and Childhood* (23).

advice manuals and sermons to works of art; "it is not so easy to find out about the lives of children."[19] Indeed, the central question of the previous generation of scholarship on childhood, did parents love their children, focuses once again on parents—i.e., adults—rather than the experience of children themselves.

It also underscores the difficulties in recapturing what Cunningham terms the "emotional past." Work on the history of emotions suggests that scholars must be careful to avoid anachronism by paying close attention to their own cultural preconceptions regarding the "proper" or normative expression of feelings.[20] For instance, in attempting to recapture early modern attitudes towards children, in general, and the death of children, in particular, we may be misreading the evidence by failing to acknowledge that what we would label an "emotion" (a term that did not become synonymous with "feeling" until about 1660)[21] might not have been expressed in a manner recognizable to us, or might have been experienced without an overt display. Using Lawrence Stone as a notable example, the editors of *Reading the Early Modern Passions* contend that, "modern readers tend to misread early modern emotion codes along specific lines, often parsing emotional control as a lack of feeling, or privileging spontaneous and passionate expressions as evidence of authentic experience."[22] It is true, as Gail Kern Paster, Katherine Rowe, and Mary Floyd-Wilson point out, that since classical philosophy, the "death of a child is a commonplace test for *apathia*," or stoicism. In Cicero's *Tusculan Disputations*, for example, the ideal stoic receives the news of his child's death with the response, "I was already aware that I had begotten a mortal."[23] But the fifteenth-century Florentine humanist, Coluccio Salutati, even as he acknowledges the superiority of the contemplative life, argues that for a man to fail to experience grief in such a case "is not only impossible, but ... undesirable."[24]

Yet uncontrolled emotions, or passions, "are potentially disruptive to both individual and social life." Accordingly, the editors of *Representing Emotions* draw on Norbert Elias's work to address how "their control becomes significant for socially dominant groups" and "for those seeking to enhance their social significance."[25] Moreover, returning our focus to children themselves, the passage from childhood to adulthood may, in fact, be demarcated in part precisely by

---

[19]   Hugh Cunningham, *Children and Childhood in Western Society since 1500* (New York: Longman, 2005), 2.

[20]   Gail Kern Paster, Katherine Rowe, and Mary Floyd-Wilson, eds, *Reading the Early Modern Passions: Essays in the Cultural History of Emotion* (Philadelphia: University of Pennsylvania Press, 2004), 11.

[21]   Stephen Mullaney, unpublished paper, cited in Paster, et al., 2.

[22]   Paster, et al., 12–13.

[23]   Cited and discussed in Richard Streier, "Against the Rule of Passions: Praise of Passion from Petrarch to Luther to Shakespeare to Herbert," 25, In Paster, et al., 23–42.

[24]   Streier, 25.

[25]   Penelope Gouk and Helen Hills, eds, *Representing Emotions: New Connections in the Histories of Art, Music and Medicine* (Aldershot and Burlington: Ashgate Press, 2005), 23.

the transition to emotional control. Carol Chillington Rutter suggests that the "grammar of emotion" learned by the schoolboy, encompassing tears, "is not an alternative to adult masculinity; it's constitutive of it."[26] In other words, children—as the essays in this volume make clear—are not simply "little adults."

Drawing on art history, literary studies, and social history, the interdisciplinary essays in this volume seek to shift the focus of discussion onto the children themselves, as well as onto familial relations, by exploring a range of intersections among gender, constructions of childhood, and the experiences of children in the fifteenth, sixteenth, and seventeenth centuries in Italy, England, France, and Spain. Rather than dividing the contributions by geography, genre, discipline, or chronology, we have chosen to group the essays around central themes of loss and celebration, education and social training, growing up and growing old. The authors choose distinctively original entry points into these themes, grounded in the particulars of childhood and gender for each subject under discussion, and utilizing an array of feminist and cultural studies perspectives.

In previous scholarship on the family, children have been used as objects to define culture and the roles of adults within the culture (as parents, tutors, wet nurses, etc.). Children have served as objects on display: son as heir, daughter grouped with ducats as a possession. The impetus for this volume arose from our interest in considering children as subjects with lived experience that is gendered. Although early modern manuals offer generic recommendations for little boys and girls (who were dressed alike in dresses in early childhood, fed the same foods and offered the same toys), gendered variations in practice—often reflected in superior infant mortality statistics for males—indicate that there were probably cultural norms that distinguished sex-specific treatment even of infants and toddlers. Certainly, the birth of a boy, who would carry the family name and patrimony and whose marriage would potentially bring in a dowry, was a greater cause for celebration than that of a daughter, who would require a dowry of her own.

Early education, generally supervised by the mother, focused on religion and morality: topics of central importance for both girls and boys, and which would no doubt include early inculcation of gender roles. By age four or five, playthings would reflect and direct children toward their future roles, with girls taught such tasks as spinning, sewing, and cooking, rather than woodworking or reading. By seven or eight, a boy would have begun his formal education, preparing for training for a trade, or following his father to help in the field. Although there were exceptions, a girl would usually remain home to receive domestic training from her mother; in Catholic families of certain classes, she might be sent to a convent for education and safe-keeping either until she was married around the age of fourteen or until she took permanent vows.

---

[26] See Carol Chillington Rutter, *Shakespeare and Child's Play: Performing Lost Boys on Stage and Screen* (London: Routledge, 2007), who maintains that "the ambitions which early modern culture expressed for its children are ones post-modernity still entertains, grapples with, contests, refashions, and turns to different ends" (xvi; also 68).

The essays in this volume grapple with ways in which constructions of childhood were inflected by considerations of gender throughout the early modern world. The contributors examine representations of early modern children and childhood in a range of sources, from paintings and poetry to legal records and personal correspondence, enabling an appreciation of the gendered negotiations of familial roles in early modern society. These essays document examples where some Renaissance children were cherished, while others were abandoned, and some children were thrust early into adult roles while others were allowed liminal space and time for what in later centuries would come to be known as "childhood." Finally, this volume sheds light on some of the ways in which, in the relations between Renaissance children and their parents and peers, gender mattered. Exploring constructions of childhood—in literature, art, and social history—enriches our understanding both of individual children and of familial relations in the early modern period, as well as of the relevance of gender to constructions of self and society, for individuals from the youngest ages and stages in all walks of life.

Conceptualizing Childhood: Loss and Celebration

The signal importance of children to the familial structure meant both that a child's arrival in the family was frequently greeted with great joy and celebration, and that the loss of a child to death in particular could have crushing social as well as personal implications for early modern parents. Focusing on parental attitudes toward children, the essays in this section consider how early modern childhood could be fractured and reconstructed through experiences of loss as well as celebration, relinquishment as well as greeting, mourning as well as recreation, while maintaining strong ties of identification between parent and child. In the opening essay of the volume, "A Comfortable Farewell: Child-loss and Funeral Monuments in Early Modern England," Patricia Phillippy examines the gendering of child loss made visible in the details, both visual and inscribed, of a range of funeral monuments, including the example of Constance Lucy, who was vocal and eloquent in commemorating her daughter and namesake, Constance, who died at the age of ten on February 14, 1596. On this monument, the single effigy, of the mother kneeling in prayer, combined with the poetic inscription, cast in the maternal voice, presents a daughter's death chiefly as a maternal loss, registering her value in the family primarily in affective terms. Phillippy's essay explores the extent to which funeral monuments can provide evidence to contemporary viewers of the depth of emotion experienced by many early modern parents for children, both living and dead, suggesting that they represent a valuable resource for the future work of excavating the subtle and intractable history of the emotions in early modern England.

In "Parents, Children, and Responses to Death in Dream Structures in Early Modern England," Carole Levin considers one of the most intense sites of cultural anxiety in early modern England: conflicts between parents and their children. Examining the popular dream book by Thomas Hill, *The Pleasant Art and Interpretation of Dreams*, which went through seven editions between 1576 and 1626, Levin suggests that "dreams, and the manner in which they were viewed, allow us to understand more about the most significant and contested cultural issues of early modern England," including the articulation of childhood and filial relationships. Levin's study of such dreams and their interpretations indicates that high mortality rates produced many dreams that reflected fear of loss, particularly of children but sometimes of parents as well, attesting to the strong bonds, whether of guilt and responsibility or of affection, between parents and children.

In "Lost and Found: Veronese's *Finding of Moses*," Naomi Yavneh examines several of the painter Veronese's versions of the "Finding of Moses" in order to consider the cultural resonance both of the orchestrated abandonment of the child and the emphasis on maternal nursing in a society which publicly supported institutions for abandoned children in coexistence with elaborate and costly lying-in ceremonies and frequent but often-ignored exhortations to maternal breastfeeding. Yavneh maintains that Veronese's visual rendition of the tale, with its representation of Pharaoh's daughter, the foster mother, as a typical patrician Venetian woman, and its allusive echoes of Veronese's own "Rape of Europa," conveys a fantasy of a foundling rescued from the darkness of an underclass for a better life, along with important cultural messages regarding Venetian ideology.

Finally, in "'Certein childeplayes remembered by the fayre ladies': Girls and Their Games," Katherine R. Larson explores attitudes toward the recreation of childhood, in the function and gendering of children's games and the interplay between the "frivolity" of child play and the adult pastimes in the early modern court. Such pastimes indicate a vision of childhood adopted and adapted by women in particular, in order to negotiate the complex social realm of adulthood at the Jacobean court. Drawing particularly upon the writings of Mary Wroth, Larson's essay illuminates the potency of playful discourses in enabling women to appropriate and redeploy ludic conventions to negotiate and communicate their experience of eroticized and politicized relationships. The gendered line between "masculine" or "manlier" sports and "the other sorte" of play regarded as appropriate for girls could be redrawn when women returned to celebratory moments from their girlhoods in order to "playe the childe again" as adults.

Imprinting Identity: Education and Social Training

The upbringing of children involved education and social training in shifting measures in early modern society, depending on the country as well as on the social class of the families involved. The essays in this section consider a remarkable range of representations of childrearing philosophies and practices across the strata of early modern society, in order to ascertain some of the ways in which constructions of childhood evolved in relation to an array of experiences of childhood. While it is general knowledge that boys would have received far more educational opportunities than girls (whether that entailed tutoring in classical languages at home or school, or placement as an apprentice), the gender of the child frequently determined, as well, the selection of childrearing philosophies or the application of practices on a daily basis. In "The Facts of *Enfance*: Rabelais, Montaigne, Paré, and French Renaissance Paediatrics," Marie Rutkoski counterpoises the burgeoning of published texts on child-rearing in sixteenth-century France with the satirical attention they received from a writer such as François Rabelais. Analyzing Rabelais's *Gargantua and Pantagruel* (1532) in relation to documented pediatric practices of sixteenth-century France, Rutkoski contends that "Rabelais exposes a cultural fascination with childhood development that mocks the medical and aristocratic community's effort to approach the subject with more pragmatism and less mysticism." Indeed, she finds that a survey of key works concerned with childhood in the period, from Rabelais to Montaigne and Paré, exposes "a cultural fault line about whether childhood development should be apprehended with wonder, or medical *savoir*."

Jane Couchman attends not only to child-rearing practices, but also to affective bonds between children and their parents and grandparents, as epitomized in the correspondence of Louise de Coligny, a prolific recorder of political and religious events in France and the Netherlands in the late sixteenth and early seventeenth centuries, in which she played a role at the highest levels. In "'Our little darlings': Huguenot Children and Child-rearing in the Letters of Louise de Coligny," Couchman indicates the extent to which the "Huguenot sensibility towards children" that emerges in the correspondence suggests that Humanist learning, the pleasures of society, fine clothes, horsemanship, music, and court dancing are all seen as compatible with the Reformed faith in bringing up children. At the same time, the essay points out that the letters document a very different program of upbringing for girls as compared to boys. Louise arranges for a solid education for her four stepdaughters—including reading and writing, foreign language study, and arithmetic, as well as dancing and lute-playing—with the clear intent of forming the girls for their roles as wives and mothers and also as actors on the national and international stage. The continuing correspondence between Louise and her stepdaughters as they grew older documents a continuing learning connection that extends from pregnancy, birth, and the raising of young children to negotiations about financial or political matters in which they were involved. In the case of her own son, Frederic-Henri, the only child of Louise de Coligny and William of Orange, Louise was no less attentive to the substance of his education, but conveyed her belief that he needed an education only men could provide, by contrast to her confidence in educating her stepdaughters herself. Once again, gender matters.

Moving from sixteenth-century French aristocracy to seventeenth-century English gentry, Sara Mendelson's essay on "Anne Dormer and her Children" offers a consideration of how one woman's correspondence with her sister offers a case study in parental expectations and parent-child relations in late seventeenth-century

England. Given the dearth of materials that include actual voices of early modern children, Mendelson discusses some of the ways in which mothers' comments, sometimes quoting verbatim from children's own speech, can shed light not only on the history of childhood per se, but on children's roles in the broader context of family dynamics and household politics. Having borne eleven children in an unhappy marriage, Anne Dormer's epistolary comments to her sister, Elizabeth Trumbull, contain detailed narratives of her daily life and her interactions with family and friends, while also including her expectations of and advice to her various children. The essay illumines the ways in which Anne Dormer's epistolary narratives frame her descriptions of her children both directly and indirectly in terms of the politics of the family as a whole, and offer a detailed look at the power of family patterns of communication and dysfunction to reproduce themselves across subsequent generations.

Focusing on prescriptive guides in "'Obey and be attentive': Gender and Household Instruction in Shakespeare's *The Tempest*," Kathryn Moncrief considers the instructional scenes between Prospero and Miranda in relation to formal strategies for the schooling of daughters in the early modern household. Moncrief is particularly interested to consider how such examples of staging education might disrupt seemingly fixed practices and ideologies. Acknowledging that this was a period of intense debate and heightened anxiety about the merits and ills of educating girls, the essay examines how the stage representations of Shakespeare intersect with the messages of educational tracts and prescriptive texts, in exploring the execution and implications of household pedagogy for girls in early modern England, which focuses upon the preparation of girls for their roles as wives and mothers.

In complementary relation to Moncrief's essay, Caroline Bicks considers not how education appears in contemporary stage drama, but rather how the education of girls is performed in the convent schools established by Mary Ward in the early 1600s. "Producing Girls on the English Stage: Performance as Pedagogy in Mary Ward's Convent Schools" explores how the gendered identities of early modern girls were produced, in a unique example of English girls on the early modern stage. Mary Ward's curriculum trained girls in theatrical performance and public speaking, both of which were central to the Jesuit curriculum for boys, with the aim of turning the girls into eloquent and pious Christian women who could then return to England to save Catholicism, one household at a time. To her critics, such public performances trained girls in the art of heretical deception and daring apostolic activity, transforming them into dangerous females not contained within the bounds of acceptable behavior or attached to or owned by any one man. Bicks's analysis highlights a larger problem that the early modern girl poses for scholars of the period, functioning as a "shifty entity, difficult to locate and analyze," because she embodies the period between childhood and marriage in stages that are multiple rather than singular. The essay proposes that by exploring the moments in which early modern girls turn into spectacles, we can glimpse the production of gendered identity in the early modern period. Bicks argues that "when the ideally contained virgin opens up and displays herself as both delightful and awful through performance, she potentially challenges ideological notions (modern and early modern) of what a girl is."

Transitional Stages: Growing Up and Growing Old

One of the challenges in examining constructions of childhood in the early modern world is that there was no single definition or set of parameters for "childhood," as such, in the period. The question of when childhood ends must be factored into any consideration of the scope of childhood experience. The essays in this section address matters of closure, or lack thereof, in exploring social and cultural parameters of "growing up"—or the departure from childhood into adulthood, and "growing old"—or the concept of "second childishness," to use Shakespeare's term. As these essays make clear, generational relationships both underscore and are emphasized by the parallels between childhood and adult identity; indeed, the volume concludes with an essay that focuses on the fluidity of parent and child roles in the end of life—a topic as relevant to the twenty-first as to the sixteenth century.

In "Boys to Men: Codpieces and Masculinity in Sixteenth-Century Europe," Carole Collier Frick points out that the sartorial boundary between childhood and adulthood was blurred in many parts of sixteenth- and seventeenth-century Europe. Dressing practices not only for boys but also for girls formally outfitted children as little adults, which for boys included the wearing of codpieces. Frick considers the use of codpieces for young boys, exploring the hypothesis that "the appearance of this prominent gendered feature of male dressing practice was a consequence of the tumultuous sixteenth century, in which it was deemed necessary to present "an uninterrupted display of overt masculinity in formal dress." Arguing that clothing practices of the wealthy elite served as a powerful visual designator of the more abstract political and social concerns and attitudes of their wearers, indicative of "changing cultural mores and compelling contemporary events," the essay focuses on the significance of codpieces as a fraught cultural symbol of masculinity in portraits of the time, assertively marking the transition from childhood to adulthood while also betraying a new sense of masculine unease in response to challenges to European sovereignty.

Analyzing the figure of the preadolescent girl in "Marvell, Boys, Girls, and Men: Should We Worry?" Diane Purkiss attends to Andrew Marvell's investment in the figure of the preadolescent girl, arguing that such representations may best be understood through a careful analysis of the cultural evolution of early modern childhood. In Marvell's lyric constructions, according to Purkiss, what is desired is not the conquest of a young girl, nor her induction into sexuality, but a particular and culturally marked moment before the genesis of masculinity can begin. Pointing out that Renaissance writers understood masculinity as in some sense "born from a childhood located in the feminine world, even as sculpted painfully from a girlish self accustomed to feminine pleasures," the essay illuminates the extent to which Marvell's constant reversion to the figure of a little girl—in a garden—as a sign of all that is private, enclosed, retired, safe from the public world of war and politics and the state, offers "nothing less than a retreat from masculine pain into a child's world of feminine pleasure, a retreat that is also and sometimes explicitly a retreat from adult sexuality," voicing a longing for precisely that safety, that maternity which masculinity must disavow. Purkiss reveals the extent to which childhood and the psyche may be caught up in the historical and cultural shaping processes of childcare practices, with implications for the gendering of constructions of childhood.

Emilie Bergmann analyzes the shifting relation between the figure of the child and responsibilities of the adult world within which the child moves, focusing on the heroic boys in three of Cervantes's theatrical works. In "Martyrs and Minors: Allegories of Childhood in Cervantes," Bergmann finds that child characters in Cervantes's early theater as well as his later narrative works "have a dual role as emblems and active defenders of Spanish Catholic cultural identity," serving as "liminal figures poised between nonexistence and adulthood," and introducing "a distinctly modern sense of destabilized identity." Comparing Cervantes's heroic boys to the street urchins in Murillo's genre paintings, Bergmann illuminates the potential for moral autonomy and spiritual heroism in even the youngest of these characters, transcending the boundariès separating childhood from adulthood.

In "Portraiture and Royal Family Ties: Kings, Queens, Princes, and Princesses in Caroline England," Julia Marciari Alexander, Deputy Director at the San Diego Museum of Art, surveys the portraits of King Charles I and his family, particularly those painted by the Flemish artist Anthony Van Dyck. Moving beyond previous critical considerations primarily of the king himself, Alexander examines some of the ways that the portraits of Charles I's family and children functioned as products of and participants in a significant shift that occurred between 1600 and 1650 in perceptions of childhood and family life across Europe. The essay considers the significance of the extent to which Charles I played out his family life on the court stage, particularly in relation to his children, whose "growing up" across a succession of portraits signified their role as "the dynastic tools of the Stuart monarchy," with the portraits themselves serving as a visual stand-in for the children in their frequent physical absence from the court. While noting the crucial distinction between aristocratic and royal children and childhood, Alexander's analysis explicates the portraits as reflections of—and agents in—the transformation of notions of family and childhood in Caroline England.

In "'Second Childishness' and the Shakespearean Vision of Ideal Parenting," Gregory M. Colón Semenza tackles the significance of "childishness" as a marker for both the beginning and the end of life, in exploring the relation between childhood and extreme old age in Shakespearean drama. Semenza is concerned to address not merely the question of what it means to be childish in Shakespeare's dramatic vision, but, rather, what might be learned about Renaissance ideals of parenting from plays about very old "children." Pointing out that an important—and gendered—trait shared by most of these characters is that "they fail spectacularly as fathers," the essay considers how Shakespeare frees his characters to exchange positions as parents and children, by suggesting that "childishness and maturity are as much states of mind or modes of behavior as biological phases of the life cycle," resulting in a "paradoxical dynamic by which 'second children' are nurtured to maturity by their more 'parental' children." Semenza proposes that if age is "largely a behavioral mode," then the "Shakespearean drama of senescence" might be regarded as "the drama of learning how to '*act* one's age' even against one's own natural impulses," a conclusion that yields interesting implications across the scope of the essays in the volume for considerations of the "performance" of childhood and the performativity of gender across generations.

Beginning from the premise embraced and supported by recent historiography that the inherently fragile existence of the early modern child might enhance his or her role as an object of value and affection, the essays in this volume attempt to capture the subjective nature of childhood by interrogating and illuminating some of the complex functions and forces of gender that shaped its construction in the early modern period. Children might be cherished or abandoned, offered an education or restricted from activities, with gender, consistently, a defining force in shaping young identities, and, thus, lives. The child-centered parenting style of the twenty-first century may seem distant from the more proscriptive period this collection treats, but the fixation of so-called "helicopter parents" with issues such as cyber-bullying, standardized testing, and the respective virtues of princesses and superheroes suggests that gender remains a central framing structure. And the role of children in forging familial, dynastic, and cultural identities, eloquently evidenced in a number of these essays, strikes a resonant note in a period of both increased multiculturalism and fundamentalism.

Greeting arrivals and grieving departures, learning lessons and playing games, growing up and growing old, early modern individuals and communities moved through childhood in deeply gendered ages and stages whose revelation in art, history, and literature, as explored in this volume, informs our understanding not just of children, but also of adults, and offers sometimes surprising frames for our comprehension of the gendering of childhood (and adulthood) in our own modern world as well.

PART 1
Conceptualizing Childhood:
Loss and Celebration

Chapter 1
A Comfortable Farewell:
Child-loss and Funeral Monuments
in Early Modern England

Patricia Phillippy

On a brass plaque in St. Margaret's Church, Westminster, the grieving parents of ten-year-old Susanna Gray memorialized their daughter, enumerating their motives for doing so. These motives were widely held in common by creators of monuments for children in post-Reformation England:

> Hallelujah
> Here under waiting for a glorious Resurrection rests
> ye body of Susanna Gray, Daughter of Henry Gray of
> Enfeild in ye Countie of Stafford Esq. She dyed ye 29
> of October: 1654 Being Neare 10. Years of Age.
> First that such virtues as She practiced may
> encourage others to imitate her
> 2: That they may not fall into oblivion.
> 3: That other may see, tis not in vaine to be
> such. Ye most impartiall of them yt knew her thought
> it Justice, to her Memory to leave this testimony
> that she was the most modest, pious, & learned
> that hath beene knowne of her yeares.[1]

The didactic character of Susanna's example, suggested in her parents' first motive, is echoed on tombs for children as well as for adults, and reflects a reformed understanding of the function of funeral monuments.[2] No longer sites for intercessory prayers for the dead, as they were in Catholic England, post-Reformation tombs were reconsidered as tributes to exemplary lives and virtues,

---

[1] Inscription from the monument.

[2] On the didactic quality of children's monuments, see Nigel Llewellyn, "'[An] Impe entombed here doth lie:' The Besford triptych and Child Memorials in Post-Reformation England," in Gillian Avery and Kimberly Reynolds, eds, *Representation of Childhood Death* (London: Macmillan, 2000), 53. See also Katharine Esdaile, *English Monumental Sculpture since the Renaissance* (New York and Toronto: MacMillan Co., 1927), 79–86, for an inclusive discussion of children on monumental works in the period.

and as genealogical records preserving family history and identity.[3] The Gray's second goal, the creation of the monument as a defense against oblivion, is also a common feature of early modern tombs, and although the résumés inscribed on monuments for adult men are usually more replete than that of ten-year-old Susanna, her portrayal as modest, pious, and (more unusually) learned echoes the monumental portraits of many adult women in the period.[4] By preventing Susanna's memory from disappearing, as her small body did, into oblivion, the monument serves as a memorial to the permanent relationships established between family members in life, but perfected in death. The tomb anticipates the reunion of parents and daughter after the Resurrection, and imagines the bonds of love between them as reinforced, rather than severed, by death.

The Grays' third avowed motive calls attention to a characteristic which this chapter argues is a chief feature of childhood tombs in early modern England. In making the difficult rhetorical and existential case that Susanna's virtuous life was not vain despite her death at a brutally young age, the memorial introduces itself into evidence: her virtues were not futile, it reasons, because the monument renders "Justice to her Memory" by offering testimony to the life which would otherwise be lost to the bereaved and to history. The brass marker substitutes for the lost child, replacing the fragility of her flesh with the brilliant permanence of the material artifact. Although adults as well as children were commemorated in opulent tombs and with precious materials in early modern England—and, admittedly, Susanna Gray's simple brass plaque would have featured among the least expensive, least opulent of memorial objects[5]—children's tombs call special

---

[3]   A royal proclamation issued by Elizabeth I in 1559 protected funeral monuments from iconoclasm based upon their value as repositories of genealogical information. For discussion, see Nigel Llewellyn, *Funeral Monuments in Post-Reformation England* (Cambridge: Cambridge University Press, 2000), 269–71; and Peter M. Sherlock, *Monuments and Memory in Early Modern England* (Aldershot: Ashgate Press, 2008), 166–95. The proclamation is reprinted in John Weever, *Ancient Funerall Monuments* (London: John Weever, 1631), 54–6. See also Sherlock, *Monuments and Memory*, 97–127, on the reconsideration of the function of monuments in the Reformation.

[4]   Numerous examples on surviving monuments and those recorded by antiquarians include these characteristics. For example, John Bennet's epitaph for his wife Elizabeth (d. 1625) calls her "A modest, chaste, religious loving Wife." See John Stowe, *Survey of London* (London: Nicholas Bourne, 1633), 796. Margaret Talbot's (d. 1620) epitaph, probably written by herself, praises "The Piety, and Vertues of her minde" (Stowe, *Survey*, 681). Women's learning is less often recalled in their epitaphs. See Peter Sherlock, "Monuments, Reputation and Clerical Marriage in Reformation England: Bishop Barlow's Daughters," *Gender and History* 16 (2004), 74, for a description of Frances Matthews's tomb in York Minister; and Frederic Chancellor, *The Ancient Sepulchral Monuments of Essex* (London: C.F. Kell, 1890), 246, for the claim made on the monument of Sir Anthony Cooke in the Church of St. Edward the Confessor, Romford, that his five daughters "know how to put together Greek with Latin,/ Distinguished by their illustrious and pious characters."

[5]   Sherlock, *Monuments and Memory*, 11, maintains that "while the largest pile of stone might require a thousand pounds or more, a modest inscription on a monumental

attention, in both their visual and textual elements, to the connection between the body mourned and the medium through which this sorrow is conveyed. The Gray monument's explicit engagement with the question of vanity—both of its subject's short life and its own memorial gesture—is typical of other monuments for children in the period. In these monuments, childhood death underscores the ephemeral and fragile qualities of all human life, and the preciousness and innocence of the deceased are literalized in the precious materials of the tomb and the imagery of its inscriptions. As these memorials substitute for and displace the bodies of children lost to death, they speak to the place and value of children in the domestic and social spaces of early modern English culture. Their efforts to stave off the vanity of childhood death and to render these losses meaningful comprise and convey a subtle history of the emotions, and an ever-changing image of the concerns attending dynastic continuity and domestic identity in the period.[6]

What is Pretty, What is Pompous

Children's effigies evolved gradually throughout the sixteenth and early seventeenth centuries, from playing subordinate, symbolic roles on parents' tombs to becoming free-standing portraits on monuments for individual children.[7] The inclusion of children, living and dead, on the tombs of their parents responds to the acknowledged function of monuments as sources of genealogical, historical, and biographical information valuable to noble and upper class families in establishing dynastic identity. These effigies and the inscriptions accompanying them, however, are rarely free of feeling, and often present children's deaths as emotional as well as dynastic losses. On the tomb of Sir Thomas Caryll in Shipley (Fig. 1.1), erected by his widow, Margaret, after his death in 1616, the recumbent effigies of husband and wife lie on an altar tomb on the face of which are portraits of three daughters and a son, the latter swaddled in his cradle. The inscription tells us, "Here underneath lyeth interred the bodye of Sr/ Thos. Caryll ... who took to wife/ Margaret ye daughter of Sr John Tufton ... by whom he had issue Edw./ deceased, Marie, married to Sr. Richard Molineux ... Philip: married to Sr. Henry Parker ... and Elizabeth deceased."[8] The figure of the child in a cradle,

---

brass or ledgerstone could be obtained for a few shillings." See also Llewellyn, *Funeral Monuments*, 163–80, and Walter Lewis Spiers, ed., *The Notebook and Account Book of Nicholas Stone* (Oxford: Walpole Society, 1919).

[6] See Llewellyn, *Funeral Monuments*, 42–8, for a discussion of the function of funeral monuments in assuring mourners of the continuity between the living and the dead. Sherlock, *Monuments and Memory*, 41–70, greatly refines this thesis.

[7] See Llewellyn, "[An] Impe."

[8] See H.R. Mosse, *The Monumental Effigies of Sussex (1250–1650)* (Hove: Combridges, 1933), 151.

Fig. 1.1   Monument for Sir Thomas and Margaret Caryll. St. Mary's Shipley
              (Sussex), after 1616. Author photo.

which ordinarily signifies death in infancy,[9] underscores the death of the only son,
Edward, as a dynastic failure, but at the same time, the tomb registers the social
capital earned by the Carylls by arranging marriage alliances for their daughters
with prominent families.[10] Unable to guarantee the family's social continuity
through a surviving male heir, the monument offers a verse inscription, possibly
written by Margaret Caryll, which stresses instead the survival of Thomas Caryll's
virtues in the historical afterlife:

> Aske not who lyes intomb'd that crime
> Argues you lived not in his time:
> His virtues answer, and to fate

---

[9]   See Jean Wilson, "Holy Innocents: Some Aspects of the Iconography of Children
on English Renaissance Tombs," *Church Monuments* 5 (1990), 57.

[10]   The Carylls were Catholics, and the inscription emphasizes their alliances with
other prominent Catholic families in the county through their daughters' marriages. See
Mosse, *Monumental Effigies*, 151–2, and Michael C. Questier, *Catholicism and Community
in Early Modern England: Aristocratic Patronage and Religion, c. 1550–1640* (Cambridge:
Cambridge University Press, 2006), 50–56.

Out liveinge him, express their hate,
For stealing 'way the life of one
Who (but for fashion) needs no stone
To speake his praise: his woorst did dye
But best parte out lives memorie.
Then view, reade, trace his tombe, praise, deeds,
Which teares, joy, love, strains, causeth breeds.[11]

The monument also recalls the death of a daughter, Elizabeth, and offers a sculptural record of her death, and those of the family's patriarch and male heir, as affective losses, realized in the domestic sphere. Joining living family members with the dead, the Caryll monument insists upon the continuity of family ties after death and looks forward to corporeal resurrection in the afterlife. Gesturing toward the Resurrection, the tomb scripts an emotional, as well as dynastic, history of the family; a history as affective as it is pragmatic, focused on the painful separations of family members by death and on their eventual reunion in paradise.

Edward Caryll's small effigy occupies an intermediate position in the spectrum of seventeenth-century monumental forms, between the stylized, symbolic depictions of children on parents' (particularly mothers') tombs and the realistic portraiture common on monuments for children themselves. If the Caryll tomb stresses dynastic identity on the one hand, and the affective ties between family members on the other, early-seventeenth-century monuments tend to replace representations of dynastic relations with those of domestic bonds. The connections between family members thus become more accessible in visual and emotional terms through images, inscriptions, and expressions that recast the public, social aspects of family identity as private, domestic affairs. This turn toward domestic intimacy is evident in the subgenre of tombs for women who died in childbirth, which gained popularity in the second decade of the seventeenth century. Nicholas Stone's monument to Arthur and Elizabeth Coke, erected in St. Mary's, Bramford, following Arthur's death in 1629 (Fig. 1.2), employs this strategy of supplanting public matters and relationships with private. Elizabeth's reclining effigy appears on an alabaster slab decorated to represent a bed, holding in her arms the profoundly swaddled form of a newborn. The impersonal, generic quality of the child's effigy stands in stark contrast to the highly refined portrait of its mother. As Judith Hurtig has shown, infant effigies on the tombs of women who died in childbirth take a deliberately stylized form which allows them to serve the conventional function of naming the cause of the subject's death.[12] By incorporating the appearance of the childbed/deathbed into the form of the altar tomb, the Coke tomb and similar monuments recreate the intimacy of the domestic setting in the public space of commemoration. In doing so, they shift attention away from the horizon of social relations, with its concern for the record-keeping

---

[11]   Quoted in Mosse, *Monumental Effigies*, 151.

[12]   Judith W. Hurtig, "Death in Childbirth: Seventeenth Century English Tombs and their Place in Contemporary Thought," *Art Bulletin* 65:4 (December 1983): 603–15.

Fig. 1.2   Nicholas Stone, Monument for Arthur and Elizabeth Coke. St. Mary's, Bramfield (Suffolk), after 1629. Author photo.

function of monuments in documenting ruptures in the dynastic continuum, toward affective bonds within families, where the deaths of mothers and children exact an emotional toll on survivors. The visual remnant of the domestic sphere in these tombs reflects the notional equivalency of the bed and the grave. This equation is voiced, for instance, in the first-person epitaph of Maria Lusher in St. Mary's, Putney, as she asks her second husband to be buried beside her (her first husband already having been interred on the other side): "You once were second to my bed;/ Why may you not like title have,/ To this my second bed, the Grave?"[13]

Confronting the stylized infant effigies on tombs such as Elizabeth Coke's, it is not difficult to assume (as critics such as Lawrence Stone and Philippe Ariès have famously maintained) that early modern parents may have limited their emotional investment in newborn children in light of the high rate of infant mortality in the period.[14] An awareness of the stylized representations of these symbolic forms, however, discounts that assumption: responding directly to Stone's thesis, Hurtig argues that the proliferation of monuments for mothers dying in childbed reflects an increased adoption of the model of companionate marriage advocated by Protestant writers in the early seventeenth century, and a concomitant elevation in "the importance and value placed upon women as wives and mothers."[15] What is clearly also at issue in these tombs, iconographically, is a willingness to encode dynastic concerns within public representations of domestic roles and relationships.

---

[13]   See Stowe, *Survey*, 784–6. Mary also wrote the epitaph for Richard Lusher's monument, near her own. Her ledger stone was rediscovered when the church was excavated in 1973. See also Henry Montagu, *Contemplatio Mortis et Immortalitatis* (London: Robert Barker, 1631), 68, discussed below. Wilson, "Holy Innocents," 57, notes the related "idea of the cradle as prefiguring the coffin," which informs Colt's rendering of Sophia Stuart's tomb, discussed below.

[14]   See Lawrence Stone, *The Family, Sex and Marriage in England, 1500–1800* (New York: Harper & Row, 1979) and Philippe Ariès, *Centuries of Childhood: A Social History of Family Life*, trans. Robert Baldick (New York: Knopf, 1962).

[15]   Hurtig, "Death in Childbirth," 615.

The changing artistic conventions of monumental forms both respond to and foster changes in perceptions of the interplay between dynastic and domestic values and their defining influence on the roles of parents and children within the family.

The thesis of parental indifference to child-loss is also deeply shaken when one compares the stylized effigies on maternal tombs with other monuments from the same decade, where the recorded devastation of husbands and fathers following the deaths of wives and children is heartfelt and profound. On a monument in St. Mary's, Battersea, Daniel Caldwall commemorates his wife, Elizabeth (d. 1620), who died in childbed at age 23, and also writes mournfully of the loss of his children:

> This stone doth tell, the Children and the Mother,
> That liv'd and dy'd all in one yeere together:
> The children first Death did deprive of life,
> Yet stai'd not there, but tooke away the Wife.
> Insatiate Death, not with the Fruit content
> But thy last malice on the Tree hast spent.

The monument for 25-year-old Elizabeth Bayly, erected in Lambeth Church by her husband, John, in 1629, also offers a textual equivalent to the Coke monument and gives voice to the sorrow attending the deaths of children, as well as mothers, in childbed:

> Reader tread soft, under thy Foot doth lye,
> A Mother buried with her Progeny:
> Two Females and a Male, the last a Sonne,
> Who with his Life, his Mother's Thred hath spun,
> His Breath her Death procur'd (unhappy Sinne,
> That thus our Joy with Sorrow ushers in.)
> Yet he being loth to leave so kind a Mother,
> Changes this Life to meet her in another.
> The Daughters first were robb'd of vital Breath,
> The Mother next in Strength of Yeeres met Death,
> The Father's only Joy, a hopeful Sonne,
> Did lose his Life when Life was scarce begun ...
> A Husband's Love, a Father's Piety,
> Dedicates this unto their Memory:
> And when he hath his Debt to Nature paid,
> In the same Grave himself will then be laid,
> That altogether, when the Trumpe shall sound,
> Husband, Wife, Children, may in Christ be found.[16]

In these stagings of the domestic tragedies wrought by the deaths of mothers and children, bereaved fathers mourn the losses of children who are not mere ciphers in the equation of dynastic identity, but are recalled as subjects in their

---

[16] Stowe, *Survey*, 792. The monument has not survived.

own right whose memories prompt loving, pious tributes. Sculptural equivalents of the lost children commemorated by John Bayly and Daniel Caldwall appear on the joint tomb of Sir Anthony Everard and his wife, Anne, at Great Waltham (Fig. 1.3). Erected by Anthony to commemorate the death of his wife, "six weeks after her lying-in" in December 1609, the tomb also remembers the three children who predeceased her, including the embracing infants indentified simply as "Anonymous and Richard."[17] The inscription goes on to report that Sir Anthony, "3 yeeres after hee had erected this monument of his deerely beloved wife," joined Anne in the grave in 1614, leaving behind him only one daughter and heir, Anne.

The increasingly lifelike, intimate, and interactive representation of children on the tombs of their parents prefigures the rise in the seventeenth century of monuments dedicated to lost children alone. In these works as a group, a foregrounding of domestic relations is also apparent. Maximilian Colt's monument for Sophia Stuart, daughter of James I and Anne of Denmark buried in Westminster Abbey after living only two days (Fig. 1.4), represents the child sleeping in her cradle, once again employing the conventional symbol for death in infancy also used on the Caryll monument. In the freestanding tomb, though, the translation of this symbolic form into three dimensions enables Colt to embody the brief life of the princess and to make a self-conscious comment upon the public presentation of family affairs. Details that underscore the private, personal aspects of the princess's birth and death are prominent in the account of her brief life:

> upon the 22nd day of June (being Sundaye) Anno 1606 betweene the howers of three and four of the clocke in the morninge … our gratious Queene Anne … was safely delivered of a Royall Daughter at Greenwich at his Majesties House there. The daye followinge being Mundaye the 23rd of the same month the Royal Babe growinge verye weake yt was baptized privately … by the name of Sophia … Allso the same nobell Infant beinge in thend overcome by the power of Death yealdid her sweete soule into the hands of the Holy geiver thereof, betweene the howers of 8 and 9 in the evening … Upon the 3rd day of August beinge Sundaye Anno 1606 the Queenes highnes was churched pryvatlye in her privie Chamber at Greenwich.[18]

The cradle comprising Sophia's tomb is turned away from visitors to the Abbey, so that the headboard becomes her tombstone, shielding her from the invasive public gaze. On the panel at her feet, unseen by visitors, Colt includes an inscription that reads, "Sophia, a royal rosebud, untimely plucked by death …/ torn from her

---

[17] For discussion, see Chancellor, *Ancient Sepulchral Monuments*, 249–58.

[18] Edward F. Rimbault, ed. *The Old Cheque-Book or Book of Remembrance of the Chapel Royal from 1561 to 1744* (London: Camden Society, 1872), 170–71. Only the infant's funeral was conducted with the pomp, somewhat incongruous to her age and sex, which marked it as a public, social event.

Fig. 1.3   Monument for Sir Anthony and Anne Everard, St. Mary and St. Lawrence, Great Waltham (Essex) (detail), 1609. Author photo.

parents to bloom afresh in the rose-garden of Christ."[19] Sophia's sleeping effigy bespeaks the privacy and intimacy of her birth and death, perceived as appropriate even to the royal family. Her death, though marked in the public forum, is experienced as a private sorrow.

The emergence of monuments for children in the seventeenth century suggests a growing perception of even very young children as subjects in their own right. John Nowel's monument for his son, Henry, in Holy Trinity, Minories, presents "a figure of a child" with an inscription recalling affectionately that the infant, born on July 23, 1598, and deceased "ex Atrophia" (from Atrophy) on August 4, 1599, was a boy of the best disposition ("optimae indolis puerulus"), born—like Virgil's Deiphobus—to a better fate ("Melioribus utere fatis").[20] The reimagining of

---

[19]   Quoted in and translated from the Latin by Joan D. Tanner, "Tombs of Royal Babies in Westminster Abbey," *Transactions of the British Archaeological Association*, 16 (1953), 38.

[20]   Stowe, *Survey*, 889. The allusion is to Virgil, *Aeneid*, 6:546; see Virgil, *Virgil, Volume I: Eclogues, Georgics, Aeneid Books I–VI*, H. Rushton Fairclough, ed. (Cambridge: Harvard University Press, 1916).

Fig. 1.4   Maximilian Colt, Monument for Princess Sophia Stuart, Westminster
                 Abbey (detail), 1606. © Dean and Chapter of Westminster.

dynastic relationships as domestic ones, evident in Nowel's memorial for his infant son and in Colt's monument for Princess Sophia, licenses a heightened emotional response to childhood death for the creators of monuments, and probably elicited similar responses from viewers, despite condemnations of excessive mourning by reformed clergy. Thomas Fuller, for instance, complains of Sophia's monument that "vulgar eyes, especially of the weaker sex, are more affected (as level to their cognizance, more capable of what is pretty than what is pompous) than with all the magnificent monuments in Westminster."[21] Fuller's rejection of the vulgarity of effusive sorrow typically genders that emotion as feminine,[22] and names the "prettiness" of the child's tomb as the chief feature prompting this emotion. His distinction between what is pretty and what is pompous condemns the material and affective preciousness of Colt's monument, casting preciousness as preciosity. The over-refinement of the monumental form and its metaphoric inscription, dedicated to a mere infant, appears to Fuller as an exercise in futility—a version of the vanity which Susanna Gray's parents intended their daughter's memorial to counter and dispel. Against this prettiness, Fuller sets the pomposity of the Abbey's "magnificent monuments"—the dignity and stately display that commemorates the heroic lives and deeds of adult men. Fuller's comments thoroughly reflect the gender divisions current in his culture: monuments that are pretty (diminutive, domestic, and emotionally evocative) are associated with the affairs of women, properly confined to the private sphere, while those that are pompous (grand, dynastic, and documentary) are resoundingly masculine, pronouncing and preserving actions performed in the public, political sphere.

Fuller's efforts to describe the deaths of infants and children as private, domestic affairs, and thereby to relegate them to the feminine realm, did little to abate the sorrows of parents, both male and female, confronting child-loss or to prevent the commemoration of these losses in monumental forms. Twenty-three years after completing Princess Sophia's monument, Maximilian Colt remembered his own daughter in an eloquent monument in St. Bartholomew the Great, London, carved "in the figure of a Rose" and reading simply:

Oritur & Moritur.
Here lyeth the body of *Abigall Coult*, the Daughter of *Maximilian Coult*, who departed this life the 19. day of March, 1629. in the 16. yeere of her Virginity.[23]

---

[21] Thomas Fuller, *The History of the Worthies*, P. Austin Nutall, ed. (London: Thomas Tegg, 1840), 2:129. See also Tanner, "Tombs," 38; and Llewellyn, "[An] Impe," 58.

[22] On excessive mourning as gendered feminine in post-Reformation England, see Patricia Phillippy, *Women, Death and Literature in Post-Reformation England* (Cambridge University Press, 2002).

[23] Stowe, *Survey*, 873. The monument has not survived.

"Blossomes yong and tender"

If, as Fuller maintains, children's tombs represent a detour from the path of dynastic commemoration—the legitimate purpose of "magnificent monuments"—into the feminized realm of domestic intimacy, one might expect women's monuments for their children to be especially demonstrative in their displays of grief.[24] While this is often true, these works also exhibit a self-conscious artistry that undermines an interpretation of their sentiments as unmediated, "raw" emotion. When Elizabeth Cooke Hoby Russell memorialized her two daughters, Anne and Elizabeth Hoby, who died at the ages of seven and nine with days of each other in February 1571, she gave voice to her overwhelming sorrow in an artful Latin epicedium inscribed within the engraved figure of a classical urn on their tomb in All Saints, Bisham.[25] Similarly, Constance Lucy was vocal and eloquent in commemorating her daughter and namesake, Constance, who died at the age of ten on February 14, 1596. As John Stowe reports, on "a Faire Marble stone in the Chancell" of Holy Trinity, Minories, a Latin elegy of ten lines accompanies "the Effigy of a Woman in Brass, praying." Playing on the Latin translations of her own and her daughter's name, Lady Lucy recalls the girl as "Ante annos Constans,/ humilis, mansueta, modesta" (Constant, humble, gentle and modest beyond her years), and employs the imagery of the faded flower, later used by Maximilian Colt, as an emblem of her loss:

> … flos formosissimus aret:
> Optima praetereunt, deteriora manent.
> Rapta immature fato, CONSTANTIA LUCY,
> Nunc jacet: & quondam lucida, luce caret.[26]
> [the most beautiful flower withers: the best passes away, and the worse remains.
> Constance Lucy, carried away unripe, now lies scattered; and shining once, now
> no longer shines.]

Although an inscription indentifies Constance as the eldest daughter of "D. Thomae Lucy Juni-/ oris, Militis Aurati, & D. Constantiae/ Uxoris" (the illustrious knight, Sir Thomas Lucy the younger and Lady Constance, his wife), the monument presents only one effigy, that of the mother kneeling in prayer. By casting the poem in the maternal voice, the monument presents a daughter's death chiefly as a maternal loss, and registers her value in the family primarily in affective terms.

---

[24] In general, the many female alliances commemorated in early modern funeral monuments suggest motives for memorial projects that extend beyond the advancement of dynastic reputation alone—a goal that has, traditionally, subordinated women's monumental works to the interests of fathers or husbands. See Patricia Phillippy, "'Herselfe livinge, to be pictured:' 'Monumental Circles' and Women's Self-Portraiture," in *The Palgrave History of British Women's Writing, 1610–1690*, Mihoko Suzuki, ed. (London: Palgrave Macmillan, 2010), 129–51.

[25] See Phillippy, *Women, Death and Literature*, 190–92; and Louise Schleiner, *Tudor and Stuart Women Writers* (Bloomington: Indiana University Press, 1994), 205–10.

[26] Stowe, *Survey*, 888. The monument has not survived. For discussion, see Phillippy, "Herselfe livinge, to be pictured," 139–46.

Constance Lucy's lament for the withering of a beautiful flower certainly conforms to Fuller's definition of "prettiness"—although the fact of its articulation in eloquent Latin verse shatters his condescending view of the "level of cognizance" of "the weaker sex." Monuments for children, more pressingly than those commemorating adults, meditate upon the fragility of the flesh and confront the troubling specter of futility in the too-swift passage from the cradle to the tomb—in Colt's phrase, "Oritur & Moritur," dead before life even begins. Inevitably, the most frequent figure for this collapse of birth and death is the fading flower.[27] In St. Mary's, Rotherhith, Nicholas and Elizabeth Reynolds commemorated three sons and two daughters (Brian, Richard, Mark, Alize, and Elizabeth)[28] with an inscription beginning hopefully, "Post tenebras, spero Lucem" (after the darkness, I hope for Light). The verses following stress the didactic lesson of the children's deaths for their elders, "the riper sort:"

> These Blossomes yong and tender, loe,
>   Blowne downe by deadly wind,
> May urge the riper sort to know,
>   Like blast shall them out find.
> For Flesh, as grasse, away doth wither,
>   No age can it eschew,
> The young and old decay together,
>   When death shall them pursue.
> No Parents, Friends, or Advocate,
>   Can him intreat to spare,
> The Faire, the Fine, or Delicate,
>   For threats he doth not care.[29]

Children of all ages, particularly female virgins, were compared to fallen flowers. When Margaret Radcliffe, maid of honor to Queen Elizabeth I, died at the age of 26 in 1599, her father erected a monument in St. Margaret's, Westminster, which complained:

> Here underneath entomb'd a Dazie lies,
> The pride of nature, with perfection fil'd;
> O woe, whom *Zephyres* blasts can ne'r make rise,
> Being by Deaths blacke storms untimely kild.[30]

Robert Herrick's epitaph for his niece, Elizabeth Herrick, inscribed on a tablet in St. Margaret's following her death in June 1630, became his first published poem

---

[27]   See Wilson, "Holy Innocents," 59–62, for some examples.

[28]   The monument does not give the ages of the children, but notes that the youngest (Elizabeth) was the last to die, in 1593, having already been married. It is likely, based on the imagery of the inscription, that some if not all of her siblings died young.

[29]   Stowe, *Survey*, 806.

[30]   Stowe, *Survey*, 812.

when it appeared in Stowe's *Survey of London* in 1633.[31] In this beautiful epitaph, Herrick complicates the common figure of the fallen child as a faded flower to comment on the value—or vanity—of funeral monuments as set against the loss inscribed within the hearts of mourners:

> In memory of the late deceased virgin
>   Mistris Elizabeth Hereicke
>
> Sweet Virgin, that I doe not set
> Thy Grave-verse up in mournfull Jet
> Or dapl'd Marble, let thy shade
> Not wrathful seeme, or fright the maid
> Who hither at her weeping howres
> Shall come to strew thy earth with flowres:
> No, know blest soule, when there's not one
> Remainder left of brasse or stone,
> Thy living Epitaph shall be
> Though lost in them yet found in me:
> Deare, in thy bed of Roses then,
> Till this world shall dissolve (as men)
> Sleepe, while we hide thee from the light,
> Drawing thy Curtains round—Good night.[32]

Even as he creates the "Grave-verse" inscribed on the marble of Elizabeth's monument, Herrick paradoxically rejects it in favor of the "living Epitaph" carried by the speaker himself which, he promises, will outlive "brasse or stone." Herrick aligns the precious body mourned with the costly materials of commemoration, but he transposes the qualities of transience and permanence adhering to flesh and stone: the monument, he maintains, is fleeting and ephemeral while the tribute of the mourning poet, with its figure of an Elizabeth sleeping rather than dead, will outlast time. The grave thus becomes a bed of roses upon which his niece lies sleeping, further strewn with the flowers—those of the mourning maidens who visit her grave and of the poet's epitaph itself. Herrick's final drawing of

---

[31]   See Tom Cain, "Herrick, Robert," *Oxford Dictionary of National Biography* (Oxford University Press, September, 2004); online edn, January, 2008, http://www.oxforddnb.com/view/article/13092.

[32]   Robert Herrick, "Upon his kinswoman Mistris Elizabeth Herrick," in *Hesperides, or, The Works both Humane & Divine of Robert Herrick, Esq.* (London: John Williams and Francis Eglesfield, 1648), 168. The inscription on the monument, which is extant, breaks each line of poetry after the second stressed foot and indents the remainder on the line below. These short lines are arranged in two columns. The tablet now bears a second inscription stating that, "this epitaph by Robert Herrick, formerly on a mural tablet in the middle of the north side of this church, was restored in memory of James Ramsey."

the curtain around this bed—the ultimate gesture of domestic intimacy—ensures Elizabeth's private, silent sleep until the Resurrection awakens her.[33]

In memorializing lost children, early modern monuments often employ the analogy at the heart of Herrick's epitaph between the precious materials with which they are constructed and the precious offspring whom they mourn. Two tombs sharing the commemorative theatre of Westminster Abbey with Colt's monument for Princess Sophia memorialize the loss of infants in forms that display this analogy (Fig. 1.5). The two pyramidal monuments stand near each other in St. Nicholas' Chapel. Both are constructed of black and white marble, the latter clearly built in imitation of and in conversation with the former. Anna Sophia (d. 1605), the infant daughter of the Christopher Harley, Count Beaumont, French ambassador to the court of James I, is commemorated with a white obelisk supported by a black cube resting on a white stone base. Nicholas Bagenall (d. 1688), son of Nicholas Bagenall of the Isle of Anglesey, "was born on the 31st day of/ December Anno Domini 1687/ And by his nurse unfortunately overlayd/ the 7th of March following."[34] The baby is remembered with a black marble pyramid above a white marble base. Both monuments are surmounted by urns, with that atop Anna Sophia's tomb containing her heart. In the same way that the heart is imagined as both the seat of the soul and synecdoche of the body, these small, costly, nonrepresentational forms serve as substitutes for the lost bodies of the precious children they recall. The absence of effigies on these tombs should not be construed as reflecting an absence of parental emotion or limit on the involvement of early modern parents with infant offspring. Colt's serene and lovely portrait of the two-day-old Sophia Stuart clearly demonstrates that even the youngest children made a lasting visual and emotional impression upon early modern parents. Parental love for children and the consequential sorrow at their deaths provide the motives for these monumental projects, and suggest a consolatory function that resides not in the religious or spiritual aspects of their textual elements—such sentiments are virtually absent from both of these tombs—but in the permanence and aesthetic pleasure of their beautiful forms.

The assertion that the nonrepresentational forms of the Harley and Bagenall monuments function as substitutes for the infant corpse, cast in material as precious but far more permanent than the child's body, finds support in the merger of effigial and nonrepresentational forms in William Wright's monument to Henry Montagu, erected by his parents in All Saints Church, Barnwell, around 1625 (Figs. 1.6 and 1.7). The son of Sidney and Paulina Montagu, the boy drowned at

---

[33]   Herrick's father's death by suicide in 1592 may have informed "an obsession with the proper rites of burial" that permeates his writing, and may be evident in his ambivalence about the permanence and legitimacy of funeral monuments in this poem: see Cain, "Herrick, Robert," in *OED*.

[34]   Inscription from the monument. See also John Dart, *Westmonasterium: Or the History and Antiquities of the Abbey Church of St. Peter's Westminster* (London: T. Bowles and J. Bowles, 1742), 1:142.

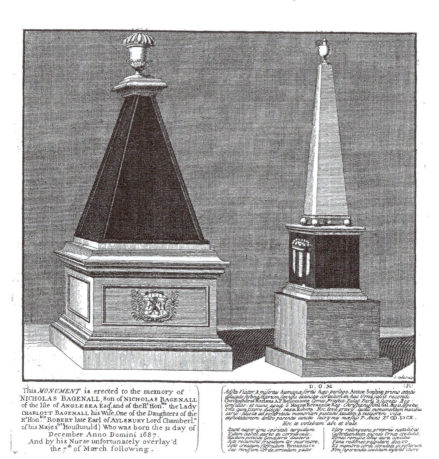

This *MONUMENT* is erected to the memory of
NICHOLAS BAGENALL, Son of NICHOLAS BAGENALL
of the Iſle of ANGLESEA Eſqᵈ and of theRᵗHonᵇˡᵉ the Lady
CHARLOTT BAGENALL his Wife, One of the Daughters of the
RᵗHonᵇˡᵉ ROBERT late Earl of AYLSBURY Lord Chamberlⁿ
of his Majeˢᵗⁱᵉˢ Houſhould) Who was born the 31 day of
December Anno Domini 1687.
And by his Nurse unfortunately overlay'd
the 7ᵗʰ of March following.

Fig. 1.5   Engraving of monuments to Nicholas Baganall and Anna Sophia,
St. Nicholas Chapel, Westminster Abbey, 1688 and 1605, from John
Dart, *Westmonasterium: Or the History and Antiquities of the Abbey
Church of St. Peter's Westminster*, 1742. © British Library Board,
shelfmark 689.ee.22.

the age of three. Like the infant memorials in St. Nicholas' Chapel, the Montagu monument is composed of an obelisk surmounting a square base and topped with an urn, but Wright places the effigy of the child within the obelisk itself. The precious material of the tomb thus enfolds and becomes the body of the departed child; the obelisk becomes his grave. The monument's inscription records the details of Henry's birth and death, and tells us that he was "tender and deere in the sight of his parents and much lamented by his friends."[35]

One such friend may have been the child's uncle, Henry Montagu, first Earl of Manchester, who shortly following the death of his nephew—and perhaps as a gesture of consolation to his grieving brother—wrote and published *Manchester al Mondo, Contemplatio Mortis & Immortalitatis*, one of the most popular treatises on the art of death of the period.[36] Published surreptitiously in 1631 from a circulating manuscript, *Manchester al Mondo* presents four meditations, "First, what Death was, and the kinds of death ... Secondly, what feares or joyes death brought ... Thirdly, when death was to be prepared for and how, [and] Fourthly death approaching, what our last thoughts should then be" (9). Comprised in equal parts of an *ars moriendi*, intended to instruct readers to die daily (96), and of a consolatory treatise, ensuring them of the certainty of life after death (121–2), the text offers a rationale for the lifelike portrait of the young Henry Montagu which appears on his monument. "Man is a future creature," his uncle writes, "his soule lookes at what is beyond this life" (24). There are three kinds of life and death, he reminds us: the death of the body, the separation of the body from the soul, and the reunion of the two at the end of the world. "Though the body sleepe a while in dust," Montagu insists, "yet shall it arise after thy likenesse" (20). To those who grieve, including the parents of his young nephew, Montagu's assurance of the Resurrection must have hit home:

> hee whom thou lovest, sleepeth, but thou wilt come to awake him: till then his couch of ease, is his coffin, the grave his bed, wherein he lies never troubled with dremes or fancies, what shall become of his body, till it rise againe. (68)

This confidence in the corporeal resurrection, in which the departed will assume the physical likenesses they bore in life, underwrites Wright's beautiful effigy of Henry Montagu. The effigy not only captures his appearance in life, but also anticipates his presence and likeness at the Resurrection. Accordingly, the base of the pedestal on which the effigy stands is decorated with waves, recalling the boy's death by drowning but also imagining his spiritual resurrection, guaranteed by baptism, in the upright effigy that appears to walk, like Christ, on water.

---

[35] Inscription from the monument.

[36] Henry Montagu, *Contemplatio Mortis et Immortalitatis* (London: Robert Barker, 1631). All subsequent citations are to this edition and appear parenthetically. The text went through 15 impressions by 1688: see "Introduction," in John E. Bailey, ed., *Manchester al Mondo* (London: Pickering and Co., 1880).

Fig. 1.6   William Wright, Monument for Henry Montagu, All Saints, Barnwell (Northamptonshire), 1625. Author photo.

Fig. 1.7   Monument for Henry Montagu (detail). Author photo.

"The Comfortable Farewell"

Stowe's *Survey of London* describes a monument, now lost, which once hung on a pillar in the middle aisle of St. Dustan-in-the-West, London. On "a faire Table in Glasse" was inscribed "The comfortable farewell of a young Infant, sighed out in his dying sicknesse, to his mournefull Parents." An epitaph at the poem's close gives the speaker's name (Simon), suggesting that this is the child's recorded, rather than imagined, deathbed speech—an incongruous one, since his description as "a young infant" seems to imply that he was too young to have spoken at his death. Preserved and now emanating from beyond the grave, Simon's calm voice consoles his own parents and others confronting the loss of their children:

> Let not my Father greeve, or Mother moane,
> That I this wretched world have soone forgone,
> Better I dye before I doe amisse,
> Than live to sinne, and be bereft of blisse;
> All I can now be charg'd with at the Tribunall Throne,
> Is sinne originall, for actuall I have none:
> And that I know my Saviour with his blood
> Hath washt away, and made my badnesse good.
> And cause I know (though knowledge I have small)
> That Jesus Christ did dye to save us all,
> I passe with joy, in Heaven to meet my King,
> With Angels and Archangels there to sing.
> Then Father mourne, and Mother weepe no more,
> I now dye rich, that might have liv'd but poore;
> For had I progrest unto mans estate,
> It is not certaine what would be my state:
> Whether a Crosse, or Blessing I should prove ...
> Yes, yes, I might perhaps have beene a slave,
> And kil'd your hearts with care, and dig'd your grave.
> But now my silly Dove-like soule doth part,
> In peace of God, and love of Parents heart;
> Sweet Innocence, my shield, I beare in hand,
> To guard me towards that most holy Land,
> Where Parents both, and Sister I shall see,
> In Gods appointed time triumphantly.
> Till then Adieu, sweet Parents, Jehovah calls away,
> My name is *Simon*, and I must obey.[37]

The ascent of the infant's dovelike soul and the assurance that his "Sweet Innocence" will earn him a place in paradise promise to comfort parents who,

---

[37] Stowe, *Survey*, 879–80. I am not aware of any freestanding glass monuments that survive from this period, although a number of monumental stained glass windows do remain. See, for example, the Hoby window in All Saints, Bisham, and the small stained glass memorial for John Donne in the chapel at Lincoln's Inn, London.

had their child lived, might have faced the uncertainty of his salvation or, worse, the fear of his damnation.[38] This remarkable speech becomes more remarkable, and more poignant, when we imagine it in its original form, inscribed upon a vulnerable pane of glass suspended above the stone floor of St. Dustan's middle aisle. The clarity of the infant's dying vision is figured in the medium in which it is conveyed. So, too, is the fragility of his young life. We can almost see his soul's ascent to heaven as a flash of light shimmering across the surface of the monumental glass, as easily as we can picture his death in the sudden crash of that same monument to the floor below.

Poised between the past which they recall and record and the future which they seek to control and embrace, early modern funeral monuments bespeak the fragility and transience of affective ties, but also attest to their resiliency. As they gesture toward a posterity to whom their family portraits offer traces of now absent ancestors, and also imagine a moment beyond posterity, when severed bonds are repaired in the Resurrection, these monumental works attest to their authors' confidence in the permanence of family relationships. They provide evidence to contemporary viewers of the depth of emotion experienced by many early modern parents for children, both living and dead, and they represent a valuable resource for the future work of excavating the subtle and intractable history of the emotions in early modern England.

---

[38] On the emphasis on children's innocence in the period, see Wilson, "Holy Innocents."

Chapter 2
Parents, Children, and Responses to Death in Dream Structures in Early Modern England[1]

Carole Levin

A sixteenth-century English dream book, Thomas Hill's *The Pleasant Art of the Interpretation of Dreams*, recounts the following: "And one dreamed having thre sonnes, two of them cutte him into peeces and eate hym and that the yonger knowinge of the matter waxed sadde and disdayned them and refusinge also that shameful matter, sayde, I wil not eate of my father." In dreaming that his sons would dismember and devour him, the father betrays his great fear of their power over him. Even hundreds of years later, this account gives one a sense of horror, for patricide is considered one of the most heinous of all crimes, and the eating of human flesh is taboo in most cultures. More importantly, this dream reveals one of the most intense sites of cultural anxiety in early modern England: conflicts between parents and their children. The dream suggests the plot of *King Lear*, where Goneral and Regan symbolically consume their father and his lands first in their over-lavish praise of him and then once they have taken over the lands that he had foolishly given them, they cast him out. But in the dream the children are male and two of them forthrightly devour their father.

The interpretation of the dream also echoes the play: "After which it h[a]ppened that his yonger soune dyed: for it signifyed by not eatyng of the father, that he should not possesse of the fathers goodes, & he also died before the father. But the other two which semed to eate hym did after death enjoy his goodes."[2] In Shakespeare's play, the children are female, and the two older sisters use flattery and pretense to get what they want, only later moving to the violence they feel

---

[1]   Much of the work of this essay was accomplished during a fellowship at the Folger Shakespeare Library and I am very grateful. Paul Hammer and Jo Carney read this essay in draft and I greatly appreciate their very helpful suggestions.

[2]   Thomas Hill, *The Pleasant Art of the Interpretation of Dreams* (London: Thomas Marsh, 1576), n.p. There are no page numbers in this edition of Hill. Though Hill does not include this in his book, in another section of Artemidorus from where this dream is detailed, he writes: "I have learned from experience that the best and most auspicious dream by far is one in which a person eats human flesh," though he goes on to say that it most unlucky to dream one eats one's own children, and nothing about being consumed by one's children. *The Interpretation of Dreams: Oneirocritica* by Artemidorus, trans. and commentary by Robert J. White (Torrance, CA: Original Books, Inc., 1990), 71, 72. The dream of the man consumed by his sons is on p. 240.

from the beginning. Cordelia had refused to participate in the fawning praise and received nothing from her father as a result just as the son who refused the gruesome practice of his brothers gains nothing but death from his virtuous decision. While the daughters of Lear are in the end destroyed by their own paternal violence, the dream interpretation leaves the devouring sons in triumph.

Yet another violent dream reported by Hill is of a poor man in a contentious relationship with his rich father. Hill assures any man who is poor with a rich father—and the manner in which the dream is recounted suggests there were many—that if he "dreameth that hee seethe his fathers head plucked up [by] a Lyon and to be deade," he will soon be able to "put away carefulnes and heavines of mynde and growe riche. ... For the heade, signifyeth the father and the plucking or drawing awaye the privation or deathe of the father, the Lyon, the sicknesse, by which the father sickninge shall dye of." With obvious satisfaction Hill avers that "he shal never be poore and nedie after." Arguments over money and inheritance resonated deeply in early modern culture, as both the intensity and ubiquity of accounts in the historical records makes clear.[3] However, while these dreams suggest significant fear and discord in the early modern family, dreams and historical accounts also include evidence of loyalty and love between parents and children, often expressed through grief over the death of a beloved family member.

In discussions of peoples in any historical period, one commonality is the recognition that people dreamed, and were concerned about the meanings of their dreams. In early modern England there were many interpretations regarding both the causes and significance of dreams and many texts offering means of interpretation. Dreams, and the manner in which they were viewed, allow us to understand more about the most significant and contested cultural issues of early modern England, one of which was the articulation of childhood and filial relationships.

In early modern England, dreams were explained in a variety of ways: some were considered natural, and were caused, for example, by eating the wrong foods; others were seen simply as fragments of the day retold. Others were seen as diabolic, perhaps the result of being bewitched, and still others might be the means by which God or the angels spoke to humans. Many believed that if one could only understand the symbolism, dreams foretold the future. Some believed that dreams held different meanings depending on one's humoral balance, astrological sign, social status, or marital status, or depending on the time of night or the time of the year in which the dream occurred. Some books dealing with the meaning of dreams were heavy tomes while others were brief broadsides; many of them

---

[3]   See for example, Barbara J. Harris, *English Aristocratic Women, 1450–1550: marriage and family, property and careers* (New York: Oxford University Press, 2002); Lawrence Stone, *The Crisis of the Aristocracy, 1558–1641* (Oxford: Clarendon Press, 1965); and Lawrence Stone and Jeanne C. Fawtier Stone, *An Open Elite: England, 1540–1800* (Oxford: Clarendon Press, 1965).

offered specific ways in which to interpret dreams. One such text was the one with which I began this essay, Hill's *The Pleasant Art of the Interpretations of Dreams*, based in part on Artemidorus's *Oneirocritica*, the ancient dream book from about 200 C.E. Hill's book was apparently widely read, or at least widely purchased; it went through seven editions between 1576 and 1626.

Thomas Hill, who described himself as a Londoner, made his living as a writer and translator, producing popular accessible books on science, conjuring tricks, and gardening, as well as on dreams.[4] Positioning his dream book as in part based on Artemidorus would give it more élan with readers concerned with showing their knowledge and appreciation of the classics, but Hill includes many examples that were not in Artemidorus's work; while the two dreams described above do appear in *Oneirocritica*, many other dreams in Hill's text do not, nor does Hill include all of Artemidorus's text. Hill's *The Pleasant Art of the Interpretations of Dreams* offers numerous dream interpretations, many of which deal with children or the relations between parents and children. Following the method of Artemidorus, Hill describes a dream and then offers its meaning, which is almost always the foretelling of some event, so that presumably if someone had a similar dream he or she would know what it portended. The structures of the dreams themselves, as well as the meanings that Hill ascribes to them, suggest that both women and men had highly conflicted attitudes toward their children, either potential or actual. Part of the anxiety about children expressed by the dreams Hill describes came from the danger of childbirth to women and from the high rate of infant and child mortality. As Sara Mendelson and Patricia Crawford so eloquently put it, "During every pregnancy, each woman feared her own death."[5] Furthermore, they feared the death of their babies. Between 20 and 50 percent of children born in the early modern period did not live to adulthood. Certainly, worry about children becoming ill or dying plagued parents not only when they were awake but also in their dreams. But dreams about children expressed other anxieties as well, dreams that also speak to the very strange dreamscape of early modern people. A number of men dreamed of themselves being pregnant; one of the strangest was that of "a certayne great wrastler [who] thought in his sleape to be greate with chylde, and after to be delivered of two blacke women children." As we have seen, dreams sometimes expressed not only fear for what might happen to one's children but fear of one's children as well and what they might mean in the dream as well. While some of the interpretations of the dreams sound rather mundane—the wrestler's dream, for example, meant that he would go blind, with each black child representing one eye going dark—the descriptions of the dreams themselves

---

[4]   For more on Hill, see F.R. Johnson, "Thomas Hill: an Elizabethan Huxley," *Huntington Library Quarterly*, 7 (1943–1944), 329–51, and Considine, "Hill, Thomas (c.1528–c.1574)," *Oxford Dictionary of National Biography* (Oxford University Press, 2004) [http://www.oxforddnb.com/view/article/13303, accessed 14 Dec 2006].

[5]   Sara Mendelson and Patricia Crawford, *Women in Early Modern England, 1550–1720* (Oxford: Clarendon Press, 1998), 152.

are strange and sometimes even horrifying. Hill's was one of the earliest printed English books on dream interpretation but many others followed, such as Thomas Tryon's *A Treatise on Dreams & Visions* and Marc Vulson's *A Court of Curiositie*.

In this essay I examine the meanings of several of Hill's dreams within the larger context of dreams parents actually had about their children, or children's actual dreams, sometimes about their parents. Because a number of Hill's accounts come from *Oneirocritica*, we cannot use them as evidence of actual people's dreams in early modern England. What can be said, however, given the popularity of the text, is that these descriptions may well have struck a nerve with the population reading Hill's text. Indeed, a number of actual early modern English dreams suggest serious anxiety, and not only over conflict about finances and inheritance. High mortality rates and religious change produced dreams that also reflected fear of loss and apprehension about salvation. But the described dreams of mothers and fathers often differed, just as the dreams about sons and daughters did. Differing gender roles and expectations played themselves out in the dream world just as they did in the waking one.

Dreams are not chosen but are beyond our control; for women, an even greater fear would be that their dreams could foretell or even cause harm to their children. Many believed that dreaming about a hare was unlucky and for a pregnant woman could cause the baby to born with a harelip.[6] Women were also warned when they were nursing their babies never to think about sexual relations, as "dreaming at night of that which their minds run on in the day, and by other filthy pollutions they infect the milk."[7]

Long before the early modern period, Artemidorus claimed that pregnant women often dreamed of dragons, which suggest some of the anxieties pregnant women must have felt, and indeed pregnant women in the pre-modern period had much to worry them. As well as their own potential deaths, fear about the number of children who died in infancy was also expressed in women's dreams. Hill's tone in presenting the dreams is relatively matter-of-fact, but there is also an overlay of great sorrow, as many of the dream interpretations describe multiple infant deaths. One dream Hill related was a multiple birth: the woman "dreamed that she saw three proper ymages or formes in the Moone." Hill explained that later she gave birth to triplets, all girls, but they "dyed in the same moneth also, that they were borne. For those three images signified the doughters, whiche one circle compassed and contayned. ... And they lived no longer because the Moone perfourmeth her course in a monethes space." The survival of children born in multiple births must have been rare indeed in the pre-modern world. As Christopher Durstan points out in his discussion of early modern England, "any abnormal pregnancy or delivery [was]

---

[6]   Stephen Wilson, *The Magical Universe: Everyday Ritual and Magic in Pre-Modern Europe* (London and New York: Hambledon, 2000), 417.

[7]   J. Wolveridge, *Speculum tatricis* (1671), 144; cited in Audrey Eccles, *Obstetrics and Gynaecology in Tudor and Stuart England* (Kent, OH: Kent State University Press, 1982), 98.

potentially fatal for both mother and child."[8] But many women survived repeated normal pregnancies, only to have their infants die. "A certayne woman thoughte in her sleepe (whyche wished to have children) that shee sawe certayne midwives stoles in whiche women use to sitte, at the travayle of chylde, swymminge on the Sea." While pregnant at the time of the dream, she was "yet not made a mother by this, for that shee brought foorth seven children, one after the other and none of theym lived but dyed in their swathing clothes."

Pregnant women's dreams frequently reveal fear over the number of children who died in infancy. In 1651, Alice Wandesford married William Thornton. Alice was apparently quite reluctant to marry; she resented the restrictions of marriage and had witnessed her older sister dying in childbed. While her sister's fate did not overtake her, only three of the nine children born to Alice survived to adulthood. Alice described a dream she had during one of her pregnancies.

> I, being great with child, dreamed one night that I was laid in childe-bed, had the white sheete spread, and all over it was sprinkled with smale dropes of pure blood, as if it had bin dashed with one's hand, which so frighted me that I tould my aunt of it in the morning; but she putt it of as well as she could, and said dreams was not to be regarded; but I kept it in my mind till my child died. (123)

Interpretation of dreams about children in Hill's book most often relate to childhood illness or death: a woman's dreaming about her eyes could be perceived as a warning about her children. Eyes, with which we see the world, enable one of our most precious senses, but in the early modern period, as today, the eye represented not only actual vision but the potential of seeing what might happen. This motif also suggested how powerfully one might know something, seeing with one's own eyes; the eye could also view a mental landscape, be the bringer of memory. Before he ever encounters the ghost, Hamlet saw his father "in my mind's eye." With poor light, much fine work, and few glasses, many people also strained their eyes. One of Queen Elizabeth's letters to Robert Dudley mentions the pain she feels in one of her eyes. Hill warns his readers that if a woman were "to dreame that her eyes bee sore" it meant "that her children shalbee sicke after."

Hill narrates an even stranger dream: "And a certayne woman dreamed: that she thought shee had an eye in her ryght pap or brest: who had a sonne that shee dearelye loved, which not longe after lost, she muche wayled for." The image of one's eye on one's breast is certainly peculiar: a mother's breast served as the source of nourishment for her infant and was what most identified her as having tender qualities, as Lady Macbeth's forceful and horrific comment about murdering a child she would have nursed reminds us. It was also for the early moderns the seat of the affections and emotions, the repository of consciousness and secrets. We know that the eye was of great and grave importance, representing not only what one could actually see but spiritually perceive as well. And the loss of an eye

---

[8]   Christopher Durston, *The Family in the English Revolution* (Oxford: Basil Blackwell, Ltd., 1989), 110–11.

in the early modern period was a grave loss indeed. One might say "Look to the safety of your eye," as a way of warning someone to take great care. Thus to dream of an eye on one's body was of grave significance, and Hill warned that if someone "dreameth to have an eye in his shoulder," he would lose the shoulder. So that by the same reason the woman lost "not her brest but the like to the breast, her sonne."

But a father too might have a strange dream about his breast that would be a forewarning also about the death of sons. If a man dreamed that "hee hath eares of cornes growen or spring out of his brest," and then someone came up to him and plucked them off "as unseemelye to him there to growe," this meant he would father two "men chyldren," but "throough an evill calamitye and myshappe," both boys would be slain. The ears of corn represented the sons, their plucking off representing their early and violent deaths. While in the mother's dream there is simply pain for the loss of the son, in the father's the sons' deaths are specifically portrayed as brutal.

If some dreams suggest the pain mothers felt over the loss of children, and some dreams the conflicts between fathers and sons, other dreams suggest the loss a father might feel over the death of a daughter. While daughters were far less valued than sons, they were also far less threatening. Men's dreams about children's death suggest the great grief they also felt at the loss of a child. Hill reported that "a certayne man thought, beynge sent into a straunge countrye on message, that in his dream he was returned home agayne: and that his wyfe after standing by him to saye litle sweetynge is dead. Who not long after receyved letters from hys wyfe, that the yongest childe hee had was dead, which was a swete childe, & to be disyred and loved of every bodye."

If some parents had nightmares about the death of their children, others may have—even inadvertently—actually caused nightmares in their children. Folk and fairy tales, filled with terrifying creatures and events, were often told to adults and children alike as they sat around the fire on a cold evening. Children were often frightened of ghosts and goblins to the point that it disturbed their sleep. Malcolm Gaskill suggests that children "soaked up stories, and not just improving fables but winter's tales of ghosts and witches, which invaded their dreams and shaped their perceptions."[9] In the fifteenth century a Bristol school-boy wrote that "Blodles and boneles stondyth by-hand the dore."[10] Sir William Cornwallis wrote in 1631 that "we heare from our nurses and olde women tales of Hobgoblins & deluding spirits that abuse travelers and cary them out of their way. We heare this when wee are children and laugh at it when we are men."[11] But given the vividness and horror of the described dreams, some men who had them were certainly not laughing.

---

[9]   Malcolm Gaskill, *Witchfinders: A Seventeenth-Century English Tragedy* (Cambridge: Harvard University Press, 2005), 12–13.

[10]   Nicholas Orme, *Education and Society in Medieval and Renaissance England* (London: Hambledon Press, 1989), 100.

[11]   Sir William Cornwallis the Younger. *Essayes*, Don Cameron Allen, ed. (Baltimore: Johns Hopkins University Press, 1946), 108.

We might wonder if Shakespeare is suggesting that Hamlet's doubts about the vision of the ghost of his father is partly motivated by an awareness that as an adult he ought not believe in such childish things, and that doing so in some sense infantilizes him.

Sometimes parents deliberately frightened children as a means of making them more obedient. Arthur Dent, writing in 1601, clearly thought this a positive approach, comparing the parent's behavior with God's: "Even as a mother when her childe is waywarde, threateneth to throwe it to the Woolfe, or scareth it with some pokar, or bull-beggar, to make it cling more unto her, and be quiet: So the Lorde oftentimes sheweth us the terrible faces of troubles and daungers, to make us cleave and cling faster unto him."[12] But others were aware that this method of obtaining good behavior might have other costs. Lewes Lavater wrote in 1572 that

> It is a common custome in many places, that at a certaine time of the yeare, one
> with a nette or visarde on his face maketh Children afrayde, to the ende that ever
> after they shoulde laboure and be obedient to their Parentes.

To press home the lesson, parents would assure their children that what they had seen were "Bugs, Witches and Hagges," creatures that commonly make children "miserablie afrayde." But Laventer did not consider it wise for parents to terrify their children into good behavior since some children "through great feare ... in the nyght crye out, when they are fast asleep."[13]

Pierre de Loyer's *A Treatise of Specters*, translated into English in 1605, makes a similar point. "Young children ... perswade themselves they see visions of Specters and Apparitions in the night, though indeede they see nothing ... feare wil make them to cover & hide themselves close under the cloths of their bed." It is little wonder that children have such nightmares: "And how can it be but that children should perswade themselves of such foolish imaginations and apprehensions in the night, seeing that even in the verie day time a man may make them to beleeve things meerely false as if they were true and certaine?" (105). Over a hundred years later Sir William Temple echoed this sentiment. "Tribe of Fairies, Elves, and Goblins, of Sprites and of Bul-beggars ... serve not only to fright Children into whatever their Nurses please, but sometimes, by lasting Impressions, to disquiet the sleeps and the very Lives of Men and Women, till they grow to Years of Discretion."[14] Adam Fox argues that with such experiences

---

[12] Arthur Dent, *The Plaine Mans Pathway to Heaven Wherein every man may clearly see, whether he shall be saved or damned* (London: Imprinted for Robert Dexter, 1601), 123.

[13] Lewes Lavater, *Of Ghostes and Sprirites Walking By Nyght* (1572), edited with introduction and appendix by J. Dover Wilson and May Yardley (Oxford: University Press, 1929), 21.

[14] Sir William Temple, "Of Poetry" (1690), in *Critical Essays of the Seventeenth Century*, vol. III: 1685–1700, J.E. Spingam, ed. (Oxford: Clarendon Press, 1909), 96.

nightmares were common for children in early modern England, that many believed the "mare" was a goblin who sat on children in their sleep."[15]

Not only did children experience fearful dreams, but many of them had dreams that expressed sadness and grief over the death of parents or surrogate parents—grandparents or parents-in-law. Just as parents' fear of the death of children was manifest in their dreams, children similarly feared and mourned the death of parents. Many young people and adults dreamed about their parents' death; for the most part these dreams expressed a complicated mixture of worry, grief, or perhaps even guilt about the relationship.

In many cases, children and young adults dreamed about the death of a parent even while the parent was still alive. In the case of both William Lilly and Richard Kay, their feelings about religion and fear of damnation conflated with anxiety about their parents and their own responsibilities. Lilly wrote later that in 1618 when he was "in the sixteenth year of my age I was exceedingly troubled in my dreams concerning my salvation and damnation, and also concerning the safety and destruction of the souls of my father and mother; in the nights I frequently wept, prayed and mourned, for fear my sins might offend God."[16] Over a century later, Richard Kay was also deeply affected by the fear of damnation. As a young man in 1740 he dreamed that he "was shut up in Hell where I imagined I kept sinking in a dark and stenchy Place." Kay felt great confusion when he awoke from the dream. He then went down on his knees to give thanks to God "that it was but a Dream, that I was yet on praying Ground, and not shut up in Hell in that miserable helpless hopeless State that Devils and Damned Souls are in."[17] In the mid-seventeenth century, Philip Goodwin argued that God would give good men frightening dreams "for the correcting of some Sin which they have committed, or whereto they are enclined."[18] Like the young William Lilly, Kay was also deeply concerned about his parents. Three years previously, when he was 21, he dreamed that his father had died and the burden of caring for his mother and heading the household had fallen to him.

---

[15]   Adam Fox, *Oral and Literate Culture in England, 1500–1700* (Oxford: Clarendon Press, 2000), 195.

[16]   Elias Ashmole and William Lilly, *The Lives of those eminent Antiquaries Elias Ashmole, Esquires and Mr. William Lilly, written by themselves; containing first William Lilly's History of His life and Times, with Notes, by Mr. Ashmole: Secondly Lilly's Life and Death of Charles the First; and lastly, the Life of Elias Ashmole, Esquire, by Way of Diary. With Several Occasional Letters, edited by Charles Burman, Esquire* (London: T. Davies, 1784), 7.

[17]   Richard Kay, *The Diary of Richard Kay, 1716–51 of Baldingstone, near Bury: A Lancashire Doctor*, edited by Dr. W. Brockband and Rev. F. Kenworthy (Manchester: The Chetham Society, 1968), 39.

[18]   Philip Goodwin, *The mystery of dreames, historically discoursed* (London, 1658), 218.

> I thought that my dear Mother who, being but a Woman, was full of her Cares and Concerns, I imagined that I who was the Head and Hope of the Family was one that she had great Dependance upon, and in the midst of all these my Cares and Concerns which had been upon me but for ten Days or a Fortnight I fancy'd myself to be alone, weeping, bemoaning my Self in my present Condition, and lamenting my Father's Death.

Just as in the previous dream discussed, Kay awoke weeping and confused but then felt great relief when he realized it was "but a dream" (12). The dream suggests that Kay's relationship with his father was easier than the one with his mother, and he feared the responsibilities that would result from his father's death.

Neither Lilly nor Kay reported that dreaming of their parents' deaths were actually omens of their parents' imminent deaths; rather, they more clearly indicated fear of what their parents' deaths would mean about the roles they would need to assume. But as we have seen, dreams were often reported as prognostications, and dreams of parents' deaths were so reported in the early modern period.

In 1635 Thomas Heywood wrote that Alexander the Great, "a man knowne to be free from all superstition," one night dreamed that "hee saw his mothers funerals solemnised, being then a dayes journey distant thence: and waking, in great sorrow and many teares, hee told this apparition to divers of his Familiars and Friends." The very next day, Heywood assured his readers, news was brought to Alexander that "at the same houre of his Dreame his mother expired."[19] While it was certainly true that there was an extremely close bond between Alexander and his mother Olympias, she actually survived her son by seven years. The story, however, would have given great authority to the belief that a child would dream of the news of a parent's death just before he or she was informed of it.

And, indeed, a man with such a reputation for high intellect and rationality as Francis Bacon believed this was possible. Bacon argued that it was worthwhile to thoroughly inquire if close family relationships such as "parents, children," might allow someone to know about the death of someone to whom they had "secret passages of sympathy" either while awake or in a dream. Bacon had first-hand experience with the phenomenon: "I myself remember, that being in Paris, and my father dying in London, two or three days before my father's death I had a dream, which I told to divers English gentlemen, that my father's house in the country was plastered all over with black mortar."[20] Elias Ashmole recorded a similar experience about his much loved father-in-law, Sir William Dugdale, later in the seventeenth century. Like Bacon, his dream was also expressed by what happened to a house that had strong emotional connotations. On February 10, 1686, he recorded in his diary: "This morning I dreamed, that being at my

---

[19] Thomas Heywood, *The Hierarchie of the blessed Angells. Their names, orders and Offices. The fall of Lucifer with his Angells* (London: Printed by Adam Islip, 1635), 223.

[20] Francis Bacon, *The Works of Francis Bacon*, II, collected and edited by James Spedding, Robert Leslie Ellis, and Douglas Denon Heath (London: Longman and Co., 1857), 666–7.

old House in Sheere-Lane, the Side of the Garret seemed to totter and fall, in so much that I thought the House itself would presently fall down. This Afternoon, about one of the Clock, my Wife's Father, Sir William Dugdale, died."[21] The head of the household could be seen in dream imagery as quite literally the house. Furthermore, "house" had multiple meanings in early modern England, suggesting the physical dwelling, the people living in the house collectively, and the lineage of ancestors and descendents. While Bacon's and Ashmole's dreams express their grief and the dreams described by Hill of sons devouring their father or a poor man's father killed by a lion are antagonistic, all of them reinforce the fundamental connections between masculinity, personal identity, and property.

A particularly fascinating woman's dream reveals the connection between parents, lineage, and tangible representations but not property: in the seventeenth century, Agnes Beaumont had a dream about her dead father in which he was represented as a tree. The dream seems to result from a conflict prior to her father's death and accusations against Agnes after he died. When Agnes was 20, her nonconformist family heard John Bunyan preach; Agnes was so moved she joined a congregation Bunyan had started in Gamlingay. While her father turned against Bunyan, Agnes became a more and more enthusiastic follower. One Sunday in 1674 she begged the reluctant Bunyan until he agreed to let her ride behind him on his horse to service. Bunyan's hesitation is understandable, for they were seen and gossip concluded there was an improper relationship between them. Agnes's father was so angry that he locked her out of their home for two days. When she promised she would no longer go to meetings unless he explicitly agreed, her father relented and the two were reconciled. But that same night he died, with Agnes the only one in the house with him. W.R. Owens suggests that her father probably died of a heart attack.[22] The family lawyer, Mr. Feery, whom Agnes had refused to marry, got his revenge upon her for spurning him, however, by accusing her of murdering her father. Agnes's older brother called for a coroner's inquest, which cleared Agnes of any wrongdoing: had she been convicted, she would have been burned to death. Soon after Agnes dreamed that in her father's yard was an old, very fruitful apple tree.

> And one night, about the middle of the night, their came a very suddaine storm of wind, and blew this tree upp by the roots, and I was sorely troubled to see this tree soe suddenly blew downe. I run to it, as it lay upon the ground, to lift it upp, to have it grow in its place againe. I thought I see it turnd up by ye roots, and my thoughts Stood lifting at it as long as I had any strength, as it lay upon the ground, first at one Arme, then at another, but could not stir it out of its place to have it growe in its place againe; at last left it, to run to my Brothers to Call

---

[21]	Elias Ashmole, *Memoirs of the life of that learned antiquary, Elias Ashmole, Esq. Drawn up by himself by way of a diary* (London: J. Roberts, 1717), 76–7.

[22]	W.R. Owens, "Beaumont, Agnes (bap. 1652–d. 1720)," *Oxford Dictionary of National Biography* (Oxford University Press, 2004), http://www.oxforddnb.com/view/article/37168, accessed 20 Nov. 2006.

helpe to set this tree in its place againe. And I thought when my Brother and his men did Come, they could not make this grow in its place againe; and, oh, how troubled was I for this tree, and soe grieved that the wind should blow that tree downe and let others stand.[23]

Agnes herself understood that the tree in her dream represented her father, and that even her brother who was so helpful to her could not bring him back; as she explained in her autobiography she had the dream "after my father was ded." Agnes would have seen her father's strength and his providing for his family as a fruitful tree—indeed, early modern family trees were often literally drawn as such—but the conflict between father and daughter was such a harsh wind that it pulled the tree down. Agnes and her beloved brother were helpless in the dream to save the tree; clearly the conflicts between the two preceding her father's death—with the attendant emotions of guilt, trouble, and grief—were key to the dream.

Thomas Hill's popular book of dreams as well as recorded actual dreams of people of early modern England demonstrate how much family and death were both on the minds of individuals and at the center of the cultural milieu. Dreams hint at the anguish over losing a child before adulthood and the fear of the power of the surviving child. Dreams also delineate for us the pain and guilt that children felt in relationship with their parents. Yet if indeed there was conflict and tension between parent and children in early modern England that we can perceive from the dreamscapes of the period, recorded dreams also testify to the deep affection as well. In 1710 Lady Wentworth wrote to her absent son that "thees thre nights I have been much happyer then in the days, for I have dreamt I have been with you."[24]

---

[23] Agnes Beaumont, *The Narrative of the Persecution of Agnes Beaumont in 1674*, edited with an introduction by G.B. Harrison (New York: Richard R. Smith, Inc., 1930), 9–10.

[24] Patricia Crawford, "Women's Dreams in Early Modern England," *History Workshop Journal* 49 (2000), 135.

Chapter 3
Lost and Found:
Veronese's *Finding of Moses*

Naomi Yavneh

In the years leading to 1580, the Venetian painter Paolo Veronese painted several versions of the "Finding of Moses," perhaps most notably for the Holy Roman Emperor, Rudolph II, nephew of Philip II of Spain. (Fig. 3.1, Veronese, *Finding of Moses* [c. 1580]).[1] Although the bibliography regarding these works is sparse, Veronese's choice to depict the episode from Exodus has been viewed as the painter's response to post-Tridentine concerns over the propriety of the type of sensuous mythological studies that the artist had most recently been commissioned to create for Rudolph, such as the "Mars and Venus United by Love" (1576–1582) currently in the Metropolitan Museum in New York. Having spent eight years at the court of his uncle, the emperor sought to emulate Philip II's collection of Titians, based largely on Ovid's *Metamorphoses*, and so commissioned another Venetian artist known for his sumptuous use of color and attention to detail. As is well-known, Veronese had previously been brought before the Inquisition (1573) because of the perceived impropriety of many of the attendees represented in a version of the *Last Supper*; the dispute was resolved by renaming the work *Dinner in the House of Levi*, but the choice of an Old Testament narrative may reflect Veronese's attempt to achieve a middle ground by representing neither a classical subject that might be deemed too lascivious nor a New Testament subject whose depiction could prove too lively or secular for the censors. In W.R. Rearick's view, "the *Finding of Moses*, with its sumptuous princess, lavish court with dwarfs and dogs, charming baby and expansive river landscape" allowed the artist to create "a theatrical spectacle that is pagan in all but name."[2] Similarly, Giles Robertson describes another of Veronese's versions of the work—that in the Gemaeldegalerie, Dresden, as "a gay record of a contemporary picnic in fine modern clothes set in a local landscape, and the subject is but the excuse for this display of finery, as so often in his work, and as indeed, led him into trouble with the Inquisition on another occasion."[3]

---

[1]   The painting, 57 cm x 43 cm, is in the Prado Museum. Other versions include a similar-sized and similarly composed one in the Mellon collection of the National Gallery in Washington, and a slightly different work in the Gemaeldegalerie, Dresden.

[2]   W.R. Rearick, *The Art of Paolo Veronese, 1528–1588.* Washington: National Gallery of Art, and Cambridge, England: Cambridge University Press, 1988, 123.

[3]   "Tiepolo's and Veronese's *Finding of Moses.*" *The Burlington Magazine*, vol. 91, no. 553 (April, 1949), 100.

Fig. 3.1   Paolo Veronese, *Finding of Moses*, c. 1580. Prado Museum, Madrid.
             © Scala/Art Resource, NY.

Although such descriptions suggest *Finding of Moses* should be viewed as a mythology in biblical garb, this essay seeks to examine the image as the product of a Venetian artist, repeatedly depicting a story with resonance for the culture of that city in the second half of the sixteenth century. The contemporary court scene of lavish luxury and exoticism Veronese chooses to depict in his *Finding* is a specifically Venetian one, as emphasized by the subtly toned but clearly recognizable view of the city of Venice in the painting's middle-left background. As I shall argue below, the paradoxical salvation of a child through his abandonment would have particular significance in a city that prided itself upon its charitable institutions and whose foundling hospital and its denizens were a central part of both the physical and cultural landscape. Moreover, the dramatic rescue by a youthful princess of a seemingly cast-off baby *from the water* to assume a position of divinely ordained authority evokes the image of Venice itself, founded and flourishing under the protection of the virginal Queen of Heaven, Mary.

While the terms "child abandonment" and "infanticide" are often conflated in our own time, at least in intent, as well as in the horrified response such actions engender, John Boswell has argued that the demarcations between the two were much clearer throughout western antiquity and into the early modern period. In *The Kindness of Strangers*, Boswell defines abandonment as "voluntary relinquishing of control over children by their natal parents or guardians, whether by leaving them somewhere, selling them, or legally consigning authority to some other person or institution."[4] Even the ancient Greek and Latin terms, *ekthesis* and *expositio*, respectively, translate more accurately, according to Boswell, as "putting out" or "offering," as "exposition" rather than "exposure" (25), reflecting the hope—if not always the reality—that these children would be saved rather than harmed by such behavior.[5]

Boswell's reading of abandonment as the alternative to infanticide, of *expositio* as exposure to the "kindness of strangers" rather than to the elements, is suggestive for the Biblical episode commonly referred to as "the finding of Moses," in which Moses' mother paradoxically seeks to save her infant from drowning by carefully placing him in a watertight basket in the Nile. The story of the child's birth, placement in the bulrushes, and subsequent discovery by Pharaoh's daughter is recounted at the beginning of Exodus in the context of the enslavement of the Israelites and Pharoah's subsequent wrath at the Jews' ever-increasing numbers. When the Israelites continue to thrive despite the harsh labor imposed upon them, Pharaoh commands their midwives to kill all male babies born to the Hebrews, declaring, "When you serve as midwife to the Hebrew women, and see them upon

---

[4] John Boswell, *The Kindness of Strangers: the abandonment of children in Western Europe from late antiquity to the Renaissance* (New York: Pantheon Books, 1988), 24.

[5] Indeed, in Boswell's view, the "conflation of abandonment and infanticide not only obscures the history of the former, which was the *alternative* to infanticide in much of Europe, but also seriously blunts the possibility of accurate demographic assessment of the impact of either one" (44).

the birthstool, if it is a son, you shall kill him; but if it is a daughter, she shall live" (Ex. 1:16).[6] Fearing God more than Pharoah, however, the virtuous and quick-thinking midwives lie, telling the king that "the Hebrew women are not like the Egyptian women: they are vigorous and are delivered before the midwife comes to them" (Ex. 1:19). Although the midwives are rewarded by God, the threat to the Hebrew children remains: not to be thwarted, Pharoah commands *all his people*: Every son that is born to the Hebrews you shall cast into the Nile, but you shall let every daughter live" (I:22, emphasis mine).

Chapter II continues with the famous account of Moses in the Bulrushes:

> Now a man from the house of Levi went and took to wife a daughter of Levi. The woman conceived and bore a son; and when she saw that he was a goodly child, she hid him three months. And when she could hide him no longer she took for him a basket made of bulrushes and daubed it with bitumen and pitch; and she put the child in it and placed it among the reeds at the river's brink. And his sister stood at a distance, to know what would be done to him. Now the daughter of Pharoah came down to bathe at the river, and her maidens walked beside the river; she saw the basket among the reeds and sent her maid to fetch it. When she opened it she saw the child; and lo, the babe was crying. She took pity on him and said, "This is one of the Hebrews' children." Then his sister said to Pharoah's daughter, "Shall I go and call you a nurse from the Hebrew women to nurse the child for you?" And Pharoah's daughter said to her, "Go." So the girl went and called the child's mother. And Pharoah's daughter said to her, "Take this child away, and nurse him for me, and I will give you your wages." So the woman took the child and nursed him. And the child grew, and she brought him to Pharoah's daughter, and he became her son; and she named him Moses, for she said, "Because I drew him out of the water." (Ex. 2:1–10)

The story of the finding of Moses is a vivid set piece—a suspenseful drama that serves to establish the legitimacy of God's chosen prophet, dragged safe from a watery grave to be raised in the household of his enemy. In the ensuing narrative, he rejects his privileged upbringing in favor of his seemingly humble but divinely elect birthright so that he may conquer his people's oppressors and lead them to the Promised Land. Typologically, of course, Moses is a figure for Christ: his placement in the ark and consequent drawing out from the water—in contrast with the multiple sons of the Hebrews cast into it by Pharoah's order—prefigure the Flight into Egypt and Herod's Slaughter of the Innocents (Matt. 2:16, discussed below). Similarly, the river evokes the waters of baptism, as does the prophet's subsequent parting of the Red Sea, a miracle itself foreshadowed by the events under discussion here.

But although the parallels between Moses and Christ are rich and suggestive, it is the women of the story who create the narrative interest and who are the actors therein. As biblical commentators have noted, the story of the clever and

---

    6   All citations, unless otherwise noted, are from the Revised Standard Version (RSV), http://quod.lib.umich.edu/r/rsv/browse.html.

God-fearing midwives serves both to establish the conflict between the Egyptian king's evil designs and God's plan for his people[7] and to set up the miraculous salvation of God's prophet (by Pharaoh's own daughter) which will ultimately lead to the delivery of God's people and the destruction of the king himself. Moses himself, however, is not yet an actor. Just as the midwives (in a deception that becomes a commonplace for patristic discussions of mendacity[8]) lie to Pharoah, so Moses' mother Jocheved (whose lineage as a daughter of Levi as well as marriage to a Levi proleptically confirm her son's priestly caste[9]), despite the king's decree, hides her goodly son for three months—as long as she can, we are told.[10] Although the text does not explain why she cannot hide him longer, considerable detail (at least by biblical standards) is given to his placement in the river: "She took for him an ark of bulrushes, and daubed it with slime and with pitch; and put the child therein, and laid it in the flags by the river's brink" (Ex. 2:3). The New English Bible translation spells out for modern readers Jocheved's intention to make the ark "watertight with clay and tar"; while she follows the letter of the king's law by placing her son amidst the river's reeds, she pays close attention to his physical safety, underscoring the distinction between Pharaoh's infanticidal casting of newborn males in the Nile and her own purpose of salvation.[11] Indeed, the baby's sister, Miriam, stands watch, "to see what would be done to him."[12] As Boswell notes, like the stories of the sacrifice of Isaac (Gen. 22:1–24) and the Judgment of Solomon (1 Kings 3:16–28), the story of baby Moses conveys, "perhaps, the complementary notions that parental love is a great good, but not inherently incompatible with relinquishing a child." Indeed, God's salvific force appears most clearly in evidence when a parent is willing to do so.[13]

---

[7] Brevard S. Childs, *The Book of Exodus: A critical, theological commentary.* Philadelphia: Westminster Press, 1974, 14.

[8] See Augustine, *De mendacia* [On Lying], for example, http://www.newadvent.org/fathers/1312.htm.

[9] The distinctions setting apart the Levites and Cohanim are not established until later in Exodus, in chapter 28:1–4.

[10] Biblical time periods are often symbolic, rather than factual. "Three months" would presumably mark the moment of transition between the newborn period, when an infant might more easily be hidden, and the period when babies begins to engage more actively with the world around them.

[11] Such conduct is in keeping with the argument of Boswell distinguishing between exposure to kill and abandonment with the hope of being found.

[12] In the interest of clarity, I have provided the names by which Moses and his family members are called later in Exodus. In fact, all the characters are referred to by their familial relationships until Moses is named by Pharaoh's daughter in Exodus 2:10.

[13] In the sacrifice (or binding) of Isaac, Abraham is about to slay his child according to God's command, when God's angel draws the father's attention to a ram caught in a thicket. Solomon is able to identify the true mother of a baby claimed by two women when she offers the child to the other woman, rather than allow the king to divide him in two.

But in the unfolding of the text, Pharoah's daughter's arrival is a moment of intense, paratactically expressed suspense well-captured in the old JPS version: "And the daughter of Pharoah came down to bathe in the river; and her maidens walked along by the river-side; and she saw the ark among the flags, and sent her handmaid to fetch it. And she opened it, and saw it, even the child; and behold a boy that wept!" (2:5–6). What will be the response of the evil king's daughter to this crying baby? Will she recognize him as one of the Hebrew sons her father has commanded to be killed? And equally significantly, is she of the same stripe as her wicked progenitor?

Most fortunately, the daughter is not the father: "she had compassion on him," even as she recognizes that "This is one of the Hebrews' children" (2:6). Miriam's cunning response to Pharoah's daughter ultimately restores the baby to his mother's arms and breasts; asking Pharoah's daughter if she should go find a Hebrew wet nurse, she returns with her mother, who will now be paid to suckle her own child. The significance of this maternal suckling seems underscored by the repetition (emphasis is mine): "Shall I ... call you a *nurse* of the Hebrew women, that she may *nurse* the child for you?" (7); "Take this child ... and *nurse* it for me" (9); "and the woman took the child and *nursed* it" (10). Only after the boy is weaned is he brought to Pharoah's daughter; he becomes her adopted son in a pattern of transition that is repeated for other exemplary biblical children destined for greatness. For example, Hannah brings Samuel permanently to the temple after his weaning (1 Sam. 1:21–4), while in the New Testament Apocrypha, Anna and Joachim similarly dedicate the weaned Mary in a story that would be familiar to sixteenth-century Venetian viewers through Titian's painting of the subject in what is now the Accademia.[14]

Before the advent of refrigeration and formula, access to fresh breastmilk—whether from a wet nurse or the child's own mother—was literally a matter of life and death. Even if discovered by a welcoming family rather than wild animals, before damage from hypothermia or exposure might take its toll, an abandoned child was likely to die unless a human nurse could be found to suckle it. But the emphasis on Jocheved's nursing seems to go beyond the obvious need to provide sustenance or even dramatic irony; maternal nursing is a praised act of virtue and parental nurture in the Bible, as evidenced by, for example, the aged Sarah's suckling of Isaac (Gen. 21:17) and Hannah's of Samuel, another child, who, when weaned, is given into the Lord's service.

Maternal nursing also has a specific religious resonance in early modern Italy, where images of the *Madonna lactans* (breastfeeding Virgin) serve to underscore both the Virgin's humility and the humanity of her son,[15] reminding

---

[14]   Titian, *The Presentation of the Virgin at the Temple* (1539), Accademia, Venice.

[15]   See, among others, Margaret Miles, "The Virgin's One Bare Breast: Female Nudity and Religious Meaning in Tuscan Early Renaissance Culture," in *The Female Body in Western Culture*, Susan Suleiman, ed. (Cambridge: Harvard University Press, 1985), 193–208; Megan Holmes, "Disrobing the Virgin: The *Madonna* Lactans in Fifteenth-Century Florentine Art," in *Picturing Women in Renaissance and Baroque Italy*, Geraldine A. Johnson

the viewer of the intercessory natures of both Mother and Child. Although the representation of the nursing Madonna had largely fallen out of fashion by the mid-sixteenth century, lactation continues to function as an iconographic signifier of *caritas* or charity, a concept central to the ideology of both Catholicism and the Venetian Republic.

The associations of maternal nursing were almost exclusively positive in the early modern period, even if the practice was not at all as widespread as treatises and advice books might suggest. Such works insist upon the infinite superiority of mother's milk, not only from the perspective of bonding and nurture[16] but because of the potentially damaging effects of imbibing the inferior qualities of an ignorant and inferior wet nurse. According to humoral theory, milk is but a whitened form of the blood that nourished the child in utero; just as that blood has formed the fetus, influencing the baby's corporeal and emotional development before birth, so the milk continues to shape the child both physically and morally after, for the child takes on the qualities of his nurse. In a lengthy discussion typical of such works, the Venetian humanist Francesco Barbaro, for example, "begs and exhorts the most noble women to [feed] her infant her own milk, for it is very important that an infant should be nourished by the same mother in whose womb and by whose blood he was conceived." He continues, explaining that, "the power of the mother's food most effectively lends itself to shaping the properties of body and mind to the character of the seed."

As in similar exhortations to maternal breastfeeding, Barbaro concedes that this best-case scenario may not be possible, and gives advice for the selection of a nurse:

> But if, as often happens, mothers cannot for compelling reasons suckle their own children, they ought to place them with good nurses, not with slaves, strangers, or drunken and unchaste women ... [By giving] their infants to the care of those who are freeborn, well mannered and especially those endowed with dignified speech," children "will not imbibe corrupt habits and words and will not receive, with [their] milk, baseness, faults, and impure infirmities and thus be infected with a dangerous degenerative disease in mind and body. (223)

---

and Sara F. Matthews Grieco, eds (Cambridge and New York: Cambridge University Press, 1997), 167–95; Naomi Yavneh, "Sofonisba Anguissola's Nursing Madonna," in Naomi J. Miller and Naomi Yavneh, eds, *Maternal Measures: Figuring caregiving in the early modern period* (Aldershot: Ashgate Press, 2000), 69.

[16]   Cf. Francesco Barbaro, *On Wifely Duties* (*On Marriage*, Book 2): "the special care and diligence of Nature can be observed, for while she has placed the nipples of other animals under their stomachs, in women she has affixed them on their breasts so that they may feed their children milk and fondle them with embraces at the same time, kiss them easily and comfortably, and, as they say, receive them to their bosoms" (221–2). Edited and translated Benjamin G. Kohl and Ronald G. Witt, with Elizabeth B. Welles, *The Earthly Republic: Italian Humanists on Government and Society* (Philadelphia: University of Pennsylvania Press, 1978).

Certainly such admonitions would enhance the significance of a narrative in which maternal breastfeeding, as we have seen, plays such a crucial role. Indeed, the medieval Jewish commentator Rashi asserts that Moses' sister asks about a nurse of the Hebrews because Pharaoh's daughter "had handed him to many Egyptian women to suckle him and he had refused to take suck—this was because he was destined to hold converse with the Shechina."[17]

Beyond the focus on the source of his physical nourishment, the orchestrated abandonment of the child has cultural resonance in a city where elaborate and costly lying-in ceremonies, along with the vociferous exhortations to maternal breastfeeding rarely heeded by the patrician class, coexisted with publicly supported institutions for abandoned children. Boswell's discussion of *expositio* makes clear that the practice was not new in the early modern period: it was frequent enough for the ancient Israelites that Ezekiel uses the metaphor of an abandoned daughter rescued, espoused, and bearing children by God to describe the relationship between God and his chosen people[18] and the practice was commonplace from classical antiquity onward. Indeed, child abandonment was so familiar to patristic writers that Tertullian, for example, used fear of having sex with one's own child as reason enough to avoid brothels.[19]

In Renaissance Venice, as in other Italian cities, illegitimate children as well as babies whose families were unable to care for or support them, were brought to a foundling hospital; at the Ospedale della Pietà (located minutes from the Piazza San Marco in the heart of the city), unwanted babies could be placed anonymously in a revolving drawer that would carry the infant into the safety of the convent without requiring the abandoner even to show his or her own face. Often, tokens suggesting the identity of the child would be left as well, in the hope of a future reunion between parent and child, and sometimes salt, to demonstrate that the child had not yet been baptized. The poignancy of Miriam's watch over her brother and her quick proposal of her own mother as wet nurse would not have been lost on a society in which abandoned children were a fixture: children from the Pietà would be seen as part of processions on Holy Days, while the musicians of its *cori*

---

[17]   *Chumash with Targum Onkelos, Haphtaroth and Rashi's commentary.* Translated and annotated by A.M. Silbermann with M. Rosenbaum. Jerusalem: Silbermann Family and Routledge & Keagan Paul, 1934, v. 2, p. 7.

[18]   Ezekiel 16:4–5: "And as for thy nativity, in the day thou wast born thy navel was not cut, neither wast thou washed in water to supple thee; thou wast not salted at all, nor swaddled at all ... but thou wast cast out in the open field, to the loathing of thy person, in the day that thou wast born." See Boswell, 146.

[19]   You expose your children, in the first place, to be rescued by the kindness of passing strangers, or abandon them to be adopted by better parents. Naturally, the memory of the cast-off relation dissipates in time, and ... in some place—at home, abroad, in a foreign land—with lust, whose realms are universal, as your companion, you easily fix unknowingly somewhere upon a child or some other relation ... and do not realize the encounter was incestuous. We are preserved from this sort of thing by the most diligent and faithful chastity ..." (cited in Boswell, 159). Justin Martyr and others also make this objection.

performed publically throughout the year.[20] One of the greatest expenses of the Pietà was in fact the payment of *balie*, wet nurses who would suckle one or more abandoned babies either on the premises or as foster children in their own homes; indeed, Brian Pullan notes that in 1559, the Pietà was responsible for paying *balie* for the care and nourishment of 1200 foundlings.[21] Jocheved's nursing of her own child might have evoked the image—possibly an urban legend—of women too poor to support their children, who abandoned their own newborns, only to have themselves rehired as the children's wet nurses.

Yet in the Catholic context of post-Tridentine Venice, the "Finding of Moses" is more than just a story from the Hebrew Bible; its typological resonance reconfigures the Jewishness of the Hebrew characters involved. As mentioned previously, the evil Egyptian king prefigures the equally pernicious Herod, king of the Jews. As opposed to the clever midwives of Exodus, the King of Matthew's Gospel tricks another type of birth attendant, the magi—kings themselves in tradition, if not in the Bible—who are going to view the child, by demanding that they reveal to him the child's location, so that "I too may come and worship him" (Matt. 2:8). As the reader knows and the magi discern in a dream, Herod plans not to adore but to destroy "the child born to be king of the Jews"; Joseph, warned in a dream of his own, flees with Mary and Jesus *to* Egypt. Herod, meanwhile, "when he saw that he had been tricked by the wise men, was in a furious rage, and he sent and killed all the male children in Bethlehem and in all that region who were two years old or under" (Matt. 2:16). This "massacre of the innocents," graphically depicted by Renaissance artists such as Veronese's contemporary, Tintoretto,[22] is explicitly described as fulfilling Jeremiah's prophetic description of "Rachel weeping for her children" (Jer. 31:15), but also evokes the newborn Hebrew boys of Exodus 1:22, thrown into the Nile.[23]

---

[20]   As Jane L. Baldauf-Berdes comments, the musicians of the Pietà "fit into Venice's social policy" by following a heavy public performance schedule throughout the year and "fulfill[ing] commitments to benefactors' legacies, such as singing anniversary masses and litanies, in a spiritual insurance system by which the state relied on its women musicians to pay for its social policies ... Cast as the angelic musicians of Christian symbolism, the chaste women musicians enhanced Venice's own methodically self-made mythology by serving as representatives of the chaste city of Venice." "Anna Maria della Pietà: The woman musician of Venice personified." In *Cecilia reclaimed: feminist perspectives on gender and music,* Susan C. Cook and Judy S. Tsou, ed. (Champaign: University of Illinois Press, 1994), 145.

[21]   Brian Pullan, *Rich and Poor in Renaissance Venice: The Social Institutions of a Catholic State, to 1620* (Cambridge: Harvard University Press, 1971), 207.

[22]   Tintoretto, *The Massacre of the Innocents*, 1582–1587, oil on canvas, Scuola Grande di San Rocco, Venice.

[23]   It is probably not coincidental that the only New Testament reference to the finding of Moses is found in the Pauline Epistle to the Hebrews—another text concerned with Christ as the fulfillment of the Old Testament—in a passage emphasizing the Christian theological virtue of Faith through the evidence of the Hebrew patriarchs and prophets: "By faith Moses, when he was born, was hid for three months by his parents, because they saw that the child was beautiful; and they were not afraid of the king's edict" (Hebrews 11:23).

The story of the three magi, celebrated in the feast of the Epiphany as the Revelation of Christ to the Gentiles, is recounted only in Matthew, whose most "Jewish" of the Gospels is structured to emphasize Jesus' status as the fulfillment of the Hebrew Bible's predictions of a coming Messiah. In this recasting of Moses' birth—to which Matthew never explicitly refers—God's chosen people the Hebrews are replaced by God's chosen people the Church of the Gentiles, seen through a Christian lens as the corrective to the blind and stiff-necked Jews who live by the Law rather than the Spirit.[24]

Viewed from this typological perspective, the role of Pharoah's daughter takes on greater prominence. According to Origen, Pharaoh's daughter can be viewed as "the Church which is gathered from the Gentiles." In such a reading, "This Church ... coming from the Gentiles finds Moses in the marsh lying cast off by his own people and exposed, and gives him out to be reared. He is reared by his own family and spends his childhood there. When, however, 'he has grown stronger,' he is brought to her and adopted as a son. We have already frequently argued in many places that the Law is referred to as Moses. The Church, therefore, coming to the waters of baptism, also took up the Law."

In such a context, weaning takes on a new meaning. The Hebrew text celebrates Pharaoh's daughter for her compassion and generosity both in saving Moses and restoring him—albeit unknowingly—to the maternal bosom, but the patristic exegetical tradition places her above both mother and sister, associated not with the childish milk (to use Paul's terminology) associated with those "unskilled in the word righteousness," but with the "solid food" of the mature, "who," we learn in Hebrews 5, "have their faculties trained by practice to distinguish good from evil" (Heb. 5:13–14).[25]

In this reading, Moses' placement in the ark is not protection but abjection: "The Law, therefore, was lying helpless enclosed in coverings of this kind, besmeared with pitch and bitumen. It was dirty and enclosed in cheap and offensive meanings of the Jews until the Church should come from the Gentiles and take it up from the muddy and marshy places and appropriate it to itself within courts of wisdom and royal houses. This Law, however, spends its childhood with its own people. With those who are not able to understand it spiritually it is little, an infant, and has milk

---

The next passage continues, "By faith Moses, when he was grown up, refused to be called the son of Pharaoh's daughter, choosing rather to share ill-treatment with the people of God than to enjoy the fleeting pleasures of sin."

[24]   Childs draws attention to the "polemical note" in the New Testament's use of Moses' story: "The pattern of the threat remained the same. The child of promise is endangered; the Gentiles announce and welcome his coming. But in the New Testament, the threat no longer comes from the pagan king of a hostile empire but from Herod, the king of the Jews. The Messiah of God has forced a wedge into the solidarity of the chosen people. Christ calls forth his most bitter opposition from within his own people" (Childs, 25).

[25]   The Christian exegetic tradition of Psalm 131 (Vulgate 130): 2 is also relevant here: "Surely I have behaved and quieted myself,/ as a child that is weaned of his mother: my soul *is* even as a weaned child" [sicut ablactatus ad matrem suam ita ablactata ad me anima mea].

as its food. But when Moses comes to the Church, when he enters the house of the Church, he grows stronger and more robust. For when the veil of the letter is removed 'perfect and solid food' [Heb. 5:12–14] is discovered in its text."[26]

This allegorical reading places us in a better position to read Veronese's painting. A courtly group of the princess and her attendants has left the city, seen in the mid-left background, to gather by the river, although no visible accoutrements suggest a bathing plan is in the offing. The most prominent figure is Pharoah's daughter, slightly to the right of the work's center, a young Venetian noblewoman, with elaborately coiffed blond hair and the large pearls that were a distinguishing feature of patrician dress. She stands slightly right of center, illuminated by a light that appears to come from above and in front of her. To her right a blond handmaiden upon whom she leans turns toward her, gesturing toward the baby, while another handmaiden similarly appears to be directing the attention of a bearded dwarf. To her left, an older, darker woman is holding up the white cloth that appears to have covered the naked Moses, who is displayed upside down from the viewer's perspective, his eyes clearly directed at the beautiful princess who returns his gaze. Although the baby's face is not clearly visible, due to his position, his body and brow are illuminated by the same light that catches the face and breast of Pharoah's daughter, and the similar fair skin tone and blond curls of the baby, along with his upward direct gaze, link princess and child as the central figures in the work. The older woman has been referred to by Rearick as another maid, but her dress, coloring, hairstyle, age, and appearance clearly distinguish her from the blond, elegantly dressed and groomed young attendants of Pharoah's daughter, suggesting that she is in fact Moses' mother.

Despite the baby's resemblance to the princess, that the woman is Moses' mother is supported by the presence at the central vertical axis of the painting of a younger, darker girl, her face—like the older woman's—in shadow, placed between Jocheved and Pharoah's daughter. This should be Miriam, the guardian of her brother and go-between for foster-mother and wet nurse/birth mother.

With her blond hair, rich gown, and extensive retinue—including a male dwarf and a male African amongst the ladies—Pharoah's daughter appears as the quintessential princess of any Venetian mythology. In fact, in many ways she resembles the heroine of, among other such works, Veronese's own *Rape of Europa*, now in the National Gallery in London (Fig. 3.2). In that Ovidian narrative we again find a princess and her retinue going down to the river to bathe; in the classical story, however, instead of finding a baby in a basket to raise as her own, the maiden is herself discovered by a god in bull's clothing, who playfully lures Europa to climb on to his back and then swims out to sea with her. The end result is not a chosen foster child sent back to its mother to nurse in a kind of "virgin birth" but the princess's rape and the consequent birth of Minos, destined for a less salubrious sort of "greatness." This far darker side to the story appears largely

[26] Origen, *Homily on Exodus.* In Ronald E. Heine, trans. *Homilies on Genesis and Exodus by Origen.* Washington, DC: Catholic University of America Press, 1982.

Fig. 3.2   Paolo Veronese, *The Rape of Europa*, c. 1570. © National Gallery, London/Art Resource, NY.

Fig. 3.3   Titian, *The Rape of Europa*, 1559–1562. The Yorck Project, http://
             commons.wikimedia.org/wiki/Commons:10,000_paintings_from_
             Directmedia.

absent from Veronese's visual representation thereof, but is thematically central to
the version by Titian now in the Isabella Gardner Museum in Boston (Fig. 3.3),
in which we find the anguished princess mid-sea, visually violated by *putti* on all
sides and proleptically positioned both for the rape to come and the birth to follow.
While the underlying violence of the Titian mythology seems incompatible with
the celebratory tone of the Exodus text as well as its salvation-oriented Christian
allegory, the birth posture of Titian's Europa serves to link her with Veronese's
Pharoah's daughter. Not only does the swath of fabric along the lower portion
of the princess's abdomen in the Veronese work give her the appearance of
pregnancy, the right hand supporting her back and left arm leaning upon her maid
evoke images of women in labor supported by companions. Pharaoh's daughter
may be the foster mother, but she looks like a typical patrician Venetian woman
whose baby almost certainly would be suckled by a wet nurse. Following Origen's
writings, in which the Law is rescued from the dirty trappings of the Letter and
raised in the Spirit by righteous Gentiles, the "drab and dingy" mother is contrasted
with the noble woman, representative in her dress as well as in the landscape
and cityscape in the background of the most Serene Republic, itself born of—or
rescued from—the sea.

The contrast between the two women's distinctive roles is suggested by their
near alignment with two trees, apparently branching out from a common base—
one with white leaves associated with the dark woman (the letter) and a living
tree with green leaves which seems to be growing out of the top of Pharaoh's
daughter's head (the spirit). While the Jews are in darkness, both Moses and the
Princess share in the illumination that is the gift of the spirit.

The typological dimension may also illuminate the presence of the dark dwarf
and the African. The connection between the slaying of the Hebrew boys in Exodus
and the massacre of the innocents in Matthew draws, as we have seen, an implicit

connection between the finding of Moses by Pharaoh's daughter and the Adoration of the Kings. Visually, the gathering around the baby in Veronese's painting (Fig. 3.4) evokes the iconography of such "Adorations," a popular subject throughout the Renaissance, when the subject of Christ's Revelation to the Gentiles becomes a vehicle to display the increasingly opulent retinues of luxuriously appointed kings, often portrayed as patrons or local dignitaries. Particularly significant for our discussion is the iconography of the magus or king, Balthasar, generally represented as African.[27] Although the black male in the lower left of the Moses painting is a servant rather than a king, his presence, bearing the ark from which the baby has been removed for display, is evocative of the later Gospel episode prefigured by the Exodus narrative, when the child will be displayed to the kings, and, by extension, the people of all nations.

Displayed by his own self-effacing and Jewish mother, Moses is "revealed" to the Gentiles, including the Princess who is herself thus linked iconographically as well as typologically with those New Testament Gentile royals, the wise men. With Venice illuminated in the background under the quintessential Venetian sky, it is clear that the abandoned child has been revealed to *la Serenissima*, as well, underscoring the Republic's role as a pious and elect City of God.

---

[27]   See , for example, Veronese's *Adoration of the Kings* (1573), located in the National Gallery in London, and his similar work of 1570, located in the Hermitage. For a discussion of the representation of the black magus, and of the blacks in Renaissance art, see Jean Devisse and Michel Mollat, *The Image of the Black in Western Art. Vol. II: From the Early Christian Era to the "Age of Discovery", Part 2: Africans in the Christian Ordinance of the World.* Trans. William Granger Ryan. New York: William Morrow and Company, 1979.

Fig. 3.4   Paolo Veronese, *The Adoration of the Kings*, 1573. © National
             Gallery, London/Art Resource, NY.

Chapter 4
"Certein childeplayes remembred by the fayre ladies": Girls and Their Games

Katherine R. Larson

In a letter written to her uncle in December 1603, Arabella Stuart concludes her description of the court's New Year's preparations with an account of the games she played with Queen Anna and her companions:

> Whilest I was at Winchester theare weare certein childeplayes remembred by the fayre ladies. Viz. I pray my Lord give me a Course in your park. Rise pig and go. One peny follow me. etc. and when I camm to Court they weare <as> highly in request as ever cracking of nuts was. so I was by the mistresse of the Revelles not onely compelled to play at I knew not what for till that day I never heard of a play called Fier. but even perswaded by the princely example I saw to play the childe againe.[1]

Picking up on Stuart's evident reluctance to participate in the games, critics have dismissed the "childeplayes" she describes as frivolous pastimes. One especially scathing assessment concludes that the queen and her ladies were "reduced to play at all sorts of childish games, to enliven the long November evenings." This scornful reading relegates the games to the province of children and implies, by extension, that they are not worth taking seriously. Why would adults condescend to play such "babyish" sports unless they were truly "oppressed with ennui, in the antique palace of Winchester?"[2]

Stuart's tantalizing allusions to a range of games popular among children in England in the sixteenth and seventeenth centuries, coupled with her surprise at being "compelled" to participate in these activities at court, can be explained in part by the timing of her letter. In the autumn of 1603, the queen acquired custody of her eldest son, Henry, then nine years old. His presence at court may well have contributed to an increased focus on childish sports.[3] Stuart is ultimately persuaded "by the princely example"—perhaps the sight of the playful young Henry—to join in the games. She goes so far as to depict her own ludic experience as a return to her

---

[1]   Arabella Stuart, *The Letters of Lady Arabella Stuart*, Sara Jayne Steen, ed. (New York and London, 1994), 193.

[2]   Agnes Strickland, *Lives of the Queens of England*, vol. 7 (London, 1844), 418.

[3]   I am grateful to Leeds Barroll for this observation.

girlhood, as she "play[s] the childe againe." The childish pastimes Stuart describes, however, which are typically played "from .10. of the clocke at night till .2. or .3. in the morning," are intimately bound up with the "confusion of Imbassages" that dominate her report: New Year's gifts planned and exchanged, audiences requested with the king and queen, and "sumptuous dinner[s]" held for aristocratic visitors and foreign ambassadors.[4] Moreover, the ladies, led by a "mistresse of the Revelles," take a prominent and active role in the sports, directing games "remembred" from their youth. Such "childeplayes," therefore, were far from trivial and demand to be considered alongside the masques and entertainments that played a strategic and authorizing role within the queen's circle.[5]

Stuart's letter raises compelling questions about the gendering of childhood pastimes in the early modern period and the political and cultural significance for women of such seemingly childish activities when they are "remembred" and replayed at court. In what follows, I will examine the function and the gendering of children's games and probe the interplay between "childeplayes" and adult pastimes in the early modern context. In the second part of the essay, I will explore how Lady Mary Wroth appropriates childish sports and ludic conventions in *The Countesse of Montgomery's Urania* and *Pamphilia to Amphilanthus* (pub. 1621) to illustrate how women used "childeplayes" not only for entertainment and solace but also as a means to negotiate the complex social realm of the Jacobean court.

Although a growing body of scholarship has helped to illuminate the rich variety of childhood and adolescent experiences in early modern England, surprisingly little attention has been paid to the recreations of girls and the gendering of games. Part of the challenge of recovering girls' games lies in the "elastic"[6] notion of early modern childhood, an experience shaped as much by social class and geographical location as by gender and age, as well as girlhood's disruption of gender categories in the period.[7] Any assessment of girlish pastimes is further complicated by what Kate Chedgzoy has called the "inherently evanescent" nature

---

[4]   Ibid., 192–3.

[5]   See Leeds Barroll, *Anna of Denmark, Queen of England: A Cultural Biography* (Philadelphia, 2001); Clare McManus, ed., *Women and Culture at the Courts of the Stuart Queens* (Houndmills, 2003); Barbara K. Lewalski, "Anne of Denmark and the Subversions of Masquing," *Criticism* 35.3 (Summer 1993): 341–56; Clare McManus, *Women on the Renaissance Stage: Anna of Denmark and Female Masquing in the Stuart Court 1590–1619* (Manchester, 2002); Louise Schleiner, *Tudor and Stuart Women Writers* (Bloomington, 1994), 107–49.

[6]   Carol Chillington Rutter, *Shakespeare and Child's Play: Performing Lost Boys on Stage and Screen* (London and New York, 2007), xiv.

[7]   Jennifer Higginbotham, *Fair Maids and Golden Girls: Early Modern Girlhood and the Production of Femininity*, PhD Diss., University of Pennsylvania, 2007. See also Deanne Williams, "Girls Own Shakespeare," paper presented at the Toronto Renaissance and Reformation Colloquium, University of Toronto, November 30, 2006.

of games and play.[8] An astonishing wealth of traces testifies to the spectrum of early modern childhood entertainments: toys, letters, diaries, autobiographies, woodcuts, portraits, plays and masques, conduct manuals, and games handbooks. To catch glimpses of young women at leisure, one has only to think of Mary Wroth's juvenile musical activities, Anne Clifford's recollections in her diary of "barley break upon the bowling green," the dramatic collaborations of Jane Cavendish and Elizabeth Brackley, or Margaret Cavendish's "Baby-Books."[9] Yet play is finally ephemeral, the product and the practice of bodies moving within specific spatial and temporal boundaries that are, in many cases, governed by rules that hold only for the duration of a particular game.

Early modern theories of play tend to script and contain girls' behavior and, as such, tell only part of the story of these lively bodies. Such discourses do, however, help to capture the moral and didactic ramifications of play in the period. If the "trew use of play," as John Harington defines it in *A Treatise on Playe* (c. 1596), is to "recreat the speryts," such pastimes always exist in tension with the more "seryows and wayghty matters" facilitated by games.[10] Pedagogical treatises insist on the value and efficiency of play in childhood education. Erasmus urges instructors to bake cookies and carve toys in the shape of letters to provide incentives for their young charges to learn the alphabet, which can be memorized "in a few days of fun and play."[11] While such "playful methods"[12] made learning more pleasant, play also provided a crucial forum for children to experiment with the skills and roles that would prepare them for adulthood.

Such role-play was decidedly gendered. In *Basilikon Doron* (1599), James I encourages Henry to practice outdoor "exercises of the bodie," albeit in moderation, thus "enabling you for your office, for the which ye are ordained."[13] Thomas Heywood's account of Queen Elizabeth's childhood, in contrast, differentiates her activities from her brother's: "when [Edward] was cal'd out to any youthfull exercise becomming a Child of his age (for study without action breedes dulnesse) she in her private Chamber betooke her selfe to her Lute or violl, and (wearyed

---

[8] Kate Chedgzoy, "Introduction: 'What, are they children?'" in Kate Chedgzoy, Susanne Greenhalgh, and Robert Shaughnessy, eds, *Shakespeare and Childhood* (Cambridge, 2007), 26.

[9] Anne Clifford, *The Memoir of 1603 and The Diary of 1616–1619*, Katherine O. Acheson, ed. (Peterborough, 2007), 137, 131; Margaret Cavendish, Duchess of Newcastle, *Sociable Letters*, James Fitzmaurice, ed. (Peterborough, 2004), 188.

[10] Sir John Harington, *A Treatise on Playe*, in Henry Harington and Thomas Park, eds, *Nugae Antiquae*, vol. 1 (London, 1804), 202.

[11] Desiderius Erasmus, "A Declamation on the Subject of Early Liberal Education for Children," in J.K. Sowards, ed., *Collected Works of Erasmus*, vol. 26 (Toronto, 1985), 339.

[12] Ibid., 340.

[13] James Rex, *Basilikon Doron*, in Charles Howard McIlwain, ed., *The Political Works of James I* (Cambridge, 1918), 48–9.

with that) to practise her needle."[14] Juan Luis Vives adds reading and the domestic tasks of spinning and cookery to his list of desirable "exercise[s]" for girls.[15] As Margaret Cavendish observes in her reflections on her childhood: "the breeding of men were after different manner of wayes from those of women."[16] To venture beyond such boundaries was to risk one's reputation. When Lala excitedly suggests boys' games like "Blow point" and "Span-counter" in response to the Prologue's announcement of "our best game" in William Hawkins's *Apollo Shroving* (1627), he mocks her, despite her evident age, for being a "Tomboy."[17]

The moral spectrum associated with games reinforced such divisions. The most convincing debates pitting "lawful" against "unlawful" sports in the period hinge on the character and station of one's playing companions and on the context, purpose, and duration of play rather than on the sports themselves. But writers still justified favored games in gendered terms, exemplified by Cavendish's insistence on the "Masculine" sports proper to a gentleman and Lawrence Humphrey's defense of "stouter and manlier" sports like "whirling, leaping, casting the darte, wrestling, [and] running" as "more commendable" for his male readers. Both contrast these pastimes with potentially effeminate recreations like "daunsing, fayninge to instrumentes, playe at dise, chesse, or tennes," which Humphrey dubiously labels the "other sorte" of play.[18]

As these examples suggest, the line dividing juvenile play from daily social performance was thin. Games both reflect and predict character: "If a person is prone to deceit, dishonesty, quarrelling, anger, violence, or arrogance," Erasmus cautions, "it is here that such flaws in his nature come to light."[19] By the time a gentleman has come of age, his skill and carriage in play stand as a marker of his civility and breeding. Vives, meanwhile, maintains that a girl's mental and physical pastimes should be strictly observed, since "she shall doe the same, when she is growne bigger and of more discretion."[20] He establishes a clear correlation between her daily "play & pastime" and the "playes and pastimes of her minde," both of which must be "set ... to honesty and vertue" and "rule[d] and measure[d]" by "her mother or her nurce, or some other honest woman of sadde age."[21] Lady Jane Grey provides some insight into the severity of such strictures when she laments that she

---

[14]   Thomas Heywood, *Englands Elizabeth* (London, 1631), 38–9.

[15]   Juan Luis Vives, *The Instruction of a Christian Woman* (London, 1585), 8–11, 15.

[16]   Margaret Cavendish, Duchess of Newcastle, *A True Relation of my Birth, Breeding, and Life*, in Sylvia Bowerbank and Sara Mendelson, eds, *Paper Bodies: A Margaret Cavendish Reader* (Peterborough, 2000), 43.

[17]   William Hawkins, *Apollo Shroving* (London, 1627), 5.

[18]   Margaret Cavendish, Duchess of Newcastle, *The Worlds Olio* (London, 1655), 63; Lawrence Humphrey, *The Nobles or of Nobilitye* (London, 1563), sigs. v.iiii.r–v.

[19]   Desiderius Erasmus, "On Good Manners for Boys," in J.K. Sowards, ed., *Collected Works of Erasmus*, vol. 25 (Toronto, 1985), 289.

[20]   Vives, 7.

[21]   Ibid., 5.

must sew, play, and dance "in such weight, measure, and number, even so perfectly as God made the world," or else face the condemnation of her parents.[22]

Play did not, of course, always take place under the watchful eye of tutors and parents, and it is in these freest moments that it assumed particular importance. While the gendered accounts of childhood activities outlined in early modern conduct literature placed strict boundaries on the kinds of activities appropriate for children, the practice and performance of play across social classes often went off-script. If games inculcated and reinforced social roles, they also provided a bounded space for the playful crossing of gender boundaries. Young women tended to be excluded from military sports like jousts and tournaments, but they often engaged in what Castiglione's Magnifico anxiously terms "robust and strenuous manly exercises."[23] "In my time," Cesare Gonzaga affirms in the same debate, "I have seen women play tennis, handle weapons, ride, hunt, and engage in nearly all the exercises that a cavalier can."[24] Joseph Strutt's account of English sports and pastimes features aristocratic women hunting, hawking, and partaking in other "masculine exercises," while village records attest to the popularity of "stoolball" and "running games" among maidservants and children at the end of the work day.[25] Young women enjoyed marbles, pick-up sticks, and drawing lots. They played a prominent role in games of confession and other *jeux d'esprit*.[26] And they could be found dancing and playing dice, chess, tables, cards, and "other sedentary games of chance and skill."[27] For John Harington, such recreation was crucial for physical and mental health and rejuvenation: "men cannot bee allways discowrsing, nor women always pricking in clowts; and therefore … it is not amisse to play at some sociable game."[28] Unusually, he extends his full list of pastimes—which includes dice, cards, tables, shooting, bowling, and tennis—to both genders.[29]

Pieter Bruegel's 1560 painting "Children's Games" provides visual insight into the breadth of juvenile games in the period and simultaneously confronts the viewer with the material and energetic bodies of these young people.[30] Girls at various stages of development are everywhere in Bruegel's painting, playing all

---

[22]   Qtd. in Anna K. Nardo, *The Ludic Self in Seventeenth-Century English Literature* (Albany, 1991), 40.

[23]   Baldesar Castiglione, *The Book of the Courtier*, Daniel Javitch, ed. (New York, 2002), 154.

[24]   Ibid., 153.

[25]   Joseph Strutt, *The Sports and Pastimes of the People of England* (London, 1801), 9; Paul Griffiths, *Youth and Authority: Formative Experiences in England 1560–1640* (Oxford, 1996), 133.

[26]   Jean-Michel Mehl, *Les jeux au royaume de France du XIIIᵉ au début du XVIᵉ siècle* (Paris, 1990), 216–17.

[27]   Strutt, liv; Mehl, 201.

[28]   Harington, 200.

[29]   Ibid., 189.

[30]   Pieter Bruegel, "Children's Games," Kunsthistorisches Museum, Vienna.

manner of games. A few sit in the foreground with a ball and jacks. Another group reenacts a wedding. Some girls play alone with dolls and musical instruments. Others play together with boys, spinning tops and joining in hide and seek and blindman's bluff. The immediate impression one has when first encountering Bruegel's visual encyclopedia of children's sports is of apparent chaos: a street and adjacent park packed with children running, chasing, competing, throwing, screaming, taunting, singing, climbing trees. Yet, whether they constitute imitations of adult activities and roles (the girls staging a wedding or the boys who have transformed a fencepost into a horse), competitive sports (tag, leapfrog, or blindman's bluff), or less formal ways of testing the limits of the body (balancing on a barrel, twirling in circles, or turning somersaults), each of the games depicted also operates within its own spatial and temporal boundaries and according to rules agreed upon by the participants.[31]

Games are highly organized activities whose imaginative structures bear marked resemblance to the hierarchies and roles grounding adult society. As François Lecercle maintains, "la société ludique forme une petite société imaginaire. C'est une microsociété régie par des règles nouvelles (celles du jeu) mais analogues aux règles sociales."[32] Whenever I play with my niece and nephew, I am reminded of the elaborateness and the precision of such rules, even if they are invented on the spot or represent significant variations from a previous incarnation of a game. Those rules must be understood and, as Johan Huizinga argues, "freely accepted" in order to be welcomed into a particular "play-ground."[33] Once within that space, the rules are "absolutely binding"[34] and hold until the boundaries of play have been dissolved. Punishments meted out for breaches of ludic decorum could themselves become brief games within the boundaries delimited by the larger sport.[35]

One allure of the game for both children and adults lies in the temporary release it provides from everyday relationships, responsibilities, and hierarchies. For children, subservient to adults in ordinary life, games offer a sanctioned space

---

[31]   My threefold categorization of children's sports follows Keith Thomas, "Children in Early Modern England," in Gillian Avery and Julia Briggs, eds, *Children and Children's Books: A Celebration of the Work of Iona and Peter Opie* (Oxford, 1989), 59–60. Alice Gomme provides a comprehensive list of sub-genres within her broader definitions of "dramatic games" and "games of skill and chance." See Alice Bertha Gomme, *The Traditional Games of England, Scotland, and Ireland*, vol. 2 (London, 1898), 460–70.

[32]   "The ludic framework generates a miniature imaginary society. This microsociety is governed by new rules (those of the game) which are nonetheless analogous to the rules governing everyday society" (my translation). François Lecercle, "La culture en jeu: Innocenzo Ringhieri et le pétrarquisme," in Philippe Ariès and Jean-Claude Margolin, eds, *Les jeux à la Renaissance* (Paris, 1982), 194.

[33]   Johan Huizinga, *Homo Ludens: A Study of the Play-Element in Culture* (Boston, 1950), 28, 10.

[34]   Ibid., 28.

[35]   See Charles Sorel, *La Maison des jeux*, Daniel A. Gajda, ed. (Geneva, 1977), 212–14; Strutt, 306.

in which to assume and experiment with social roles and to critique and even transform social mores. As Montaigne aptly notes, *"the playing of children is not really play, but is to be judged as their most serious actions."*[36] A preliminary game leading to the election of a leader or a ludic sovereign who will govern the ensuing activities often marks the entrance into the playing space. Children typically resort to hand gestures, rhymes, or other rituals to determine who is going to be "It" in a game of tag, but there is also evidence that they used more formal election processes. Selection of the ludic sovereign is a crucial part of the game of "Questions and Commands" that Strutt documents: "a king, elected by lot, commanded his comrades what they should perform."[37] Adults too are captivated by the suspension of ordinary identities and conventional hierarchical markers enabled by play. As the banquet begins in Book Four of Stefano Guazzo's *The Civile Conversation* (trans. 1586), Lord Vespasian renounces his rank to coincide with Lady Jane's election as queen of the games.[38]

For early modern adults, the function of the ensuing game and the roles assumed within it depended in part on the setting. Games could offer a nostalgic return to the perceived innocence of childhood and a pleasurable escape from everyday responsibilities. In other cases, however, and sometimes simultaneously, games could facilitate the negotiation of political or erotic relationships and create alternative avenues for agency.[39] As I have demonstrated elsewhere, the abdication of traditional hierarchical markers demanded by ludic contexts opened up important opportunities for women's participation, leadership, and speech that were not always confined solely to the ludic context.[40] Games provided "playgrounds"[41] for adults no less serious than the playing spaces of children.

Indeed, games can transcend limits of age as well as gender. The boundaries between children's games in the period and the leisure activities of older youth and adults were often difficult to determine. In *La Maison des jeux* (1657), Charles Sorel creates a separate category for children's games, which he calls "les premiers Jeux ... de mesme qu'ils sont pratiquez dans les premiers degrez de

---

[36]　Michel de Montaigne, "Of Custom," in Jacob Zeitlin, ed., *The Essays of Michel de Montaigne*, vol. 1 (New York, 1934), 94.

[37]　Strutt, 310.

[38]　Stefano Guazzo, *The Civile Conversation of M. Steeven Guazzo*, vol. 2 (New York, 1967), 121.

[39]　On the politics of games, see Leah S. Marcus, *The Politics of Mirth: Jonson, Herrick, Milton, Marvell, and the Defense of Old Holiday Pastimes* (Chicago, 1989); Nardo, *The Ludic Self*; and, more recently, Gregory M. Colón Semenza, *Sport, Politics, and Literature in the English Renaissance* (Newark, 2003).

[40]　Katherine R. Larson, "Conversational Games and the Articulation of Desire in Shakespeare's *Love's Labour's Lost* and Mary Wroth's *Love's Victory*," *English Literary Renaissance*, 40.2 (Spring 2010): 165–90.

[41]　Huizinga, 10.

nostre vie, & qu'ils servent à entretenir cét âge dans sa gayeté naturelle."[42] Toys like tops, balls, and kites feature prominently among these activities, as do tag and running games played with or without a blindfold. The bulk of Sorel's pastimes, however, fall into an ambiguous category, which he terms "Jeu meslez": mixed games. These activities are appropriate "autant aux enfans qu'à la jeunesse plus élevée, & mesmes aux personnes d'âge meur."[43] Witty *jeux d'esprit* and wordplay are common among these sports.

Sorel emphasizes that it is not so much the content of such games that is more "spirituels que ceux des petits enfans."[44] Rather, it is the "usage" of the game that changes. The function and the gravity of a game shift depending on the age, gender, and social status of its players and the context of play. Not all games are, of course, appropriate for children, while others are too "enfantins" (childish) for adolescent or adult players.[45] But Sorel's creation of the ambiguous category of "Jeu meslez" points to a slippage in ludic culture that makes it nearly impossible to assign many games exclusively to the sphere of either children or adults.[46] Indeed, several of the games Sorel includes in his list of "premiers Jeux" appear in accounts of adult Christmas pastimes at the English court, notably versions of tag and blindman's bluff. The games played by adults are always to some extent implicated in early modern "childeplayes."

The pastimes referenced in Arabella Stuart's letter encapsulate this ambiguity. "I pray my Lord give me a Course in your park," "Rise pig and go," "One peny follow me," and "Fier" constitute variants of popular children's games which could have been played by adults, children, or a combination of the two. Traces of these activities have been preserved in games handbooks and in the exhaustive studies of English pastimes undertaken by Alice Gomme and Joseph Strutt, which document the rules and scripts of a wide range of popular children's games in their most pervasive forms. The titles Stuart uses in her letter have not, to my knowledge, survived intact. Because many games circulated orally, the names attached to them varied, sometimes quite widely. "Fier," for example, which Stuart claims never to have heard of, could easily refer to a circle game like "Fire and No Smoke" or "Fire, Air, and Water."[47]

---

[42]   "first games, in that they are played during the first years of our lives and serve to maintain those at that stage in their natural gaity" (my translation). Sorel, 204–5. See also Francis Willughby, *Francis Willughby's Book of Games: A Seventeenth-Century Treatise on Sports, Games and Pastimes*, David Cram et al., eds (Aldershot, 2003), 187–94.

[43]   "both for children and for adolescents, and even for those of a more mature age" (my translation). Ibid., 208.

[44]   "challenging than those of small children" (my translation). Ibid.

[45]   Ibid., 207. On the distinct aspects of adolescent experiences in the period, see Ilana Krausman Ben-Amos, *Adolescence and Youth in Early Modern England* (New Haven, 1994); Griffiths, *Youth and Authority*.

[46]   See also Willughby, 251–2.

[47]   For descriptions of these games, see Gomme, vol. 1, 122; Willughby, 196.

"Rise pig and go" and "One peny follow me" have been more difficult to identify. Francis Lancelott helpfully includes "Rise pig and go" alongside "juvenile sports" like "Merry trotter" and "Run, bull, and fetch it," though without detailing the specifics of play.[48] A picture of young boys "tossing and swinging themselves upon a Merry-totter"—essentially a rope suspended from a branch or a beam to create a swing—appears in *Orbis Sensualium Pictus* (1659) with an illustration of other "Boyes-Sport[s]" like "scourging a Top" and "play[ing] ... with Bowling-stones."[49] Pennies and pigs crop up regularly in boys' games that require throwing marbles and stones at targets and spinning tops.[50] In the context of the court's New Year's activities, however, particularly given that the ladies were participating in and leading the sports, "Rise pig and go" and "One peny follow me" likely represented circle games. This hypothesis is reinforced not only by the motions of rising, following, and chasing implied by their titles, but also by the fact that the children's game "Pig in the Middle" was itself a variant of "Bull in the Park," which required the participant labeled the "Bull" to force his way out of the ring of players after asking a series of questions before being chased around the circle.[51]

Although Gomme notes that "the game of 'Course of the Park' has not been described,"[52] the recurrence of "parks" in circle games of the period connects "I pray my Lord give me a Course in your park" to a popular pastime known by several different names, including "Hunting a Deere in My Lords Park," "Drop Handkerchief," and "Kiss in the Ring." Variants are still extant. Players gather together in a circle holding hands, "their faces looking all towards the center." One player runs around the outside of the circle, "and gives some one of them a little tap, or lets fall a glove behind him or any other marke they agree upon. Hee that is thus touched, must bee let out of the circle, and must run after the other that touched him," with the goal of tagging that person before they make it around the circle. Crucially, the pursuer must follow the other player's moves exactly as he "leads him about the circle and crosse it, running under their armes backwards & forwards &c." If the chaser fails, "hee must bee imprisoned in the circle or Parke." If, however, the chaser catches up, it is the other player who is imprisoned. Player two then walks around the circle and selects an unsuspecting new companion. The "park" fills up with punished players, and the game ends when "the circle comes

---

[48] Francis Lancelott, *The Queens of England and Their Time* (New York, 1858), 663.

[49] J.A. Comenius, *Orbis Sensualium Pictus*, trans. Charles Hoole (London, 1659), 276–7.

[50] See, for example, the descriptions of "Peg-in-the-Ring," "Penny Cast," "Penny Prick," and "Pig-ring" in Gomme, vol. 2, 38–40. See also Willughby, 205. Strutt features marbles and tops in his account of "manly Pastimes imitated by Children" and records an anecdote in which Prince Henry determines to transform a "stack of corne in proportion not unlike to a topp wherewith he used to play" into a "goodly topp." Strutt, 300, 305.

[51] Gomme, vol. 1, 50–51. See also Iona and Peter Opie, *Children's Games in Street and Playground* (Oxford and New York, 1984), 237–9.

[52] Gomme, vol. 1, 81.

to bee so streight that it wont hold all the prisoners."[53] Some versions included rhymes, songs, or a series of questions.[54]

As the variant name "Kiss in the Ring" suggests, circle games like "I pray my Lord give me a Course in your park" often had a flirtatious context. In Gomme's account of "Kiss in the Ring," it is a kiss, rather than the prospect of imprisonment, that becomes the goal (or, depending on the perspective of the player, the punishment!).[55] Strutt draws attention to the erotic charge of the game, known in his account as "Cat after Mouse": "When this game is played by an equal number of boys and girls, a boy must touch a girl, and a girl a boy, and when either of them be caught they go into the middle of the ring and salute each other; hence is derived the name of kiss in the ring."[56] Circle games, which, like *jeux d'esprit*, often featured kisses as rewards and punishments, provide valuable evidence of the gendering of Stuart's "childeplayes" and are suggestive of the extent to which adults too could capitalize on the erotic context sanctioned by such sports. As the *OED* reminds us, the word "game" connoted not only "amusement, diversion, pastime," but also "[a]morous sport or play."[57]

Mary Wroth, a prominent member of Queen Anna's circle, participated actively in entertainments at the Jacobean court and would have been well acquainted with games like those Stuart describes. Her writings devote considerable attention to gendered pastimes and attest to the strategic potential of such activities for negotiating court relationships. Wroth situates her female protagonists as skilled players who derive authoritative subject positions from their recreations. In *Love's Victory* (c. 1619), Dalina and Musella preside over the games that form the structural backbone of the tragicomedy. The young women in *Urania*, meanwhile, participate in a wide range of sports: riding, hawking, hunting, walking, fishing, darts and archery, masques and dancing, drawing lots, storytelling and conversation, wordplay, and singing. Pamphilia herself is a formidable singer and a "harty hunteress" who was "so fond of that sport, as she loved it more then any delight."[58]

Wroth relies on these activities metaphorically to convey her protagonists' otherwise inexpressible emotions, as hunting blurs with the pain of "being hunted by afflictions" (1.181) and fishing prompts a meditation on the "smart of [Cupid's] hooke" (1.289). In many cases, moreover, games not only offer a vocabulary for representing intimate and painful experience, but also facilitate the disclosure of

---

[53] Willughby, 189–90.

[54] See Gomme, vol. 1, 109–12.

[55] Gomme, vol. 1, 305–10.

[56] Strutt, 302.

[57] *OED*, "game," *n.* I.3.a. and I.3.b.

[58] Lady Mary Wroth, *The First Part of the Countess of Montgomery's Urania*, Josephine Roberts, ed. (Tempe, 1995), 326; Lady Mary Wroth, *The Second Part of the Countess of Montgomery's Urania*, Josephine Roberts, ed., completed by Suzanne Gossett and Janel Mueller (Tempe, 1999), 394. Subsequent parenthetical references will be to these editions.

those thoughts and desires within Wroth's writings.[59] The "foolish sport" played by Alarina and her suitor in *Urania*, for example, which features details like the drawing of lots to determine the order of play and a ludic punishment, moves from Alarina's ambiguous statement, "I thought on him I loved" to a full confession of her affections: "''Twas you,' said I" (1.218–19).

Children's games constitute an important subset among these pastimes. Pamphilia confides that she has in her sadness "many houres sate looking on the fire, in it making as many sad bodies, as children do varietie of faces" (1.147), while the love-struck Leonius "start[s]" at the word of the shepherd youth "as children doe at Bugbeares" (1.429). Despite her interest in the leisure activities of young women, Wroth is rarely explicit in depicting girls at play. Instead, she devotes her most detailed explorations of "childeplayes" to boys' sports. She likens the "unguided" and "unrul'd" ship that Philarchos encounters to "the Boates boyes make of paper, and play withal upon little brookes" (1.534) and describes another "fine barck" interrupting the pastimes of six youths "sporting by the river side, playing with the water ... [and] catching little fish" (2.218). This attention to boys' play is to some degree related to the changing roles of her female protagonists, who join in "sporting" with boys in the second part of the romance in a maternal capacity (2.384, 2.305–6). These scenes, however, also reflect the tendency in the period of boys to be grouped with women as similarly feminized, eroticized, and subservient.[60]

Wroth uses these juvenile activities to explore the tyranny and cruelty that becomes integral to her depiction of the child-monarch Cupid. Despite their conventional association with "innosent and pretty" (2.218) activities, "childeplayes" can be startlingly violent. Think of Valeria's account of the young Martius "mammock[ing]" a "gilded butterfly" in *Coriolanus*.[61] Such sports, usually attributed to boys, are not uncommon in accounts of childhood play, where the line between amusement and torture can be thin.[62] Wroth's allusions to childhood sports do not shy away from this aspect of play. In Part Two of her romance, for instance, she develops an extended simile likening a growing company to boys striving to make the biggest snowball. Their competition has a sinister edge. Once the snowball has "come to the bignes of rolling itt furder, [it] must bee ther made like a trophy of their childish victory over the purly suffering

---

[59]   See Larson, "Conversational Games." On the importance of theatrical entertainments for Wroth, see Heather L. Weidemann, "Theatricality and Female Identity in Wroth's *Urania*," in Naomi J. Miller and Gary Waller, eds, *Reading Mary Wroth: Representing Alternatives in Early Modern England* (Knoxville, 1991), 191–209.

[60]   See Higginbotham, 3–4; Hattie Fletcher and Marianne Novy, "Father-Child Identification, Loss and Gender in Shakespeare's Plays," in Kate Chedgzoy, Susanne Greenhalgh, and Robert Shaughnessy, eds, *Shakespeare and Childhood* (Cambridge, 2007), 49–50.

[61]   William Shakespeare, *Coriolanus*, in Stephen Greenblatt et al., eds, *The Norton Shakespeare*, (New York, 1997), 2801–2.

[62]   See Strutt, 307.

snowe, whos softnes can nott withstand the childrens cruellty" (2.22). The scene underscores the inherently competitive nature of many pastimes. Far from freeing their participants from hierarchical relationships, games in fact depend on them.

Play's potential for cruelty and violence, coupled with its reliance on power and authority, becomes a defining feature of Wroth's characterization of Cupid in *Urania* and *Pamphilia to Amphilanthus*. In sonnet P38 in the 1621 version of her sonnet sequence, Wroth's speaker apologizes for underestimating Cupid by differentiating his power from a child's: "[We] led with folly, and by rashnes blind/ Thy sacred powre, doe with a childs compare."[63] Despite this dismissal of childish activities, Wroth depicts the encounters between her protagonists and the "wanton" (P64, 5) and "wayward" (P58, 13) child-monarch in terms of coercive and often torturous play: "childlike, wee can nott his sports refuse" (P64, 14), Pamphilia laments.

Cupid becomes for Wroth a decidedly vicious ludic sovereign, a "Lord Love" who tyrannizes his followers with his "Baby government" (*Urania* 2.16; 1.490–91). As a "froward Childe" and "Peevish Boy," Cupid epitomizes Erasmus's deceitful player, "Jugl[ing] and play[ing] faulce with all men" (1.490–91; 2.44). Yet he holds indisputable power over his "childlike" followers, "sporting with some like wantons, in ernest with others like strict Judges" (2.16). His "baby game[s]" (1.341) are anything but pleasant. Steriamus characterizes them in *Urania* "rather [as] racks and tortures then delights, unlesse you will call them playes, as Dogges and Horses are taught by stripes and blowes, and such pastime I have in love, and so love playes with mee" (1.416). Again conflating play and physical pain, Wroth ultimately likens the desires sparked by the "fire of love" to the experience of children who "play ... with fire till they burne their fingers" (2.82).

In *Pamphilia to Amphilanthus*, Wroth reinforces this characterization of Cupid through the structure of her poems. She situates the labyrinthine *corona* that lies at the heart of her sequence as a ludic punishment designed to expiate Pamphilia's faults and secure her sovereign's mercy. Much of the tension in the published version of *Pamphilia to Amphilanthus* lies in the conflict between Pamphilia's "will" and Cupid's, exemplified by Pamphilia's tortured acquiescence to Cupid's machinations in "Am I thus conquer'd?" (P16). As the sequence progresses, however, Pamphilia resigns herself increasingly to Cupid's authority. She foregrounds her subjection in the politically charged language of P76, which precedes the *corona*: "O pardon, Cupid I confess my fault/ Then mercy grant mee in soe just a kind/ For treason never lodged in my mind" (P76, 1–3). Highlighting Pamphilia's determination to make amends, the poem recalls contemporaneous descriptions of ludic penalties. Consider Lady Jane's punishment of Lord Hercules in *The Civile Conversation*:

---

[63]   Lady Mary Wroth, *Pamphilia to Amphilanthus*, in Josephine Roberts, ed., *The Poems of Lady Mary Wroth* (Baton Rouge, 1983), 106. Subsequent references will be to this edition and will follow Roberts's numbering of the poems.

wee thinke it good everie one, to moove certaine questions to Lorde Hercules, which he alone, (for punishment and satisfaction of his faulte, which by generall consent he hath deserved) shall fullie aunswere unto.

And when he hath sufficientlie satisfied our mindes … we are content then to restore him againe to our former grace, and favourablie entertaine him once againe into our companie.[64]

In P76, Pamphilia agrees to "give a crowne unto [Cupid's] endless prayse/ Which shall thy glory, and thy greatnes raise" (P76, 12–13).

Her expiation takes the form of an Italianate poetic experiment bounded by the challenging rule that the last line of each sonnet must become the first line of the next. None of the ludic punishments described in *The Civile Conversation* or *La Maison des jeux* demand that their participants compose something as intricate and difficult as a *corona*. However, many of them rely on an analogous degree of wordplay. In *La Maison des jeux*, Sorel presents a group of young women who, bored with the conventional penalty of "que de baiser ou de souffrir d'estre baisées," demand the more interesting punishments offered to the male players: "de faire quelque petit compliment, de chanter quelque couplet de chanson, … ou autre chose semblable."[65] Many of these exercises required participants to build their contribution on the same letter, series of adjectives, or verse deployed by the previous player. Francis Willughby's description of the game called "Capping of Verses" exemplifies the tricky circularity that was a common requirement of such sports."[66] Even as it looks back to her uncle and father's poetic experiments, therefore, Wroth positions her *corona* within a ludic framework, as a witty penalty designed to placate a ludic sovereign.

My reading of Wroth's *corona* is enhanced by the intriguing fact that a diversion known as "the game of the labyrinth" was circulating in Europe in the sixteenth and seventeenth centuries. Innocentio Ringhieri includes the game in his collection of sports alongside pastimes like "the game of the ceremonies of Cupid," "the game of the lover," "the game of jealousies," and "the game of chastity."[67] The game shares a number of features with other eroticized circle games of the period. The players begin by joining hands, alternating between male and female participants, to form a circle, here designated a "labyrinth" rather than a "park." Two participants assume the roles of Theseus and Ariadne, who stand at the entrance to the enclosed space. Another player, designated as Cupid, governs the

---

[64]   Guazzo, vol. 2, 172–3.

[65]   Sorel, "only to kiss or to endure being kissed"; "to give a small compliment, to sing a verse from a song, or something similar" (my translation), 307.

[66]   "A begins any verse, as: In nova fert animus mutates dicere formas. B is to say another that begins with the same letter As verse ended with, which was S. B: Si mea cum vestris valuissent vota Pelasgi. Then A must repeat a verse that begins with an I, and so by turns." Willughby, 202.

[67]   Innocentio Ringhieri, *Cento givochi liberali, et d'ingegno* (Bologna, 1551), sigs. 74r–76r. My thanks to Emilia Barbiero and Marianna Ricciuto for their help with translation.

labyrinth itself, which Ringhieri calls "the school of love." A group of six female players joins Cupid within the labyrinth, while six male players wait outside the circle. As the players enter, they are asked a series of questions and challenged to escape the labyrinth. Those who fail are forced to endure penalties. Successful players, in contrast, exchange kisses with their chosen partner and declare their affections before going their separate ways, returning to Theseus and Ariadne. After the players have braved the labyrinth three times, the circle breaks up and the participants form couples to begin a dance.

The game of the labyrinth stands as a fascinating intertext to Wroth's *corona*. It is not clear whether Wroth ever read Ringhieri's work; the manual is not listed among the extant records of the Sidney family library.[68] Ringhieri's decision to include the game in his collection, which was reissued in 1553 and 1580, however, coupled with its reappearance in Sorel's *La Maison des jeux* in the mid-seventeenth century, testifies to its popularity; Wroth could well have encountered a version of it at court or through continental accounts from her father and cousin. Wroth begins her *corona* by describing Pamphilia's experience within the labyrinth in terms that recall Ringhieri's description of the entanglements and obstacles suffered by delinquent players: "In this strang labourinth how shall I turne?/ Wayes are on all sids while the way I miss" (P77, 1–2). She again presents her sufferings as enforced upon her by Cupid—"I must thes doubts indure with out allay" (11). Bounded by its formal circularity and by the central metaphor of the confining labyrinth, the playing space of the *corona* becomes for Pamphilia, as for Ringhieri, a "school of love." Prompted by her "Tuter" Cupid, she begins to embrace a love "Made of vertu, join'de by truth, blowne by desires/ Strengthned by worth" (P81, 14; P84, 5–6). Wroth situates Pamphilia in these poems as a confident speaker who seeks to convert Amphilanthus and her audience to her doctrine of constant and virtuous love: "[True love] doth inrich the witts, and make you see/ That in your self, which you knew nott before" (P82, 9–10). If Ringhieri's female players acknowledge and kiss their lovers only to continue on through the labyrinth alone, Pamphilia combines the passionate expression of her desire with the determination to embrace constancy.

The *corona*'s ludic elements challenge the apparent interiority of the published sonnets and intensify their political relevancy. Pamphilia's syntactical ambiguity and apparent refusal to address Amphilanthus directly in the 1621 sequence have perplexed critics trying to trace the interchange between Pamphilia and her beloved. The concrete relationship between Pamphilia and Amphilanthus that is so much more overt in the Folger manuscript becomes discernable in the published version if one reads the *corona* as a trace of the playing bodies that animate courtly confession games and circle games like Ringhieri's.[69] The beauty of ludic

---

[68] My thanks to Germaine Warkentin for assistance regarding the Sidney family library.

[69] On the eroticized embodiment evident in Folger MS V.a.104, see Ilona D. Bell, "Wroth's Private Sonnet Sequence," paper presented at the Renaissance Society of America

spaces is that they enabled players to articulate their desires without risking their reputations. Games "provided an acceptable vehicle for bringing young people of both sexes together and allowing them a degree of social, even sexual, intimacy," while protecting their "erotic sparring" within a deliberately ambiguous playing space.[70] The ludic conventions that inform the framework of the 1621 sequence help to veil the poems' erotic content without negating it completely. Fittingly, the point in the published sequence at which Wroth's syntax becomes muddiest, in the *corona*, also represents the moment when Pamphilia articulates the maturation of her love.[71]

Even as it provides a space that facilitates self-expression, Wroth's *corona* artfully makes use of ludic conventions to encapsulate the competitive and unstable world of court relationships. The *corona*'s ludic framework reinforces the political resonances of Wroth's labyrinth, which Ann Rosalind Jones has read as a "figure both elegant and sinister for the entrapping anxiety of courtiers in quest of favor."[72] In the *corona*, Pamphilia affirms Cupid's "government" (P86, 8) as "commander of all harts,/ Ruller of owr affections kinde, and just/ Great King of Love" (P89, 9–11). Given the intimate access that Wroth enjoyed to the queen's circle and her resultant awareness of the currency of courtly games and entertainments as a means of securing and maintaining court favor, it is not inconceivable that her flattering appeal to Cupid should function equally as a playful petition to her sovereigns. As Margaret Hannay has argued in relation to Philip and Mary Sidney, "the courtier's desire to receive 'favor'—in some tangible form like a title, estate, grant, or monopoly—might be recast" quite profitably within a Petrarchan framework.[73] By conflating the politicized genre of the sonnet with that of the game, Wroth intensifies her request. Pamphilia's declaration to Amphilanthus in P79 that, if he should "Please [Cupid], and serve him, glory in his might,/ ... firme

---

Conference, Chicago, April 4, 2008, and "Mary Wroth's Crowning Glory," paper presented at the Renaissance Society of America Conference, Los Angeles, March 21, 2009.

[70] Richard Firth Green, "*Le Roi Qui Ne Ment* and Aristocratic Courtship," *Courtly Literature: Culture and Context*, Keith Busby and Erik Kooper, eds (Amsterdam and Philadelphia, 1990), 213.

[71] See Mary Moore, "The Labyrinth as Style in *Pamphilia to Amphilanthus*," in Clare R. Kinney, ed., *Mary Wroth, Ashgate Critical Essays on Women Writers in England 1500–1700*, vol. 4 (Aldershot, 2009), 61–77; Elaine Beilin, "'The Onely Perfect Vertue': Constancy in Mary Wroth's *Pamphilia to Amphilanthus*," *Spenser Studies* 2 (1981): 229–45.

[72] Ann Rosalind Jones, "Designing Women: The Self as Spectacle in Mary Wroth and Veronica Franco," *Reading Mary Wroth: Representing Alternatives in Early Modern England*, Naomi J. Miller and Gary Waller, eds (Knoxville, 1991), 150. See Margaret P. Hannay, *Mary Sidney, Lady Wroth* (Aldershot, 2010) for an important rereading of longstanding critical assumptions that Wroth was isolated from or in disfavor with the court.

[73] Margaret P. Hannay, "Joining the Conversation: David, Astrophil, and the Countess of Pembroke," *Textual Conversations in the Renaissance: Ethics, Authors, Technologies*, Zachary Lesser and Benedict S. Robinson, eds (Aldershot, 2006), 116–17.

hee'll bee, as innosencye white" (9–10), functions equally to convey the hope that Wroth's loyalty might be rewarded with reciprocal "firme[ness]."

The transformation promised by the *corona* does not detract from the childish torments that continue to haunt Wroth's speaker. The poems convey Pamphilia's continued subjection through a bizarrely masochistic idealization of Cupid's childish persecutions. Here, his "flames ar joyes" (P78, 14), the pains of love a "pleasing sting" and "hapy smarting": "Such as although, itt pierce your tender hart/ And burne, yett burning you will love the smart" (P80, 11–14). Nor does Pamphilia emerge from her labyrinthine school fully cured. Unlike Guazzo's Lady Jane, Wroth does not provide Pamphilia with a favorable judgment. The goodwill conventionally associated with the successful completion of the ludic punishment is left implicit; expected, but ultimately, as are so many of Pamphilia's appeals, unanswered. The *corona* concludes by returning her to the place from whence she began, even as she tries to rise above her amorous suffering: "In this strange labourinth how shall I turne?" (P90, 14).

The circular structures of both *corona* and labyrinth, commandeered by the ludic sovereign Cupid, bring us back in turn to the "babyish" circle games with which I opened this essay. Mary Wroth's writings testify to the potency of such playful discourses. Although *Urania* and *Pamphilia to Amphilanthus*, like *Love's Victory*, finally offer only a trace of young women at play in early modern England, the discursive significance of games and ludic conventions in these texts demonstrate the seriousness of such activities and the extent to which women could appropriate and redeploy ludic conventions to negotiate and to communicate their experience of eroticized and politicized relationships. If games afforded women opportunities to return to their girlhoods and "playe the childe againe," the "remembr[ance]" of such pastimes represented not simply nostalgic entertainment, but a conscious entrance into a hierarchical "play-ground" where the stakes could be just as high as those lying beyond the space of the game.

Works Cited

Barroll, Leeds. *Anna of Denmark, Queen of England*. Philadelphia: University of Pennsylvania Press, 2001.

Beilin, Elaine. "'The Onely Perfect Vertue': Constancy in Mary Wroth's *Pamphilia to Amphilanthus*." *Spenser Studies* 2 (1981): 229–45.

Bell, Ilona D. "Mary Wroth's Crowning Glory." Paper presented at the Renaissance Society of America Conference. Los Angeles, March 21, 2009.

———. "Wroth's Private Sonnet Sequence." Paper presented at the Renaissance Society of America Conference. Chicago, April 4, 2008.

Ben-Amos, Ilana Krausman. *Adolescence and Youth in Early Modern England*. New Haven: Yale University Press, 1994.

Bruegel, Pieter. "Children's Games." Kunsthistorisches Museum, Vienna.

Castiglione, Baldesar. *The Book of the Courtier*. Trans. Charles S. Singleton. Ed. Daniel Javitch. New York: W.W. Norton & Co., 2002.

Cavendish, Margaret, Duchess of Newcastle. *Sociable Letters*. Ed. James Fitzmaurice. Peterborough: Broadview Editions, 2004.

———. *A True Relation of my Birth, Breeding, and Life*, in Sylvia Bowerbank and Sara Mendelson, eds, *Paper Bodies: A Margaret Cavendish Reader*. Peterborough: Broadview Editions, 2000.

———. *The Worlds Olio*. London, 1655.

Chedgzoy, Kate. "Introduction: 'What, are they children?'" in Kate Chedgzoy, Susanne Greenhalgh, and Robert Shaughnessy, eds, *Shakespeare and Childhood*. Cambridge: Cambridge University Press, 2007.

Clifford, Anne. *The Memoir of 1603 and The Diary of 1616–1619*. Ed. Katherine O. Acheson. Peterborough: Broadview Editions, 2007.

Comenius, J.A. *Orbis Sensualium Pictus*. Trans. Charles Hoole. London, 1659.

Erasmus, Desiderius. "A Declamation on the Subject of Early Liberal Education for Children" (*De pueris statim ac liberaliter instituendis declamatio*), in J.K. Sowards, ed., *Collected Works of Erasmus*, vol. 26. Trans. Beert C. Verstraete. Toronto: University of Toronto Press, 1985.

———. "On Good Manners for Boys" (*De civilitate morum puerilium*), in J.K. Sowards, ed., *Collected Works of Erasmus*, vol. 25. Trans. Brian McGregor. Toronto: University of Toronto Press, 1985.

Fletcher, Hattie and Marianne Novy. "Father-Child Identification, Loss and Gender in Shakespeare's Plays," in Kate Chedgzoy, Susanne Greenhalgh, and Robert Shaughnessy, eds, *Shakespeare and Childhood*. Cambridge: Cambridge University Press, 2007.

Gomme, Alice Bertha. *The Traditional Games of England, Scotland, and Ireland*, 2 vols. London: David Nutt, 1894.

Green, Richard Firth. "*Le Roi Qui Ne Ment* and Aristocratic Courtship," in Keith Busby and Erik Kooper, eds, *Courtly Literature: Culture and Context*. Amsterdam and Philadelphia: John Benjamins Publishing Company, 1990.

Griffiths, Paul. *Youth and Authority: Formative Experiences in England 1560– 1640*. Oxford: Clarendon Press, 1996.

Guazzo, Stefano. *The Civile Conversation of M. Steeven Guazzo*. Trans. George Pettie and Barth Young, 2 vols. New York: AMS Press Inc., 1967.

Hannay, Margaret P. "Joining the Conversation: David, Astrophil, and the Countess of Pembroke," in Zachary Lesser and Benedict S. Robinson, eds, *Textual Conversations in the Renaissance: Ethics, Authors, Technologies*. Aldershot: Ashgate, 2006.

———. *Mary Sidney, Lady Wroth*. Aldershot: Ashgate, 2010.

Harington, Sir John. *A Treatise on Playe*, in Henry Harington and Thomas Park, eds, *Nugae Antiquae*, vol. 1. London: Vernor and Hood, 1804.

Hawkins, William. *Apollo Shroving*. London, 1627.

Heywood, Thomas. *Englands Elizabeth*. London, 1631.

Higginbotham, Jennifer. *Fair Maids and Golden Girls: Early Modern Girlhood and the Production of Femininity*. PhD Diss., University of Pennsylvania, 2007.

Huizinga, Johan. *Homo Ludens: A Study of the Play-Element in Culture*. Boston: Beacon Press, 1950.

Jones, Ann Rosalind. "Designing Women: The Self as Spectacle in Mary Wroth and Veronica Franco," in Naomi J. Miller and Gary Waller, eds, *Reading Mary Wroth: Representing Alternatives in Early Modern England*. Knoxville: The University of Tennessee Press, 1991.

Lancelott, Francis, *The Queens of England and Their Time*, 2 vols. New York: D. Appleton and Co., 1858.

Larson, Katherine R. "Conversational Games and the Articulation of Desire in Shakespeare's *Love's Labour's Lost* and Mary Wroth's *Love's Victory*." *English Literary Renaissance* 40.2 (Spring 2010): 165–90.

Lecercle, François. "La culture en jeu: Innocenzo Ringhieri et le pétrarquisme," in Philippe Ariès and Jean-Claude Margolin, eds, *Les jeux à la Renaissance*. Paris: Librairie Philosophique, 1982.

Lewalski, Barbara K. "Anne of Denmark and the Subversions of Masquing." *Criticism* 35.3 (Summer 1993): 341–56.

Marcus, Leah S. *The Politics of Mirth: Jonson, Herrick, Milton, Marvell, and the Defense of Old Holiday Pastimes*. Chicago: University of Chicago Press, 1989.

McManus, Clare. *Women on the Renaissance Stage: Anna of Denmark and Female Masquing in the Stuart Court 1590–1619*. Manchester: Manchester University Press, 2002.

McManus, Clare, ed. *Women and Culture at the Courts of the Stuart Queens*. Houndmills: Palgrave Macmillan, 2003.

Mehl, Jean-Michel. *Les jeux au royaume de France du XIIIe au début du XVIe siècle*. Paris: Fayard, 1990.

Montaigne, Michel de. "Of Custom," in Jacob Zeitlin, ed. and trans., *The Essays of Michel de Montaigne*, vol. 1. New York: Alfred A. Knopf, 1934.

Moore, Mary. "The Labyrinth as Style in *Pamphilia to Amphilanthus*," in Clare R. Kinney, ed., *Mary Wroth, Ashgate Critical Essays on Women Writers in England, 1550–1700*, vol. 4. Aldershot: Ashgate, 2009.

Nardo, Anna K. *The Ludic Self in Seventeenth-Century English Literature*. Albany: State University of New York Press, 1991.

Opie, Iona and Peter Opie. *Children's Games in Street and Playground*. Oxford: Oxford University Press, 1984.

Rex, James. *Basilikon Doron*, in Charles Howard McIlwain, ed., *The Political Works of James I*. Cambridge: Harvard University Press, 1918.

Ringhieri, Innocentio. *Cento givochi liberali, et d'ingegno*. Bologna, 1551.

Rutter, Carol Chillington. *Shakespeare and Child's Play: Performing Lost Boys on Stage and Screen*. London and New York: Routledge, 2007.

Schleiner, Louise. *Tudor and Stuart Women Writers*. Bloomington: Indiana University Press, 1994.

Semenza, Gregory M. Colón. *Sport, Politics, and Literature in the English Renaissance*. Newark: University of Delaware Press, 2003.

Shakespeare, William. *Coriolanus*, in Stephen Greenblatt, Walter Cohen, Jean E. Howard, and Katharine Eisaman Maus, eds, *The Norton Shakespeare*. New York: W.W. Norton & Co., 1997.

Sorel, Charles. *La Maison des jeux*. Ed. Daniel A. Gajda. Geneva: Slatkin Reprints, 1977.

Strickland, Agnes. *Lives of the Queens of England*, vol. 7. London: Henry Colburn, 1844.

Strutt, Joseph. *The Sports and Pastimes of the People of England*. London: Methuen & Co., 1801.

Stuart, Arabella. *The Letters of Lady Arabella Stuart*. Ed. Sara Jayne Steen. New York and London: Oxford University Press, 1994.

Thomas, Keith. "Children in Early Modern England," in Gillian Avery and Julia Briggs, eds, *Children and Their Books: A Celebration of the Work of Iona and Peter Opie*. Oxford: Clarendon Press, 1989.

Vives, Juan Luis. *The Instruction of a Christian Woman*. London, 1585.

Weidemann, Heather L. "Theatricality and Female Identity in Wroth's *Urania*," in Naomi J. Miller and Gary Waller, eds, *Reading Mary Wroth: Representing Alternatives in Early Modern England*. Knoxville: University of Tennessee Press, 1991, 191–209.

Williams, Deanne. "Girls Own Shakespeare." Paper presented at the Toronto Renaissance and Reformation Colloquium, University of Toronto, November 30, 2006.

Willughby, Francis. *Francis Willughby's Book of Games: A Seventeenth-Century Treatise on Sports, Games and Pastimes*. Ed. David Cram, Jeffrey L. Forgeng, and Dorothy Johnston. Aldershot: Ashgate, 2003.

Wroth, Lady Mary. *The First Part of the Countess of Montgomery's Urania*. Ed. Josephine Roberts. Tempe: Arizona Center for Medieval and Renaissance Studies, 1995.

———. *Love's Victory*, in S.P. Cerasano and Marion Wynne-Davies, eds, *Renaissance Drama by Women: Texts and Documents*. London and New York: Routledge, 1996.

———. *Pamphilia to Amphilanthus*, in Josephine Roberts, ed., *The Poems of Lady Mary Wroth*. Baton Rouge: Louisiana State University Press, 1983.

———. *The Second Part of the Countess of Montgomery's Urania*. Ed. Josephine Roberts. Completed by Suzanne Gossett and Janel Mueller. Tempe: Arizona Center for Medieval and Renaissance Studies, 1999.

PART 2
Imprinting Identity:
Education and Social Training

Chapter 5

The Facts of *Enfance*:
Rabelais, Montaigne, Paré, and French Renaissance Paediatrics

Marie Rutkoski

When Louis XIII of France was born in 1601, a crowd of people pushed their way into the delivery room to see the new heir to the throne, causing the midwife to express concern at the number of people surrounding the baby.[1] Henri IV snapped at the woman, "Shut up, shut up, Midwife! Don't worry about it! That child belongs to everybody: everyone must enjoy him!"[2] Louis would state at 13 years old that he never really had a childhood, claiming that "it is not with kings as with ordinary men, but they are born complete—nurtured, reared, educated, and accomplished."[3] Yet the journals of his doctor, Jean Héroard, belie Louis's claim to have been a ready-made, socialized adult, showing a child who at a tender age threatened to kill his governess and, while practicing his letters, doodled a pigeon, a bird of paradise, and a swan.[4] Héroard documented how the many stages of the boy's childhood held the court's fascination. As the boy's father said they would, everybody at court enjoyed him, observing with great interest his nursing problems, precocious sexuality, games, and toilet training. Héroard treated him in accordance with paediatric and child-rearing manuals of the time, from ordering that the newborn be given a bit of wine for stimulation, to his criteria for selecting the boy's nurse, to deciding when he should begin to punish the prince physically.

Héroard's treatment of the young prince also displays a consistency with an attitude that pervades paediatrics at the time: pragmatism. A man who was careful to note down the hour when the prince woke up, what he ate (such as plum jam), and how his face appeared, Héroard regularly chose to document the prince's actions

---

[1]   Elizabeth Wirth Marvick, *Louis XIII: The Making of a King* (New Haven: Yale University Press, 1986), 8. Marvick cites as her source Louise Bourgeois, *Récit véritable des naissances de messeigneurs et dames les enfans de France* (Paris, 1626).

[2]   Ibid.

[3]   Marvick, xiii. Her source is Hardouin Le Bourdays, *Discours sur l'ordre tenu de Leur Majestes en entrant dans la ville du Mans* (Le Mans, 1614).

[4]   Madeleine Foisil, "Louis XIII: L'enfance et l'adolescence d'après le Journal de Jean Héroard." *Journal de Jean Héroard*, Madeleine Foisil, ed. (Librarie Arthème Fayard, 1989), 85, 175.

rather than explore their mystical significance or potential wondrous nature.[5] French paediatrics tended to keep an interest in wonder and the *insolite* at arm's length, choosing skepticism over ready belief in unusual births, and empiricism over interpretation when confronted with physically abnormal children.

And yet it is precisely accounts of such atypical children that expose a lingering interest in wonder, even as doctors and other writers espouse science. It is well understood that there was a considerable fluidity between mysticism and science in the European Renaissance, as in the case of a French text that proposes to predict a child's health problems according to its astrological sign (children born under the sign of Aries, Arcandam claims, "shalbe void of hedach, but greatly troubled with the strang ayre, gravell and stone").[6] Of note, however, is Renaissance French paediatrics' effort to dismiss mysticism in its various forms, and its inability to do so wholly. I focus on three generically different texts, François Rabelais's *Gargantua and Pantagruel* (1532), Michel de Montaigne's "Of a Monstrous Child," and Ambroise Paré's *Oeuvres* to suggest that they rest on a cultural fault line about whether childhood development should be apprehended with wonder, or medical *savoir*.

In mid-sixteenth century Montpellier, where François Rabelais studied medicine, a professional if small organization of physicians was established, leading to a decades-long push towards the incorporation of medical practice and, thus, the delegitimizing of unqualified healers.[7] This trend towards professional medicine, combined with a continued reference to medieval and classical sources, may account for the marked consistency between the paediatric practices of Jean Héroard, Jacques Guillemeau, Laurence Joubert, and Vallambert.[8] The increased professionalization of medicine explains the doctor Fontaine's indictment of those who try to heal children with remedies based on "false imaginations."[9] "Such abuse is intolerable when acted upon anyone," he writes, "but particularly so upon children, in the case of a disease that people pretend doctors do not understand."[10]

---

[5]   The prince asked for plum jam on August 16, 1603, and was given it after the Queen approved. *Journal de Jean Héroard*, 449.

[6]   *The Most Excellent Profitable, and pleasaunt Booke of the famous Doctor and expert Astrologian Arcandam, or Aleandrin, to finde the Fatall destiny, constellation, complexion & naturall inclination of euery man and childe, by his birth VVyth an addition of Phisiognomy, very pleasa[n]t to read. Now newly tourned out of french into our vulgar tongue, by William Warde* (London: Thomas Marshe, 1578), sig. B74.

[7]   Laurence Brockliss and Colin Jones, *The Medical World of Early Modern France* (Oxford: Clarendon Press, 1997), 177–88.

[8]   Shulamith Shahar notes that the sixteenth century witnessed a surge in pediatric material that frequently referred to medieval writers, *Childhood in the Middle Ages*, trans. Chaya Galai (London: Routledge, 1992), 77.

[9]   I.A.Q. Fontaine, *Discours de la Picote, ou Petite Verole, vraye peste des petits enfans Par M. IAQ Fontaine Docteur Medecin* (Aix: Printed by Iean Tholosan, 1602), sig. B1v.

[10]   Ibid. Fontaine writes in French, "Ces abus ne sont tolerables en aucune personne, mais principalement en celles des petits enfans, en la maladie desquels on se vente que les medecins n'entendent notte." The translation is mine.

The title of Laurence Joubert's *Eurreurs Populaires au Fait de la Medecine et Regime de Sante* declares its interest in purveying medical truth, and is quick to debunk superstitions about childbirth and the care of newborns. Joubert addresses and dismisses a number of these popular beliefs, in which both women and children are objects of analysis. It is impossible, he states, to predict how many children a woman will have by looking at the umbilical cord after she gives birth to her first child.[11] It is equally wrong, he writes, to think that anyone can ascertain if a woman is pregnant by studying her urine, and that a newborn baby's rash is due its conception during the period of its mother's menses.[12] He deplores how "old matrons" can never seem to shake belief in a superstition they take for truth. Instead it stays with them "like an oil stain."[13] Joubert here pinpoints women as the culprits of medical moonshine, and it seems fairly clear from the preponderance of paediatric texts written by men that one facet of the sixteenth-century shift toward professional medicine was the cultivation of that field as a masculine domain. Although in 1609 Louise Bourgeois began publishing on a related field, midwifery, she is an outlier, and one might hear King Henri's words to her after she delivered his son—"Shut up, shut up, Midwife!"—as an echo of Joubert's impatience for "old matrons" whose pretensions to medical authority needed to be silenced. Women caretakers of children appear in paediatric texts of the period, but largely as subjects and agents of a male doctor's advice. It was common to give explicit directions on how to select an appropriate wet nurse, for example, and when they feature as active caretakers of children in paediatric texts their role is limited. In Guillemeau's manual, nurses' medical intervention is restricted to simple issues that involve no treatment more difficult than rubbing a baby's mouth with violet syrup, and Guillemeau's interest in nurses is in their emotional, rather than medical, influence over a child.[14]

Though they do not agree on every detail, texts written by renowned late sixteenth- and early seventeenth-century French doctors reveal sympathy of thought in content as well as method. Following Bartholomaeus Anglicus and Aldebrandin of Sienna, Guillemeau and Vallambert agree about where a cradle is ideally situated: in a room that is not too bright, and has temperate air.[15] These doctors as well as Paré also advocate that a mother should nurse her own child,

---

[11]   Laurence Joubert, *Eurreurs Popvlaires av Fait de la Medecine et Regime de Sante* (Avignon, 1578), sig. S1r.

[12]   Joubert, sigs. K6v–K7r, Z4v.

[13]   Joubert, sig. Z5v.

[14]   Jacques Guillemeau, *The Nursing of Children. Wherein is Set downe, the ordering and goverment of them, from their birth. Together: with the means to helpe and free them, from all such diseases as may happen unto them. Written in French by James Guillimeau the French Kings Chirurgion in Ordinary* (London: A. Hatfield, 1612), sigs. Mm2r, Lll v, Tt2v.

[15]   Guillemeau, sig. Mm4r. Simon de Vallambert, *Cinq Livres, De la Maniere de nourrir et Gouverner les Enfans des leur naissance* (Poitiers: de Marnesz and Bouchetz, 1565), sig. D6r. Shulamith Shahar, *Childhood in the Middle ages*, trans. Chaya Galai (London: Routledge, 1992), 40.

Guillemeau adding that he would like women to imitate Blanche of Castille who, angry when she discovered that somebody else had nursed her son, put her fingers down the baby's throat, causing him to vomit the other woman's milk.[16] Several doctors (Vallambert, Paré, Guillemeau) suggest rubbing a child's gums with honey.[17] Guillemeau thought that no pain was greater than teething, and Héroard would stay awake at night when the prince's teeth were coming in, holding the boy's hand.[18] Most doctors of the period approached the subject of paediatrics with meticulous care, Héroard perhaps being the quintessential example.

Although monstrous or strange births form a significant part of some doctors' consideration of children (as with Paré), they are quick to point out the questionable nature of some tales. Guillemeau writes that in Rascat, a child with two horns was heard crying in the womb 14 days before its birth, but he suggests the implausibility of this tale by noting that an infant does not cry in the womb.[19] Sometimes there seems to be a delight in recounting such stories, as when Joubert tells a story about a woman's delivery of 363 chick-sized babies only in order to dismiss it. Though he does not explicitly state whether he believes the tale to be true, he appears humorously skeptical. The woman's supposed plight, he writes, could have only occurred if she had been a giantess.[20]

Although published well before the heyday of French publications on paediatrics, Rabelais's story of a giant's incredible birth and childhood nonetheless draws on conceptions about child-care that persisted into the late sixteenth and early seventeenth centuries. When Gargamelle goes into labor, the midwives "found some fleshy excrescences, which stank, and they were sure this was the baby."[21] Certainly, Rabelais indulged in scatological humor where he could, but in this instance he seems to cast a sly eye at sixteenth-century medicine's treatment of a newborn as, in Évelyne Berriot-Salvadore's words, "un corps excrémentiel."[22] According to Renaissance paediatrics and its consideration of a system of humors, the infant took part in the feminine nature of its mother's body, and was described as all softness, tenderness,

---

[16] Vallambert, sig. A2r. Ambroise Paré, *The Workes of that famous Chirurgion Ambrose Parey Translated out of Latine and compared with the French by Th. Johnson* (London: Th. Cotes and R. Young, 1634), sig. Gggg4r. Guillemeau, Kk1v.

[17] Vallambert, sig. D7r, E2r. Paré, sigs. Gggg4r and Lllll6r. Guillemeau, Mm2r.

[18] David Hunt, *Parents and Children in History: The Psychology of Family Life in Early Modern France* (New York: Basic Books, Inc., 1970), 123.

[19] Guillemeau, sig. Kk3r.

[20] Joubert, sigs. P1v–P2r.

[21] François Rabelais, *Gargantua and Pantagruel*, trans. Burton Raffel (New York: Norton, 1990), 21.

[22] Évelyne Berriot-Salvadore, "L'enfant dans le discours médical de la Renaissance," *Autour de l'enfance*, Évelyne Berriot-Salvadore and Isabelle Pébay-Clottes, eds (Biarritz: Atlantica, 1999), 93–8, 97.

and humidity.[23] The infant is also depicted as perpetually filthy. Guillemeau advises that a nurse, when inspecting a baby, should "looke whether the fundament bee well opened, and whether there bee any filth bred there or no."[24] He also notes that some infants may have problems urinating. In this case, he suggests, a nurse should try sucking the end of the baby's penis and applying herbs to his stomach: "If the bladder of the child be too full of urine, his bellie will be hard, and strout out; and then let the Nurse sucke the end of his yard, and presse downe his bellie a little, towards the bladder: lay to his bellie water Cresses, and Pellitorie of the wall fried."[25] Vallambert writes that a nurse must not mind the smell of a baby's excrement, advises washing the child in slightly salty water when its skin is "en humidité et ordure," and outlines an extensive regimen for bathing a child.[26] Even as Gargamelle's excretions are taken for her baby, her actual child becomes a caricature of the infants depicted in paediatrics manuals. Gargantua urinates and defecates everywhere, and the apex of his childhood is when he discovers the perfect ass-wipe (a goose held between the legs), taking care to describe his various experiments with other materials and animals and how they interacted with his "matière fécale."[27]

Given Rabelais's interest in the triumph of the low over the high, he was perhaps naturally interested in Gargantua's bottom and what came out of it. The carnivalesque spirit that Mikhail Bakhtin famously attributed to Rabelais expresses itself in "the peculiar logic of the 'inside out' (*à l'envers*), of the 'turnabout,' of a continual shifting from top to bottom, from front to rear, of numerous parodies and travesties, humiliations, profanations, comic crownings and uncrownings."[28] The ass-wipe, David Frame writes, is an example of just such a phenomenon, as objects commonly used as face-wipers are applied to Gargantua's bottom.[29]

Rabelais wields *logique à l'envers* throughout *Gargantua and Pantagruel* to accomplish a particular kind of reversal: the uncrowning of textual authority. After describing the birth of Gargantua via his mother's ear (an orifice rather at the opposite end of the business of labor, and so yet another site for the inversion of logic) Rabelais comments, "I'm not sure you're going to believe this strange birth. If you don't, I don't give a hoot—but any decent man, any sensible man, always

---

[23]   Évelyne Berriot-Salvadore, *Un Corps, Un Destin: La Femme Dans la Médecine de la Renaissance* (Paris: Honoré Champion Éditeur, 1993), 185. See also Berriot-Salvadore, "L'enfant," 95.

[24]   Guillemeau, sig. Mm2r.

[25]   Guillemeau, sig. Uu1v.

[26]   Vallambert, sigs. A2v, G2r, G3v–G4v.

[27]   François Rabelais, *La vie treshorrificque du grand Gargantua*, Françoise Joukovsky, ed. (Paris: Flammarion, 1993), 88.

[28]   Mikhail Bakhtin, *Rabelais and His World*, trans. Helene Iswolsky (Cambridge: Massachusetts Institute of Technology, 1969), 11.

[29]   Frame, 109.

believes what he's told and what he finds written down."[30] Rabelais mocks the mannerism of credulity: the man who believes what he reads signals (or attempts to signal) that his moral, class, and intellectual status is sound.[31] Rabelais also, following this passage, tweaks the nose of a reader and citer of classical texts, reminding the incredulous that they need only turn to classical precedents to find examples of unusual births in, for example, Pliny's *Natural History*.[32] This gesture towards a textual source is painted as the recommendation of one fraud by another: "I'm hardly the kind of established liar that [Pliny] was," writes Rabelais with something like openly false modesty.[33] He turns to hawking his own work above all others in Book 2, writing,

> Just show me a book—in any language and on any subject you can think of—which can do such things, have such powers, display such virtues, and I'll fork over a good half-pint of tripes. No, my friends, no. This book we've been talking about simply has no equal, it is incomparable, utterly original.[34]

As Carla Freccero observes, Rabelais at once mocks a Renaissance desire to establish a genealogical inheritance of classical writing, and efforts (like his own) to shrug off the weight of textual authority.[35] Despite his claim to the nonpareil, Rabelais does not exempt himself from his indictment of textual authority, but rather encourages his readers to see him as another liar amongst many, one whose words must be taken with a barrelful of salt even (especially) when he swears, "I consign myself—body and soul, guts and bowels—to a thousand basketfuls of good devils if in this entire tale I put down a single untruthful word."[36]

Rabelais's work swells with textual allusions to such an extent that one of his English Renaissance readers, Gabriel Harvey, used the words "Gargantua" and

---

[30]   *Gargantua and Pantagruel*, 21. "Je me doubte que ne croyez assurement ceste estrange nativité. Si ne le croyez, je ne m'en soucie, mais un homme de bien, un homme de bon sens croit tousjours ce qu'on luy dict, et qu'il trouve par escript." *La vie treshorrificque du grand Gargantua*, 61. Bakhtin calls Gargantua's birth "unexpected and completely carnivalesque," adding, "The child does not go down, but up," 226.

[31]   What Raffel translates as "any decent man, any sensible man" is "un homme de bien, un homme de bons sens." "Un homme de bons sens" clearly pertains to the intellect, while "un homme de bien" is more vague. The construction "un homme de bien" suggest many things: good manners, good morals, good origins, good style, and wealth.

[32]   *Gargantua and Pantagruel*, 22.

[33]   *Gargantua and Pantagruel*, 22.

[34]   *Gargantua and Pantagruel*, 134.

[35]   Carla Freccero, *Father Figures: Genealogy and Narrative Structure in Rabelais* (Ithaca: Cornell University Press), 12.

[36]   *Gargantua and Pantagruel*, 134. As Samuel Kinser notes, Rabelais was fond of paratextual comments that refer to how his book will be read and interpreted, and shows an interest in the mediation of author, printer, and public. *Rabelais's Carnival: Text, Context, Metacontext* (Berkeley: University of California Press, 1990), 17–18, 37.

"Pantagruel" to describe the habit of haunting print shops.[37] The value of making such allusions seems largely to rest in putting them in the stocks. Rabelais continually deflates textual authority, even his own. But one particular kind of writer that Rabelais satirizes is prominent amongst others: the medical authority. The satirization of the promulgating of medicine or what passes for it pervades the novel.[38]

In a particularly scathing glance at female medical authority, Gargantua's unusual birth owes much to the malpractice of "a dirty old hag who was said to be a great doctor," whose decision to give Gargamelle an astringent causes her womb to "stretch loose at the top, instead of the bottom," squeezing the baby up and through her body.[39] Yet the midwife (and, by extension, her colleagues) is not the only object of ridicule. Alluding to Pliny's praise of flax in his *Natural History*, Rabelais's Third Book concludes by devoting several chapters to the "marvelous" herb Pantagruelion, which, in addition to being incombustible and able to contain air currents, can cure burns, kill ear-dwelling vermin, soothe arthritis, and "is a sovereign remedy for colicky horses."[40] Even the chapter devoted to Gargantua's ass-wipe, while not precisely a joke at medicine's expense, still mixes pharmacy with laughter. Barbara Bowen writes,

> All the plants essayed by the child Gargantua as toilet-paper substitutes are present in herbals from antiquity through the Renaissance with a variety of medicinal properties, most frequently connected with diarrhea or other intestinal problems; part of the comedy here must be in Gargantua's use, raw, on one end of his body, of leaves which are normally cooked and absorbed at the other end.[41]

A man who gave up being a monk in order to become a doctor, Rabelais calls upon Galen's medical works, advising his readers, "Just like the dog, you ought to be running with your educated nose to the wind, sniffing and appreciating such magnificent volumes."[42] Galen was a prominent source for several French Renaissance doctors, including those interested in child-care, and Rabelais possessed the 1525 Aldine publication of his work.[43] But his invocation of Galen

---

[37]   Anne Lake Prescott, *Imagining Rabelais in Renaissance England* (New Haven: Yale University Press, 1998), 202.

[38]   Bakhtin, 186.

[39]   *Gargantua and Pantagruel*, 21.

[40]   *Gargantua and Pantagruel*, 371. Bakhtin, 186.

[41]   Bowen, 138.

[42]   *Gargantua and Pantagruel*, 8.

[43]   On Galen and child-care, see John Boswell, *The Kindness of Strangers: The Abandonment of Children in Western Europe from Late Antiquity to the Renaissance* (New York: Pantheon Books, 1988), 146; Guillemeau, sigs. Mm3r and Mm4v; Shahar, 40; On Rabelais's interest in Galen, see Donald M. Frame, *François Rabelais: A Study* (New York: Harcourt Brace Jovanovich, 1977); Barbara C. Bowen, *Enter Rabelais, Laughing* (Nashville: Vanderbilt University Press, 1998), 135; and Vivian Nutton, "Rabelais's Copy of Galen," *Etudes Rabelaisiennes*, vol. 22, 181–7.

has a comic twist. These "magnificent volumes" are not cited to show Galen's biological expertise, but his culinary taste: the achievement of his works, it seems, is having proven that marrow "is more delicious than a vast quantity of other things," and "is nature's perfect food."[44]

It is not quite enough to note what is transparently so: Gargantua is not treated in accordance with paediatric advice in the period, neither in terms of what he eats (vast rather than carefully measured quantities), how he is allowed to behave, or what he drinks.[45] The manner in which he passes his childhood is what remains relevant, and that manner is pure extravagance, a continual exaggeration on Renaissance paediatrics' themes. Describing Gargantua's toddler period, Rabelais makes a claim for the baby's normalcy: "those years went by just as they do for ordinary children. He drank, ate, and slept; he ate, slept, and drank; he slept, drank, and ate." And, despite being perhaps the only case of a birth via a mother's ear, Gargantua is a figure who regularly recalls sixteenth-century child-care advice, whether it pertains to the excretions of the infant body and how to deal with them, or the administration of wine as medicine. Vallambert allows wine as a kind of cordial for weak infants, but counsels against liberal or regular use of it.[46] Giving wine to children, he writes, has long been a controversy, with Aristotle forbidding wine until age 21, Galen until age 14, and Gordon until age 4. Though many agree with Gordon, Vallambert writes, he sides with Galen.[47] Several doctors seem willing, like Vallambert, to allow a small quantity of wine to an infant if medically needed: a spoonful of lukewarm wine mixed with sugar was commonly administered as medicine to children.[48] But Gargantua is born demanding his portion of wine. At the moment of his birth, he cries, "Drink! Drink!"[49] He never seems to cease asking for wine, and neither do the adults around him cease to administer it: "whether he was jumping up and down in a rage, or bawling his eyes out, or screaming, they'd bring him wine to set him right again, and just like that he'd be peaceful and happy."[50]

Although many of the paediatrics manuals treated here postdate Rabelais's novel by several decades, the doctors were all drawing (as did Vallambert when discussing the debate about whether to give children wine) from sources that Rabelais knew well, and knew at a time when doctors were trying to establish

---

[44]   *Gargantua and Pantagruel*, 8.

[45]   Emile Roy, "Un régime de santé du XVe siècle pour les petits enfants, et l'hygiène de Gargantua," *Mélanges offerts à Emile Picot I* (Paris: Société des Bibliophiles, 1913), 151–8, 154–5.

[46]   Vallambert, sigs. D8v and M1r–v.

[47]   Vallambert, sig. M2r.

[48]   Jacques Duval, *Des hermaphrodits Accovchemens des Femmes, et Traitement qui est requis pour les releuer en santé, & bien éleuer leurs enfans* (Rouen: David Gevffroy, 1612), sig. R8v. Héroard also gave wine to the newborn Louis XIII, Marvick, 11.

[49]   *Gargantua and Pantagruel*, 21.

[50]   *Gargantua and Pantagruel*, 23.

medicine as a professional field of expertise. This effort is indicated by a certain symptom in paediatrics texts from the latter half of the sixteenth and the beginning of the seventeenth centuries: an emphasis on regimen—on knowing, for example, how many baths a day and how much wine (if any) to give an infant. Through the use of satire that never lets textual authority rest, Rabelais explodes this pragmatism as the care of Gargantua resembles and yet goes well beyond typical ideas of French Renaissance child care.

Most of Rabelais's efforts to defer to medicine as a revered practice waver between several points on the spectrum of laughter, from coy feint to snide remark to blatant absurdity. But Montaigne's "Of a Monstrous Child" attempts to submit its subject to the realm of science and medical experts. What the essay leaves, however, is a lasting impression of its cognitive dissonance. Its stated effort to ignore the mystical potential of the conjoined twins it treats becomes subverted by its own words, and by its very structure.

Montaigne, who read Ambroise Paré's *Oeuvres* (1575) and its section devoted to the *insolite* ("On Monsters and Prodigies"), pursued opportunities to see monsters of various kinds for himself, and reveals an early modern impulse to interpret a child's deformed body even as he refrains from subscribing to it.[51] In a rare moment of attempted interpretive restraint, Montaigne devotes a brief essay, "Of a Monstrous Child," almost entirely to a physical description of conjoined twins with one head. His first sentence situates his account in the realm of science, and promises to withhold commentary: "This discourse shall passe single, for I leave it to Physitions to treate of."[52]

This opening sentence is an Aristotelian gesture. In his *Generation of Animals*, Aristotle discussed monsters in a scientific fashion and believed that monsters

---

[51] Paré's *Oeuvres* may have been intended to deal only with the science of medicine, and indeed the largest portion of it describes medical procedures, diagnoses, etc. But moments in "On Monsters and Prodigies" seem to deal more with the imagination and social performance. Paré, for example, describes strange children born according to whatever their mothers happened to be thinking of or looking at during conception, and he debunks beggars who fake repulsive medical conditions to garner donations. Paré is a well known source of Montaigne's, and an example given in the *Oeuvres* is repeated in the *Essais*: Montaigne echoes Paré's account of a girl born covered with hair because her mother looked at a painting of a bearded St. John during conception. Montaigne, "On the Power of the Imagination," *The Essayes*, trans. John Florio and intro. Desmond McCarthy, 3 vols. (London: J.M. Dent, 1928). Paré, *On Monsters and Marvels*, trans. and intro Janis L. Pallister (Chicago: Chicago University Press, 1982), 38. The curious essayist not only read accounts of monsters, but also saw them face-to-face. In the same essay that describes the conjoined twins, "Of a Monstrous Child," Montaigne also gives an account of a man he went to see in Medoc, a shepherd who had no genitals but three holes from which he perpetually urinated. "Of a Monstrous Child," *The Essays*, II.440.

[52] Montaigne, "Of a Monstrous Child," *The Essayes*, II.440. "Ce conte s'en ira tout simple, car je laisse aux medecins d'en discourir." *Essais*, Joseph-Victor le Clerc, ed. (Paris: Lefèvre, 1844), 432.

are not contrary to nature as a whole—only to nature in its generalities.[53] But Montaigne's promise to leave the subject of the child's strange form in the hands of medical experts is not to be trusted. The essay, though brief, is hardly "tout simple," as the original French declares. The essay is not "simple" or, in John Florio's 1603 English edition, "single," but double-sided, ambivalent. It textually repeats the form of the one-headed, two-bodied child; though its title (a sort of head) promises an essay on *a* monstrous child, the body of the essay portrays conjoined twins. The narrator himself comes to resemble what he describes. Montaigne seems divided as to whether he has beheld a child or children, alternating between the use of singular and plural pronouns to describe the infant(s).[54] Not only is the essay more complex than it purports to be, but Montaigne also proves not quite able to leave the interpretation of this double child to the doctors. He notes that many people might interpret the child's body to predict political developments. Such analysis, he suggests, is mere superstition, and monsters are nothing special—at least, they are no more special than any other creature. With an Augustinian appreciation of the breadth of God's creation, Montaigne writes,

> Those which we call monsters are not so with God, who in the
> immensitie of his worke seeth the infinitie of formes therein
> contained. And it may be thought, that any figure [which] doth
> amaze us, hath relation unto some other figure of the same kinde,
> although unknown unto man.[55]

While Montaigne rejects the urge to find a secret meaning in a monster's body, and tries to defuse the electrical current of the *insolite* that surrounds a monster, he finishes (contradictorily, as is his wont) by being unable to escape thinking of a

---

[53]   Norman R. Smith, "Portentous Births and the Monstrous Imagination in Renaissance Culture," *Marvels, Monsters, and Miracles: Studies in the Medieval and Early Modern Imaginations*, Timothy S. Jones and David A. Springer, eds (Kalamazoo: Studies in Medieval Culture, 2002): 267–83.

[54]   Florio's translation rather minimizes Montaigne's deliberate vacillation between describing one child and two children. Florio uses singular pronouns to indicate the child except in one case: "They were joyned face to face, and as if a little child would embrace another somewhat bigger," 439. Florio may, however, indicate awareness of Montaigne's wavering between the single and the double by translating the first sentence as "This discourse shall passe *single*" (my italics).

[55]   Dudley Wilson writes, "For Augustine, as for Job, a large part of the universe is indeed inexplicable, and our attitude towards it should be that of wonder rather than that of analyst and explainer," *Signs and Portents: Monstrous births from the Middle Ages to the Enlightenment* (London: Routledge, 1993), 26. Montaigne, "Of a Monstrous Child," *The Essayes*, II.440. The original French is as follows: "Ce que nous appellons monstres ne le sont pas à Dieu, qui veoid en l'immensité de son ouvrage l'infinité des formes qu'il y a comprinse: et est à croire que cette figure qui nous estonne se rapporte et tient à quelque aultre figure de mesme genre incogneu à l'homme," *Essais*, 434.

monster as a signifier for hidden meaning.[56] Montaigne again resembles the double child. His opinion, melded though in opposition in this short essay, wants to move in two different directions. While conjoined twins may not signal a particular event to Montaigne, and he stresses that they are probably not unique or strange but have a duplicate or relative ("of the same sort"; "*du mesme genre*") in the world, they still index the unknown: "And it may be thought, that any figure [which] doth amaze us, hath relation unto some other figure of the same kinde, although unknown unto man." His claim recalls Augustine, who gestures to the unknown as he writes that a "portent" (*portenta*, classed by Augustine in the same group as *monstra, ostenta*, and *prodigia*) "happens not contrary to nature, but contrary to what is known of nature."[57]

Montaigne's essay is noteworthy for its effort at pragmatism—its deference to medical experts, and the empirical, eyewitness-style report he attempts to give. But it is remarkable for its inability to banish wonder from a realm that he claims should be judged by science. Montaigne is unable to tell his tale simply, but instead structurally reproduces the monster he saw, engendering in his reader a wonder about the unseen child, a wonder that Montaigne invokes when he acknowledges that this strange child represents the unknown.

Paré is a doctor who strove to debunk misconceptions and provide clear meticulous evidence, from accounts of disproving the supposed ailments of beggars to detailed anatomical drawings. His *Oeuvres* provide a number of visual examples of abnormal positions infants sometimes take in the womb, and his tone when discussing such deliveries is peppered with such empirically matter-of-fact phrases as "I have felt," "I have found," "I have found," and "I observed."[58] Yet the death of one infant leaves Paré unusually flustered. For Paré, the death of a child was usually a matter of simple autopsy. For example, when called upon to determine the death of an eight-month-old baby, Paré and other doctors studied the corpse. Noticing the baby's swollen gums, Paré cut into them and decided, in consultation with his colleagues, that the child had died because his teeth had not been strong enough to push through the skin.[59] It is a death that presents a simple scientific explanation. But one death promotes a sense of wonder in Paré. When discussing the unusual fetal positions he has encountered in his practice, Paré describes a very special one: "And, moreover, I protest before God that I found a childe being yet alive in the body of his mother (whom I opened so soone as shee was dead) lying all along stretched out,

---

[56] Wilson briefly discusses this essay and notes Montaigne's cynicism about prognostication in it, 76. But he does not notice how Montaigne cannot quite help thinking of the conjoined twins as a signal of the unknown.

[57] Augustine, *The City of God against the Pagans*, trans. Eva Matthews Sanford and William McAllen Green, 7 vols. (Cambridge: Harvard University Press, 1965), 21.8 (pp. 57 and 51).

[58] Paré, Ffff6v, Gggg1r.

[59] David Hunt, *Parents and Children in History: The Psychology of Family Life in Early Modern France* (New York: Basic Books, Inc., 1970), 121.

with his face upwards, and the palmes of his hands joyned together, as if he were at prayer."[60] The strength of Paré's words suggests he is shaken: "moreover, I protest before God," he swears. But perhaps a stronger testimony to this case's subversion of Paré's sense of pragmatic *savoir-faire* is his exclusion of a visual representation of this infant's position among the many others he provides in the same section of the book. Organizationally, the case of the praying child is associated by proximity with the breech positions both verbally and visually described. Why, then, does the doctor who produced an enormous, incredibly detailed book that became a bestseller and a foundational text in Renaissance medicine neglect to include a drawing of a position that, given the strength of his reaction, impresses him greatly? By occluding a visual portrayal of the praying infant, Paré promotes the occult nature of his birth, suggesting that wonder is a quality that inevitably touches French Renaissance efforts to approach paediatrics with pragmatic eyes.

The idea that paediatrics was seen as a special practice of medicine is not at all clear. Fontaine, for example, objects to those who do not realize that "the bodies of little children are a medical subject just like those of men."[61] On the one hand, Fontaine seems to promote the necessity of treating children with all the serious medical attention afforded to adults. On the other hand, his insistence that "children are like men" suggests that treating children is not necessarily different from other medical practices. Material that we might label as paediatrics was regularly folded into texts (such as Guillemeau's and Joubert's) that treated obstetrics or, in the case of Paré, into vast tomes that encompassed many medical subjects. But it is nonetheless the case that Renaissance France witnessed an increased textual interest in the care of children. The medical profession developed an investment in itself as a profession, one that was a bulwark against popular misconceptions about children's health. In print, at least, paediatrics was a male-dominated profession that sought to sideline "old matrons" who propagated such misconceptions, and so an emphasis on habit and pragmatic approaches held sway. One can see this in the repeated mentions of the word "regime" in pediatric texts, and how this use hearkens back to earlier texts Renaissance doctors likely would have known, such as Bartholomaus Metlinger's *Regime of Life for Young children* (1457) and Heinrich von Louffenburg's *Regimen of Health for Young Children* (1429).[62] An effort at consolidating an approach to child-care was being made in Renaissance France, and that approach relied on *savoir-faire* rather than suspicion. Yet texts so different as a novel, an essay, and a medical manual suggest that paediatrics inevitably had to acknowledge, even as it tried to dismiss, the quality of wonder.

---

[60]   Paré, Gggg1r.

[61]   Fontaine, sig. B1v.

[62]   Paré, sig. H6v. Joubert, title page. Évelyne Berriot-Salvadore argues that the birth scene in *Gargantua and Pantagruel* attests to the author's interest in the multiplication of obstetrics texts and paediatrics in the vulgar tongue, and offers Metlinger's text as one such example. "L'enfant," 93.

Chapter 6

"Our little darlings":
Huguenot Children and Child-rearing in the
Letters of Louise de Coligny

Jane Couchman

… no one can love, estime, cherish and honor you more than your mama, who kisses your hands a hundred times, and those of our little darlings. May God bless them.[1]

This is how Louise de Coligny closed a letter she wrote to her stepdaughter Charlotte-Brabantine de La Tremoille in July 1601. The same sentiments recur with variations in all her letters to Charlotte-Brabantine: The "little darlings" are Charlotte-Brabantine's children Henri, Charlotte, and Frédéric de La Tremoille. As Evelyne Berriot-Salvadore has written, "Louise de Coligny seems to be the emotional centre around whom a warm and supportive family developed."[2] We are fortunate that Louise's letters to Charlotte-Brabantine, along with letters written to Charlotte-Brabantine by her older sister Elisabeth de Bouillon, some letters from their other siblings, and from Charlotte-Brabantine's husband the Duke de La Tremoille, and letters exchanged among the children and their parents, have been preserved in the La Tremoille family archives.[3]

Louise de Coligny's correspondence has long been consulted as a source of information about political and religious events in France and in the United Provinces of the Netherlands in the late sixteenth and early seventeenth century, in which she played a role at the highest levels. She was the daughter of Gaspard de Coligny, the fourth wife of William "the Silent" of Orange Stadthouder of the United Provinces of the Netherlands, the stepmother of Maurice of Nassau, who became Stadthouder after his father's death, and a cousin of Henri IV of France.

---

[1] Marchegay, 186. Letters from Louise de Coligny are cited from Louise de Coligny, *Correspondance*, Paul Marchegay and Léon Marlet, eds (Genève: Slatkine, 1970, réimpression de l'édition de Paris, 1887) and, where applicable, from Jane Couchman, "Lettres de Louise de Coligny aux membres de sa famille aux Pays-bas et en France," *Lettres de femmes XVIe–XVIIIe siècles*, Elizabeth Goldsmith et Colette Winn, eds (Paris: Champion, 2005). Unless otherwise indicated, all translations from sources in French are mine.

[2] Evelyne Berriot-Salvadore, *Les femmes dans la société française de la Renaissance* (Genève: Droz, 1990), 139.

[3] Archives nationales de France, Chartier de Thouars 1 AP 333, 337, 340, 342.

She corresponded with the Earl of Leicester and Elizabeth I and was a friend of Queen Marie de Medicis, to name only the most prominent of her contacts.[4]

But children figure just as centrally in her letters and in her life as does her exercise of informal political influence. In her correspondence, and in their extant letters as well, we can observe her relationships with the children who came under her care, particularly her four stepdaughters, her son, and her stepgrandchildren. The letters depict a Huguenot sensibility towards children which is both affectionate and firm, but far from austere. Charming sketches of the children and their activities are combined with discussions of health and discipline. Humanist learning, the pleasures of society, fine dresses and jewelry, horsemanship, music, and court dancing are seen as quite compatible with the Reformed faith. Though the letters describe, not surprisingly, a different program for girls and for boys, this well-educated woman ensured that her stepdaughters and granddaughters received as enlightened an upbringing as she.

Is this the beginning of a "modern" sensibility about children? Historians are of course constantly revisiting the findings of Philippe Ariès, studying early modern families in their social contexts, and showing that earlier practices which might seem strange to us reflect in fact a concern for the best interests of children, for their upbringing, and for their salvation.[5] Certainly, the activities and well-being of the children are central concerns for Louise and for her stepdaughters, as well as for the children's fathers and uncles. As for the children, they emerge in their own words and in the words of their relatives as delightful in their sometimes stubborn assertion of themselves as individuals. These sources, along with other letters and memoirs of Huguenot noblewomen in late sixteenth- and early seventeenth-century France, provide a lively supplement to prescriptive documents such as catechisms and consistory records.[6]

---

[4] Jules Delaborde, *Louise de Coligny, Princesse d'Orange* (Genève: Slatkine Reprints, 1970) réimpression de l'édition de Paris, 1890, Tomes I et II; Jane Couchman, "'... give birth quickly and then send us your good husband ...': Form, Persuasion and Informal Political Influence in the Letters of Louise de Coligny," *Women's Letters across Europe 1400–1700: Form and Persuasion*, Jane Couchman and Ann Crabb, eds (Burlington, VT: Ashgate, 2005), 149–69.

[5] Philippe Ariès, *L'enfant et la famille sous l'Ancien Régime* (Paris: Seuil, 1964); Olwen Hufton, "Le travail et la famille: La maternité," *Histoire des femmes en occident: XVIe –XVIIIe siècle*, Natalie Zemon Davis and Arlette Farge, eds (Paris: Plon, 1991) 50–63; François Lebrun, "Parents et enfants"; Rosemary O'Day, *The Family and Family Relationships, 1500–1900: England, France and the United States of America* (New York: St. Martin's Press, 1999); Stephen Ozment, *Ancestors: The Loving Family in Old Europe* (Cambridge: Harvard University Press, 2001); Linda A. Pollock, "Parent-Child Relations," *Family Life in Early Modern Times, The History of the European Family*, David I. Kertzer and Marzio Barbagli, eds, vol. I (New Haven and London: Yale University Press, 2001) 192–219, 303–7.

[6] See Nadine Kuperty-Tsur, "Rhétorique parentale et religieuse: les voies de la transmission des valeurs de la réforme aux enfants," *Les deux réformes chrétiennes:*

Louise de Coligny's Children

When William of Orange was assassinated in July 1584, he was survived by 12 children born to his four wives. Several of the children were already adults and others were settled with family members.[7] Louise took responsibility for their infant son Frédéric-Henri (1584–1647), and for four of her youngest stepdaughters: Louise-Julienne (1576–1644), Elisabeth (1577–1642), Charlotte-Brabantine (1580–1631), and Amélie-Antwerpienne (1581–1657), daughters of William and his previous wife, Charlotte de Bourbon-Montpensier.

Caring for the children after William's death was not a simple undertaking. The family was in a precarious financial situation because of the complexity of William's estate, which was heavily encumbered with debts incurred during the revolt William had led of the United Provinces against the Spanish. Louise wrote frequently to her brother-in-law Jean de Nassau, now the head of the family, about her serious concerns for the children's health and well-being. Unable to access any funds that might have been in William's estate, she had money sent from her properties in France, but that source was soon exhausted. In October 1581, she reminded her brother-in-law where the youngest of William's 12 surviving children were:

> My son, Monsieur the Count of Nassau [Maurice, 18, his father's heir as Stadhouder] is well, thank God, and is about to depart for Zeeland. My daughters

---

Propagation et diffusion, Myriam Yardeni and Illana Zinguer, eds (Brill: Leiden, 2004) 153–71; Évelyne Berriot-Salvadore, "L'éducation de la vraie chrétienne," *Les Femmes dans la société française de la Renaissance*, 61–82; Barbara Pitkin, "'The heritage of the Lord': Children in the theology of Jean Calvin," *The Child in Christian Thought*, Marcia J. Bunge, ed. (Grand Rapids: Eerdmans, 2001) 160–93, 186–7; and Jeffrey R. Watt, "Calvinism, childhood, and education: the evidence from the Genevan Consistory," *Sixteenth Century Journal* 2002, XXXIII/2, 439–56.

[7] William's surviving children were: Philippe-Guillaume and Marie with Anne of Egmont; Anne, Maurice, and Émilie with Anne of Saxe; Louise-Julienne, Elisabeth, Catherine-Belgica, Flandrine, Charlotte-Brabantine, and Amélie-Antwerpienne with Charlotte de Bourbon; and Frédéric-Henri with Louise de Coligny. At the time of William's death there were several offers to care for the younger children. Anne went to live with her stepsister Marie in Buren; Émilie went to Dillenburg to live with her father's family; Catherine-Belgica went to live with her godmother, William's sister Catherine, Countess of Schwarzburg; Flandrine was already staying with her mother's cousin, the Abbesse of the convent of the Paraclete. Elizabeth I of England offered to take Louise and Elisabeth; the Duchess of Bouillon offered to take Charlotte-Brabantine, and the Electrice of the Palatinate wanted to take Amélie-Antwerpienne, but the States General of the United Provinces refused their offers. See Susan Broomhall, "Lettres de Louise-Julienne, d'Élisabeth et d'Amélie de Nassau à leur soeur Charlotte-Brabantine de Nassau (1595–1601)," *Lettres de femmes: Textes inédites et oubliés du XVIe au XVIIe siècle*, Elizabeth C. Goldsmith and Colette Winn, eds (Paris: Champion, 2005), 135–40, for a fuller account of what became of all of William's children.

> Mlle d'Orange [Marie] and Anne are in Buren. Little Catherine-Belgica is with
> the Countess of Schwarzburg, my sister. The others are with me, and are quite
> well, as is my son, except for Louise, who has been extremely ill for six weeks,
> so much so that the doctors are very concerned. I do what I can, and will continue
> to do so, with God's help.[8]

On December 19, 1584, she wrote again:

> ... my dear brother, the affairs of this grieving family are in such a pitiable
> state that, if a remedy is not soon forthcoming through your prudence and good
> counsel, I can forsee only great confusion. ... for I have been here for five
> months with four of my step-daughters and my son ... without having received
> a penny from the estate.[9]

Many of her letters from the 1580s and 1590s document her attempts to raise funds
to support her young children from the States General of the various Provinces
of the Netherlands. She enlisted the help of other relatives and friends, including
the Earl of Leicester, who was in the Netherlands as Elizabeth I's representative.
She wrote to Leicester in November 1586, asking him to recommend to the States
General that she receive some income from land that had belonged to William,
so that she could "be spared that most extreme of sicknessess, poverty."[10] It was
not until April 1592, eight years after William of Orange's assassination, that the
States General of the United Provinces finally allocated an annual pension to her
for the care of the children who were with her.

The children's health and the precariousness of their young lives remained a
concern throughout Louise's letters and those of her stepdaughters. Louise wrote
to her brother-in-law in January 1588: "As for my son, he is well at the moment,
after having been ill after we returned from Frisia. My little daughters are also
well, they are growing taller and learning their lessons well.[11] In April 1589,
she wrote:

> ... My dear brother ... , all the news I'll give you is that your little nieces and
> my son, your nephew, are well. [My son] has been ill with fevers all winter, but
> right now he is feeling better. I hope that God will preserve for me this dear
> token from My Lord his father. He is all the consolation I have, and my unique
> pleasure.[12]

When Charlotte-Brabantine gave birth to her first child, her sister Louise-Julienne
acknowledged the fragility of the newborn child:

---

[8]   Marchegay, 42, Couchman, 102–3.

[9]   Marchegay, 12–13.

[10]   Marchegay, 41.

[11]   Marchegay, 42–3.

[12]   Marchegay, 45 .

I pray God that, as it has pleased Him to give him [Henri] to you, it will please Him also to conserve him to you, and to give to both of you the grace to receive much contentment from him and to raise and nourish him so that he may one day serve the glory of God and the good of all of Christianity.[13]

These loving parents were not spared the early deaths of some of their children. When Charlotte-Brabantine's daughter Elisabeth died at the age of three in 1604, the elder Elisabeth wrote to the grieving mother: "Dear sister, it's not a beloved niece whom I mourn, it's a child for whom I weep with the true love of a mother."[14]

The Question of Salvation

In writing about the children's well-being, these parents reflect the potentially paradoxical beliefs which Huguenot parents negotiated in their childrearing. They believed that God's grace and election, which can neither be merited nor rejected, were essential to the survival and the salvation of their children. They also believed that parents were responsible for bringing up the children, following the Proverb: "Train up the child in the way he should go: and when he is old, he will not depart from it" (Proverbs 22:6). According to Calvin, parents who believed they were among those whom God had chosen could expect that their children would also be among the elect. At the same time, education was both a duty of parents and a right of children; the children needed to learn about their Christian election so that their faith and gratitude would be strengthened and they would be able to respond appropriately to the gift of election.[15]

In her dedication of her *Mémoires* of her husband's life to their son, Philippe (1579–1605), Charlotte d'Arbaleste Du Plessis Mornay (1548–1590) explains the goals of Huguenot education:

My son, God is my witness that, even before your birth, he gave me the hope that you would serve him. ... With this intention, your father and I have taken care to nourish you in the fear of God, which we have, insofar as we could, given you to drink with your milk; we have also made sure ... that you were instructed in good letters and, by His grace, we met with some success, so that you could not only live, but even shine forth in His Church.[16]

---

[13] Louise-Julienne to Charlotte-Brabantine, Broomhall, 170.

[14] Elisabeth to Charlotte-Brabantine, cited in Berriot-Salvadore, 152. The previous year, Elisabeth had lost a daughter soon after her birth.

[15] Pitkin, "'The heritage of the Lord': Children in the theology of Jean Calvin," 162, 171, 182, 188. As Kuperty-Tsur explains it, Charlotte Du Plessis Mornay's account "is both a matter of the act of grace and the duty to educate," "Rhétorique parentale et religieuse," 159.

[16] Charlotte Du Plessis Mornay, *Mémoires de Madame de Mornay*, vol. I, Mme de Witt, ed. (Paris: Rénouard, 1868), 1.

Charlotte Du Plessis Mornay rejoices in the precious gift of the child, and is confident that he is among God's elect, just as his parents are. She accepts their duty to raise him in the Reformed faith, while also acknowledging that God alone, by His grace, decides the future of the child.

> We can believe that, as he is our God, he will also be our children's God, for he has promised this. But even though he will lead them to election through his mercy, we must not, for our part, neglect to lead them through the parental care of their education, making them inheritors through knowledge, and teaching them to understand how much they owe to the grace we have received from Him.[17]

Charlotte Du Plessis Mornay wrote her *Mémoires* so that young Philippe could learn from the example of his father's life, both as a model of conduct to be imitated and as an illustration of the operation of God's grace.

In Louise de Coligny's correspondence, religious education and salvation are, to some extent, taken for granted, and certainly do not receive the coherent explication that is found in Charlotte Du Plessis Mornay's *Mémoires*. The children report that they are learning psalms and religious poems and reassure their parents that they are saying their prayers regularly. Charlotte de La Tremoille, aged about seven, wrote to her mother: "... I will do everything you tell me to do, and I will pray God to give you good health ... and to give me the grace to be very well-behaved."[18] But we have more information about other aspects of the children's lives and education than about their religious upbringing.

Charlotte de Bourbon's Daughters: Educating Noble Huguenot Girls

Louise de Coligny was part of a community of Huguenot noblewomen actively involved in learning and in political life, which extended backward in time to Louise de Savoie and Margaret de Navarre, and forward through their daughters and granddaughters.[19] As a result both of their elevated rank and their families' Reformed religious views, these women received a solid education.[20] Louise was educated by her mother Charlotte de Laval and by her stepmother Jacqueline d'Entremonts, and had as her models female relatives such as Eléonore de Roye and Jeanne d'Albret, with whom she and her family had close associations. Louise

---

[17]   Ibid., 8–9.

[18]   Charlotte to Charlotte-Brabantine, Berriot-Salvadore, 487.

[19]   Nancy L. Roelker, "The appeal of Calvinism to French noblewomen in the sixteenth century," *Journal of Interdisciplinary History*, 1972, 391–407, and "The role of noblewomen in the French reformation," *Archiv für Reformationsgeschichte*, 1972, 168–95.

[20]   Berriot-Salvadore, 63: "In the reformed milieu, women's education cannot appear as a moral dilemma, since learning doesn't lead to evil, but to the truth of the divine message. Thus, there is no need for a specific pedagogical project: the education of women, like the education of the poor and humble, is a praxis which impregnates daily life."

probably also participated with her brothers in the lessons they received from their tutor Legresle. The men of their families respected these women for their contributions to the Huguenot cause. Calvin exchanged letters with several of them and counted on them to support and expand the Reformed Church in France.

Most of what we know about how Louise de Coligny educated the four stepdaughters who lived with her, Louise-Julienne, Elisabeth, Charlotte-Brabantine, and Amélie-Antwerpienne de Nassau, comes from the letters they exchanged with her and among themselves after they left home to be married.[21] In fact, one of the first lessons the girls learned from their stepmother was the importance of letters as a way of keeping in touch with distant relatives and of having an impact on events that mattered to them. Even when writing to her brother-in-law immediately after William's death, Louise included letters which three of the sisters had written in support of her request for assistance. Marie wrote:

> My uncle, we have suffered such a great loss, my sisters and I, that we do not know whom to turn to except yourself. We humbly ask that you will be a good father and a good uncle to us, so that we may continue in the religion in which our father has nourished us until now.[22]

From their letters, we can see that Louise had formed the girls for their roles as wives and mothers and also as actors on the national and international stage. She introduced them to the precepts of their faith, to the Gospels, and to regular prayers. In preparation for the advantageous marriages she arranged for them, they all learned to read and write in French and in at least one other language. Amélie and Charlotte-Brabantine learned Italian, while Louise-Julienne and Elisabeth learned German.[23] All the girls learned arithmetic and were trained to take care of the noble households for which they would eventually be responsible. Soon after her marriage to the Duke of Bouillon, Elisabeth, aged 18, wrote to Charlotte-Brabantine: "Your sister is very good at managing her household", a skill which she attributes to the lessons of "Madame my step-mother."[24] Societal graces were not ignored. All the girls learned to dance, and Charlotte-Brabantine enjoyed playing the lute.[25]

---

[21]   See Susan Broomhall and Jacqueline Ghent's perceptive article "In the name of the father: Conceptualizing the *Pater Familias* in the letters of William the Silent's children," *Renaissance Quarterly* LXII, 4 (Winter 2009), 1130–66.

[22]   Delaborde, 139–40.

[23]   Elisabeth to Charlotte-Brabantine, Elisabeth de Nassau, duchesse de Bouillon, *Lettres d'Élisabeth de Nassau, duchesse de Bouillon, à sa soeur Charlotte-Brabantine*, P. Marchegay, ed. (Les Roches-Baritaud, 1875), 28. A dialogue written in Italian for Amélie is published in P. Marchegay et H. Imbert, *Lettres missives originales du XVIe siècle* (Niort, 1881), 428.

[24]   Elisabeth to Charlotte-Brabantine, Marchegay, 39. This was apparently unusual; her new family was most impressed. Berriot-Salvadore, 136, n.42.

[25]   Elisabeth to Charlotte-Brabantine Marchegay, 35, 39.

Just as important, the girls developed close relationships with their stepmother and their siblings, and shared in their letters all aspects of their family life, pregnancy, birth, delight as children learn to walk and talk, concern over childhood illnesses, mourning for the death of a child, loneliness during the frequent absences of husbands at court or at war, and negotiations about financial or political matters in which they were involved.

Frédéric-Henri of Orange-Nassau: Educating a Son

Of all the children in Louise's charge, her own son Frédéric-Henri (1584–1647) was the dearest to her, but by no means the easiest to raise. He was William of Orange's third son, and Louise de Coligny's only child, born on January 3, 1584, nine months after his parents' marriage and six months before his father's assassination. Confident in raising her stepdaughters herself, Louise was aware that her son needed an education only men could provide. So she consulted her old friend Philippe Du Plessis Mornay, writing to him that her friends had described his son to her, and had "given me such a good report of the great promise of such a fine youth that it made me very much wish to raise my own son in imitation of him."[26] Du Plessis Mornay responded by sending her a document he called: *Advice on the instruction of a young man whom one wishes to nourish with good letters, sent to Madame the Princess of Orange, at her request, for her son.*[27]

At the outset, Du Plessis Mornay stresses that "Children's inclination, which comes from God, can do more than any art we may provide," He recommends that a tutor be chosen to correspond with "the quality of the child" so as to "accommodate [his] studies to [his] nature and [his] vocation."[28] "Inclinations," "quality," "nature," and "vocation" are all gifts from God. The child should learn to confess his faults and to "fear God, the center and the end of wisdom"; he should exercise charity and be offered models of good behavior to observe, for "children take on the color of good or of evil without thinking about it." Here Du Plessis Mornay echoes a debate about the nature of the child: does he or she possess at birth a certain "inclination," a personality and talents which are his own and which must be awakened, or is the child born with a completely unformed personality, learning by imitation from what he finds in his surroundings? In the passages cited, Du Plessis Mornay seems to combine the two. In any case, he does not suggest, nor does Calvin, that children require severe punishments because of original sin.

---

[26]   Marchegay, 95. Du Plessis Mornay's son was of course young Philippe Du Plessis Mornay, whom we met earlier in his mother, Charlotte's, *Mémoires*.

[27]   Philippe Du Plessis Mornay, "Advis sur l'institution d'un enfant que l'on veult nourrir aulx lettres, envoyé à madame la princesse d'Orange, à son instance sur le sujet de son fils," *Mémoires et correspondance*, tome V, Genève, Slatkine, 1969, réimpr. de l'édition de Paris, 1824–1825, 65ff.

[28]   Ozment, *Ancestors*, 69. Pitkin, "The heritage of the Lord," 164.

Du Plessis Mornay does not mention that the boy should learn the Catechism, probably because he could assume that the boy's mother would already have seen to that aspect of his education.[29] The only biblical text Du Plessis Mornay recommends is the book of *Proverbs*, which appears after a long list of Greek and Latin authors in a section dealing with the languages the child should learn. Otherwise, the education proposed is thoroughly humanist. Du Plessis Mornay proposes that the child be given "some history books and others, in which there are pictures, which please at that age." From them, he will learn Latin, Greek, and Hebrew, but one at a time, not all at once, otherwise "he will be confused." In this way, the child will learn "grammar, rhetoric and dialectic." He will learn his lessons by heart, he will be able to recite them "with confidence," and he will often translate from one language to another. Duplessis Mornay is in agreement with other contemporary theoreticians that "until 14 years, it is memory that rules." This is thus the time to learn languages and histories.[30] "From then on, the judgement must be exercised," and this is the time when mathematics should also be taught. In all cases, the child learns better if his teacher finds ways to make him want to do so. The child will also learn to paint, and will learn the terminology related to various crafts and occupations. He will be "brought up with compagnons suitable to his birth" and will practice "games and exercises appropriate to his age." When she received this advice, Louise de Coligny wrote to thank Du Plessis Mornay, but with regret that she could not put it into practice in the Netherlands, a place she describes as "sterile in men capable of educating young men."[31] To remedy this situation, she encouraged the humanist Joseph Justus Scaliger to accept a position at the University of Leyden. When he did so, she established a household in that city while her son attended classes for a short period of time.[32]

Frédéric-Henri's university studies were cut short by a more pressing ambition Louise had for her son. Since his birth, she had dreamed of establishing him at the court of Henri IV of France, a reasonable ambition because of her own ties of family and friendship with the king and others at court.[33] In January 1598, when he

---

[29]   There is no mention of a Catechism or of a Confession of Faith. See Pitkin, "The heritage of the Lord," 187. The evidence from the Genevan Consistory indicates, however, that both parents were involved in the religious education of their children; Watt, "Calvinism, childhood and education," 146–7. See also Pollock, "Parent-child relations," 202.

[30]   The sources do not agree on the precise "ages" relative to child development. See Pitkin, "The heritage of the Lord," 164, and François Lebrun, "Parents et enfants," *Histoire de la famille*, t. 2, *Le Choc des Modernités*, André Burgière, Christine Klapisch-Zuber, Martine Segalen, Françoise Zonabend, eds (Paris: Colin, 1986), 148–53.

[31]   Marchegay, 95.

[32]   Anthony T. Grafton, *Joseph Scaliger: A Study in the History of Classical Scholarship*, 2 vols. (Oxford: Oxford University Press, 1983, 1993).

[33]   See, for example, a letter from Henry of Navarre to Maurice of Nassau, April 26, 1589: "[Gaspard de Coligny's] daughter, your step-mother, was cared for with the late Queen, my mother [Jeanne d'Albret] as dearly as my sister and me, when we were all together." *Lettres missives de Henri IV*, t. 9, suppl., 660. See also Delaborde, 226–8.

was 13 years old, Louise was finally permitted by the States General of the United Provinces to take her son to the French court, where he was warmly received. Louise wrote to Charlotte-Brabantine of Frédéric-Henri's progress in his riding lessons with Antoine de Pluvinel, Henri IV's celebrated master of equitation.[34] The young man prepared to join the king's entourage, for which Louise incurred considerable expense.[35] She was particularly proud of her son's performances in court ballets. In December 1598, she described to Charlotte-Brabantine "a ballet which was danced at Saint-Germaine at the baptism of Alexander Monsieur in which your brother danced, and was one of the most important, and who received the most praise."[36] Alexandre Monsieur was Henri IV's son by his mistress Gabrielle d'Estrées. Louise expresses no discomfort with the fact that her son had participated in court dances to mark the public baptism of the king's mistress's child.

Louise hoped to stay at the French court with her son. However, she was obliged to respond to the wishes of her stepson, Maurice de Nassau, now Stadhouder of the United Provinces of the Netherlands, who was grooming Frédéric-Henri to be his heir. Maurice and the States General of the United Provinces ordered Frédéric-Henri to return to the Low Countries, where he lived with the soldiers, was given a company to lead, participated in battles, and developed habits of which Louise strongly disapproved. She remarked that he had inherited the stubbornness of his father's family.[37] In October 1600, when she thought Frédéric-Henri might return to France for the marriage of Henri IV to Marie de Médicis, she was delighted. She wrote to Charlotte-Brabantine: "I am very pleased, mostly because he won't spend the winter in the idleness of the Hague, where they waste their time in excessive debauchery. Your cousin Ernest leads him into this … I am angry at him."[38] Soon after, Louise settled in The Hague, mainly to be near her son, about whom she was constantly concerned. She particularly wanted to see him well married. She wrote to Charlotte-Brabantine that if that happened she would "die for joy."[39] Although she did not live to see it, Frédéric-Henri became Stadhouder of the United Provinces and Prince of Orange in 1625, married and had children, continuing the Orange-Nassau dynasty.

Grandchildren

When her stepdaughter Charlotte-Brabantine's first child, Henri de La Tremoille, was born in December 1598, Louise de Coligny wrote to the new mother:

In September 1595, Henri IV had formally invited Frédéric-Henri to live in France and to enjoy all the honors to which his birth entitled him.

[34] Marchegay, 139.

[35] Marchegay, 136.

[36] Marchegay, 143–4.

[37] Marchegay, 168, 203, Couchman, 126.

[38] Marchegay, 173.

[39] Marchegay, 320.

My daughter, a son! I weep for joy. Well, I have no words to express my pleasure, for it is beyond all words and all speech. ... God be praised that you have given birth so fortunately! but I would like to have seen you and to have heard what you said in your labor, and I very much want to know how you've been feeling since then. ... I am dying to see this grandson, and how your little hands hold him.[40]

During Charlotte-Brabantine's second pregnancy a year later, her husband was away in Paris, but kept in touch by letter. "It is amazing." writes Evelyne Berriot-Salvadore, "to meet this great lord—at the very moment when Henri IV was naming him a Peer of France—busy ordering a cradle, baby clothes and a drinking cup for 'the little person' soon to be born."[41] On the occasion of Charlotte de La Tremoille's birth, Louise wrote to her stepdaughter: "So you have given me a grand-daughter! My goodness, I imagine she is very pretty! ... I am dying to see you with your little ones, whom I kiss in my imagination a million times."[42]

Louise's grandchildren are immediately identified by their parents and grandmother as individuals, gentle and affectionate, lively and turbulent. Little Henri de La Tremoille figures often in his grandmother's letters. In one of them she promises: "When I am in Paris, I will send him a little horse made of coconut fibre."[43] When his mother is away, Louise writes to Henri himself to inquire after his siblings and his mother "as the oldest, I write to you for all three and kiss you all in my imagination."[44] (He was seven years old.) Claude de La Tremoille writes to his wife after she has left on a trip, describing the reactions of each of the children to her departure: "it's unbelievable how much Charlotte cried" also little "Babet" (Elisabeth) and "Atreri" (Frédéric), but Henri, the eldest, held back his tears.[45] During his mother's absences, little Henri wrote regularly to her, reporting on his progress in his studies and on his siblings.

Elisabeth de Bouillon's children are also indulgently loved. She writes to Charlotte-Brabantine that her eldest daughter "Lolo" (Louise) "amuses us all the time" ... "she gets naughtier every day; I wish you could have her in your dressing room for an hour a day, she would make a fine mess."[46] Visiting with Elisabeth de Bouillon, Louise writes to Charlotte-Brabantine:

---

[40] Marchegay, 145, Couchman, 118.

[41] Berriot-Salvadore, 146, referring to letters from Claude de La Tremoille to his wife, Aug. 29, Sept. 13, Oct. 17, Oct. 19, 1599.

[42] Marchegay, 166.

[43] Marchegay, 181, Couchman, 124–5.

[44] Marchegay, 230.

[45] Berriot-Salvadore, 150.

[46] Elisabeth to Charlotte-Brabantine, Broomhall, 167. At two and a half, Louise had: "begun to speak Limousin, and a language so particular to her that aside from two or three people, no one understands her. I'm sure that if you saw her I would soon teach you to understand her, and as a result you'd spend a cheerful hour with her." Berriot-Salvadore, 150.

... their daughter [Louise] ... is as beautiful as can be ... she has taken to me so warmly that I'm bursting with pride, for they all say that she has never been fond of anyone except me. She doesn't pay attention to her father or her mother, there's only her grandma. It's so intense that I'm afraid it won't last; still, I'll do everything I can to keep her good will.[47]

As early as April 1603, Louise wrote to Charlotte-Brabantine: "My daughter, you must give me one of your daughters."[48] In July 1607, Louise welcomed the seven-year-old Charlotte de La Tremoille to The Hague, where she stayed until 1610. Obviously, the pleasure Louise took in raising her stepdaughters extended to her granddaughter. Elisabeth reported to Charlotte-Brabantine: "Madame my step-mother can't praise your daughter enough. She says she has the nicest spirit and the prettiest little face she's ever seen, and that she's the perfect image of Brabantine. My dear, you must acknowledge God's grace in giving you such perfect children."[49]

We learn something about Charlotte's earlier education in a letter she wrote to her mother, probably in which she boasted that she had learned "seventeen psalms, all Pibrac's quatrains, and all Zamarial's eight-line poems, and what's more I know Latin."[50] Pibrac and Zamarial were well-known moralists; the works Charlotte had memorized deal with the theme of the vanity of earthly pleasures. However, in another letter written at about the same time, she announces that she has had her ears pierced so that she can wear "pendant ear-rings."

In her letters, Louise kept Charlotte-Brabantine up-to-date about her daughter's activities: "... our little sweetheart ... can always get her way with her uncles. She was the belle of the ball that was held when the Countesses of Nassau and Culembourg were here."[51] Charlotte learned Flemish, worked on her handwriting, and received dancing lessons "to make her a bit more graceful."[52] Questions of discipline are mentioned in several of Louise's letters, and Charlotte wrote herself to her mother in February, 1609:

Madame, I am very sorry not to have been obedient to you, but I hope that from now on you will not have reason to be upset with me, since up to now I haven't been very good, but I hope to be, so that you will have reason to be pleased, and Madame my grandmother and Messieurs my uncles will not find me ungrateful ... For New Years, ... Madame [Louise] gave me a diamond and ruby brooch, Monsieur le Prince d'Orange [Philippe-Guillaume] gave me

[47] Marchegay, 156.
[48] Marchegay, 210.
[49] Delaborde, 124.
[50] Berriot-Salvadore, 487. The references are to the *Quatrains* of Guy de Faur de Pibrac, and to the *Octonaires sur la vanité et l'inconstance du monde* by Antoine de la Roche Chandieu, known as Zamariel.
[51] Marchegay, 244.
[52] Marchegay, 236.

earings, His Excellence [Maurice of Nassau] gave me three dozen pearl and ruby buttons, my uncle [Frédéric-Henri] gave me a dress made of cloth of silver … .[53]

Once again we see that Huguenot piety does not exclude certain luxuries!

In January 1610, Charlotte-Brabantine sent her daughter some fine dresses, which prompted Louise to write back about the pedagogical methods she was employing with her granddaughter:

> … you certainly made your daughter proud by sending her such lovely dresses. I hope you will be content with her, for she has an admirable spirit which, thank God, is not inclined to bad things; but she still can't stop to learn what we want her to learn. But what of it? We have to use both patience and fear, because there is still a lot of childishness in her. … and we don't spare the rod when she needs it. It's true that we don't use it until we have to, for I would prefer that reason, rather than the cane, made her do what she should. … It's obvious that she only likes playing, and I'd much rather she be like that, than that she apply her mind to silly affectations, as so many others do. … You should be delighted and rest assured that I treat her as I would my own child, and you shouldn't be afraid that she's a problem for me. On the contrary, it brings me much pleasure to be able to instruct a young person to whom I am so attached.[54]

As Du Plessis Mornay had done when writing about her son's education, Louise emphasizes the child's God-given gifts: "she has an admirable spirit." Louise understands motivation and uses corporal punishment when she judges it to be necessary, but only as a last resort when patience, fear, and reason have not sufficed.[55] Since the child is already one of the elect, there is no need to beat the devil out of her.

When it was nearly time for Charlotte to return to her mother, Louise wrote "I don't know which of us will be the most upset, for in truth I think it will be harder for me to live without her than for her without me."[56] Louise took other young women into her household subsequently. In January 1619, she sends greetings to Charlotte-Brabantine from another granddaughter who was staying with her,

---

[53] Berriot-Salvadore, 495.

[54] Marchegay, 266.

[55] In general, Protestant families preferred not to use corporal punishment. See Pollock, "Parent-child relations," 199; Ozment, *Ancestors*, 70. Henri IV, recommended that his son, the future Louis XIII should be whipped, "knowing well that in my case there was nothing in the world that would benefit him more: for at his age I was whipped soundly," Madeleine Foisil, "Un roi de France père de famille et éducateur: Henri IV," *Autour de l'enfance*, Évelyne Berriot-Salvadore and Isabelle Pébay-Clottes, eds (Biarritz: Atlantica, 1999), 282.

[56] Marchegay, 253. In 1626, Charlotte married James Stanley, 7th Earl of Derby. She became famous for her gallant defense of their property, Lathom House, against the Parliamentary forces in 1644 and 1646. See Sonja Kmec, "'A stranger born': Female usage of international networks in times of war," in *The Contending Kingdoms: France and England 1420–1700*, ed. Glenn Richardson (Burlington, VT, and Aldershot, UK: Ashgate, 2008) 147–60.

"little Angélique," daughter of Émilie and the pretender to the Portuguese crown.[57] A month later, she writes that Angélique "... has been very ill with a great continuous fever for three days. I am anxious about her, for I would very much regret losing her, she brings me great pleasure and she is getting prettier every day."[58] Dictating her will on her deathbed, Louise leaves money for Angélique "to take her back to her country," and asks her son Frédéric-Henri to "arrange for little Angélique of Portugal to be nourished and brought up until she is married" at which point she asks her son to give her fifteen thousand livres tournois as a dowry.

Conclusion

In her childrearing practices with her stepdaughters, her son and her granddaughter, we can observe that Louise de Coligny is putting into practice the basic notions proposed by her friends Philippe and Charlotte Du Plessis Mornay. The belief that the children, like their parents, are among God's elect is the foundation of their education. The parents have a duty to see that the children become "inheritors [of God's kingdom] through knowledge"[59] as well as through grace, and to ensure that good models of behavior are provided for them. However, since God has chosen them, they are not in need of discipline to eradicate original sin. A strong humanist education for boys, and reading, writing, and speaking more than one language for girls, are seen as quite compatible with their Reformed faith. And, unlike the children of Calvin's Geneva, both boys and girls enjoy the luxuries and pleasures of this world: riding, dancing, music, and fine clothes. The children for whom Louise de Coligny was responsible also developed loving relationships with her and with each other, and learned to support each other through difficult as well as joyful times.

---

[57]   Marchegay, 319.

[58]   Marchegay, 322.

[59]   Charlotte Du Plessis Mornay, 8.

Works Cited

Primary Sources

Berriot-Salvadore, Evelyne. "Une éducation maternelle", pièces justificatives. *Les femmes dans la société française de la Renaissance.* Genève: Droz, 1990, 481–502.

Broomhall, Susan. "Lettres de Louise-Julienne, d'Élisabeth et d'Amélie de Nassau à leur soeur Charlotte-Brabantine de Nassau (1595–1601)." *Lettres de femmes: Textes inédites et oubliés du XVIe au XVIIe siècle.* Ed. Elizabeth C. Goldsmith and Colette Winn. Paris: Champion, 2005, 135–77.

Coligny, Louise de. *Correspondance.* Ed. Paul Marchegay et Léon Marlet. Genève: Slatkine, 1970, réimpression de l'édition de Paris, 1887.

Couchman, Jane. "Lettres de Louise de Coligny aux membres de sa famille aux Pays-bas et en France" in *Lettres de femmes XVIe–XVIIIe siècles.* Ed. Elizabeth Goldsmith and Colette Winn. Paris: Champion, 2005, 89–133.

Du Plessis Mornay, Charlotte d'Arbaleste. *Mémoires de Madame de Mornay.* Ed. Mme de Witt. Paris: Rénouard, 2 vols. 1868–1869.

Du Plessis Mornay, Philippe, *Advis sur l'institution d'un enfant que l'on veult nourrir aulx lettres, envoyé à madame la princesse d'Orange, à son instance sur le sujet de son fils. Mémoires et correspondance,* tome V. Genève: Slatkine, 1969. Réimpr. de l'édition de Paris, 1824–1825, 65–71.

Nassau, Élisabeth de, duchesse de Bouillon. *Lettres d'Élisabeth de Nassau, duchesse de Bouillon, à sa soeur Charlotte-Brabantine.* Ed. P. Marchegay. Les Roches-Baritaud, 1875.

Secondary Sources

Ariès, Philippe. *L'enfant et la famille sous l'Ancien Régime.* Paris: Seuil, 1964.

Berriot-Salvadore, Evelyne. *Les femmes dans la société française de la Renaissance.* Genève: Droz, 1990.

Broomhall, Susan, and Jacqueline Ghent. "In the name of the father: Conceptualizing the *Pater Familias* in the letters of William the Silent's children." *Renaissance Quarterly* LXII, 4 (Winter 2009), 1130–66.

Couchman, Jane. "'… give birth quickly and then send us your good husband …': Form, Persuasion and Informal Political Influence in the Letters of Louise de Coligny." *Women's Letters across Europe 1400–1700: Form and Persuasion.* Ed. Jane Couchman and Ann Crabb. Burlington VT, and Aldershot, UK: Ashgate, 2005, 149–69.

Delaborde, Jules. *Louise de Coligny, Princesse d'Orange.* Genève: Slatkine Reprints, 1970. Réimpression de l'édition de Paris, 1890, Tomes I et II.

Foisil, Madeleine. "Un roi de France père de famille et éducateur: Henri IV." *Autour de l'enfance.* Ed. Evelyne Berriot-Salvadore and Isabelle Pébay-Clottes. Biarritz: Atlantica, 1999, 279–94.

Grafton, Anthony T. *Joseph Scaliger: A Study in the History of Classical Scholarship*, 2 vols. Oxford: Oxford University Press, 1983, 1993.

Hufton, Olwen. "Le travail et la famille: La maternité." *XVIe–XVIIIe siècle: Histoire des femmes en occident*. Ed. Natalie Zemon Davis and Arlette Farge. Paris: Plon, 1991, 50–63.

Kertzer, David I., and Marzio Barbagli. *Family Life in Early Modern Times, The History of the European Family*, vol. I. New Haven and London: Yale University Press, 2001.

Kmec, Sonja. "'A stranger born': Female usage of international networks in times of war," in *The Contending Kingdoms: France and England 1420–1700*. Ed. Glenn Richardson (Burlington, VT, and Aldershot, UK: Ashgate, 2008, 147–60.

Kuperty-Tsur, Nadine, "Rhétorique parentale et religieuse: les voies de la transmission des valeurs de la réforme aux enfants." *Les deux réformes chrétiennes: Propagation et diffusion*. Ed. Myriam Yardeni et Illana Zinguer. Leiden: Brill, 2004, 153–71.

Lebrun, François, "Parents et enfants." *Histoire de la famille*, t. 2, *Le Choc des Modernités*. Ed. André Burgière, Christine Klapisch-Zuber, Martine Segalen, and Françoise Zonabend. Paris: Colin, 1986, 141–53.

O'Day, Rosemary. *The Family and Family Relationships, 1500–1900: England, France and the United States of America*. New York: St. Martin's Press, 1999.

Ozment, Stephen. *Ancestors: The Loving Family in Old Europe*. Cambridge: Harvard University Press, 2001.

Pascal, Eugénie. "La lectrice devenue scriptrice: Lecture épistolaire dans les réponses d'Élisabeth à Charlotte-Brabantine de Nassau." *Lectrices d'Ancien régime*. Ed. Isabelle Brouard-Arends. Rennes: Presses Universitaires de Rennes, 2002.

Pitkin, Barbara. "'The heritage of the Lord': Children in the theology of Jean Calvin." *The Child in Christian Thought*. Ed. Marcia J. Bunge. Grand Rapids: Eerdmans, 2001, 160–93.

Pollock, Linda A. "Parent-Child Relations." *Family Life in Early Modern Times, The History of the European Family*, vol. I. Ed. David I. Kertzer and Marzio Barbagli. New Haven and London: Yale University Press, 2001, 192–219, 303–7.

Roelker, Nancy L. "The appeal of Calvinism to French noblewomen in the sixteenth century." *Journal of Interdisciplinary History*, 1972, 391–407.

———. "The role of noblewomen in the French reformation." *Archiv für Reformationsgeschichte*, 1972, 168–95.

Watt, Jeffrey R. "Calvinism, childhood, and education: the evidence from the Genevan Consistory." *Sixteenth Century Journal* 2002, XXXIII/2, 439–56.

Chapter 7
Anne Dormer and Her Children

Sara Mendelson

As historians of childhood have frequently lamented, first-person narratives by early modern children are among the rarest of treasures. The problem of evidence is particularly acute for the lives of young children. In her recent survey of the historiography of childhood, Margaret King has called the period from birth to adolescence the "silent years."[1] Yet while there is a dearth of personal documents by children themselves, we can learn a great deal from indirect sources. First and foremost among these are the observations of early modern mothers. At their best, family correspondence and other personal documents offer a detailed picture of children's lives as viewed by adults: we can watch women teaching their sons and daughters in real time, commenting on their development, and sometimes quoting verbatim from children's own speech.

A case in point is the correspondence of Anne Cottrell Dormer, a seventeenth-century Englishwoman from a wealthy family with close connections to the English court. Through letters written by Anne and her relations during the 1680s, we can explore the lives of children of the English gentry through the eyes of their mother and other members of the Cottrell and Dormer families. Anne Dormer's letters to her sister Lady Elizabeth Trumbull, now part of the Trumbull Papers,[2] were written while Elizabeth was living as a diplomat's wife in Paris and then Constantinople between 1685 and 1691. The letters offer information about material culture, daily activities, health and medicine, friendly and neighborly relationships, political turmoil before and after the Glorious Revolution, and the horrors of an abusive marriage. They also feature vivid and detailed references to Anne's children.

Embedded within Anne Dormer's letters are multiple voices in addition to her own. There are conversations with her husband or assorted friends and relations. Occasionally she records remarks made by her youngest children, Fanny [Frances] and Clem [Clement], who were living at home with her at the time the letters were written. These little scenarios are usually framed in terms of the politics of the family as a whole. Even the youngest members of the household are portrayed

---

[1]   Margaret King, "Concepts of Childhood: What We Know and Where We Might Go," *Renaissance Quarterly* 40, no. 2 (2007), 389.

[2]   Anne Dormer, Letters to her sister, Lady Elizabeth Trumbull, and two letters to her son, John Dormer, 1685–1691, British Library, Additional MS 72516, fols. 156–241 (hereafter cited as Dormer, Letters).

as players in a drama which replicates the patterns established by the main protagonists, Anne Dormer and her husband, Robert.

To gain a deeper understanding of Anne and Robert Dormer's interactions with their children, we need to step back one generation to see how the two parents constructed their own experiences of childhood. Anne Cottrell was born in 1648 during the English Civil War, the oldest daughter of Sir Charles Cottrell, Master of Ceremonies to Charles I and Charles II. As prominent royalists, Cottrell and his wife fled to the Netherlands shortly after Anne's birth. Left with a nurse in England, Anne probably lived with her aunt Clayton, wife of the Master of Merton College, Oxford. Both her sister Elizabeth and her brother Charles Ludowick were born in the Netherlands in 1652 and 1654, respectively.

Some time before Sir Charles returned to England in 1660, his wife died and he acquired a mistress, Lady Jane Salkeld, whom Anne and her sister viewed as a kind of wicked stepmother. In their letters, the two siblings referred to Lady Salkeld as "the serpent" who had invaded their familial Garden of Eden. Anne's husband later deplored the fact that Anne had had no real mother to watch over her while she was growing up. As he told her, "it was greate pitty I had lost my Mother, for had I had a mother shee would never have lett a crew of such young fellows as Mr Colt have come to the house ... ." In the early 1660s Anne spent some time in a London girls' school. Once Sir Charles Cottrell set up house in Spring Gardens, St. James' Park, the girls lived with him and their brothers until they were married. Here the sisters forged a passionate friendship which was to last for the rest of their lives. For Anne, the relationship with Elizabeth remained a stronger bond than that of marriage or even motherhood.[3]

Anne and Elizabeth were married within two years of each other, Anne in 1668 at age 20, Elizabeth in 1670 at 17. Anne married Robert Dormer (1628?–1689), a middle-aged widower who had inherited a large estate at Rousham, Oxfordshire. Elizabeth married William Trumbull, a lawyer who later became a successful diplomat and politician. After postings to Paris and Constantinople during the 1680s, he served as lord of the Treasury, member of the Privy Council and finally Secretary of State in 1695, the year Anne Dormer died.

The Trumbull marriage was a romantic union of two seemingly equal partners. Elizabeth willingly accompanied her husband on two dangerous foreign missions, first to the French court at Paris during the 1685 massacre, and then to an equally hazardous posting at the Ottoman court at Constantinople. The couple was still exchanging passionate love letters as late as the 1690s. The only flaw in their happiness was their inability to have children.

In stark contrast, Anne Dormer suffered more than 20 years of spousal abuse.[4] Her husband, Robert, had inherited a family fortune while still a youth. Freed from

---

[3]   For details of Anne Cottrell Dormer's life, see Mary O'Connor, "Anne Dormer." *Oxford Dictionary of National Biography* (2004).

[4]   On Anne Dormer's marriage, see Mary O'Connor, "Interpreting Early Modern Woman Abuse: The Case of Anne Dormer," in *Quidditas* 23 (2002), 51–67, and the same

parental discipline, Dormer had sown his wild oats on the continent, a mode of life which left him rootless, bored, distrustful of women and opposed to any activity which entailed self-discipline or hard work.[5] His marriage to his first wife, Katherine Bertie, produced one child, Robert, born in 1659. A decade later the elder Dormer became infatuated with 20-year-old Anne Cottrell, whom he married and with whom he had 11 children over the course of the next 18 years.

At some point after 1685, Dormer drew up a list of all the children born to him and his two wives. The list reads as follows:

children of Robert Dormer "written by his own hand"
[by Katherine Bertie]   Robert 7 May 1659
[by Anne Cottrell]   John 16 Jan 1669
                     Charles 25 Feb 1670
                     William 23 Feb 1671
                     Anne 3 July 1673, dyed 4 Oct 1681
                     Katherine 11 Jan 1674, dyed 21 March next
                     Robert 26 Oct 1676
                     Phillip 24 Nov 1677
                     Clement 6 Jan 1678, dyed 22 Feb 1679/80
                     James 16 March 1679
                     Frances 9 March 1681
                     Clement 14 Feb 1684/5

Eight of Anne's eleven offspring, seven sons and a daughter, were still alive during the late 1680s.

Robert Dormer saw himself as the archetypal patriarch, an absolute monarch within the family domain. As he understood his role, his wife and children were to serve as his obedient subjects or rather as his private possessions. As Anne wrote in 1688, "… prid[e] makes him think a Wife can not be kept too much a slave … ." As for Dormer's possessiveness, "one of the first maxims he layed downe to me was, that if he had a Wife was either handsom or anything else that was agreeable, he would have it all to him self."[6] So extreme was his jealousy, as Dormer explained to his new wife, that "it would not trouble another man more to see his wife in bed with another man then it would him if his wife were pleasing to any but himself … ."

---

author's "Representations of Intimacy in the Life-Writing of Anne Clifford and Anne Dormer," in *Representations of the Self From the Renaissance to Romanticism*, P. Coleman, J. Lewis, and J. Kowalik, eds (Cambridge: Cambridge University Press, 2000), 79–96.

[5]   Anne feared that Italy would have the same unfortunate effect on Jack as it had had on her husband: "I beseech God bless Jack and send him safe home and through Italy free from those mischiefs that place did his unhappy father …," Dormer, Letters, fol. 205v. She also blamed Restoration London for exacerbating her husband's cynicism about women; see Dormer, Letters, fol. 197v.

[6]   Dormer, Letters, fol. 191v.

To Elizabeth, living in Constantinople, Anne remarked ironically that there was "not a greater slave in Turky then I am here ... ."[7]

Anne's children were taught to regard their father's edicts as absolute laws with no court of appeal. Anne's stepson Robert was the first to discover the high price to be paid for slighting his father's wishes. During the early 1680s, Robert formed a romantic attachment which was neither initiated nor approved by his father. At the same time, Robert was drawn into debt through his association with profligate companions. Although he had reached his majority in 1680, he was cut off from his father's largesse with a stipend of 100 pounds a year, a fraction of his former expectations as the oldest male heir. Anne continued to get on well with her stepson, but Dormer and his first son became permanently estranged.

Anne's father and her brother-in-law, Sir William Trumbull, were quick to take advantage of the breach between father and son. By 1683, Trumbull had persuaded Dormer to settle his considerable fortune on John [=Jack] Dormer, his eldest son by his second wife.[8] Jack and his siblings henceforth became pawns in the struggles between Robert Dormer and his wife, for Anne was always fearful that her husband's anger might be turned against his second family as well as his first. As Anne wrote to her sister regarding Jack, "I know the misplacing a word or running out five pound shall put him in the same rank of favour with his elder Brother whom he [Dormer] never asks after nor concerns himself no more then if he had not beene ever anything to him, he payes his hundred pound a year and that is all the trouble he is at for him."[9]

At times Anne Dormer pondered the pros and cons of separating from her husband. Yet she always held in the forefront of her mind the probable fate her children would suffer as a result of her own defection. For their sake, she felt constrained to carry on with the marriage so long as Dormer would allow her to live with him. As she reminded her sister, "I must not exasperate him [her husband] for I and my poore children are in his power."[10]

Each of Anne's eight surviving children is mentioned in her letters. Elizabeth received periodic news bulletins about Anne's five younger sons who were at school or involved in arrangements which kept them away from home. Anne thought she had reason "to hope well of every one of my boyes ... ."

> Charles grows indeed a fine sober well inclined youth and handsom enough
> Will [William] I heare very well [o]f and Robin [Robert] is like to be very well
> favoured a[nd has a] sweete disposition but Phill [Philip] will be the schollar
> [of them] all and jemmy [James] is not like[ly] to come much be[hind] him ... .

All she wanted from her younger sons was "but the pleasure to see them do themselves good ... ." It is clear from Anne's comments here and elsewhere that

---

[7]   Dormer, Letters, fol. 176v.
[8]   Rousham MSS Sir Charles Cottrell to Robert Dormer #1682–1683.
[9]   Dormer, Letters, fol. 189v.
[10]   Dormer, Letters, fol. 181v.

her sons were not spending their youth away from home because of a lack of parental love and concern. On the contrary, Anne's fear that too much affection would ruin their characters was given as the main reason for James's "going so soone from home … ." Living with the family, James had been "so greate a favorite and so unreasonably humored he was in the way of being utterly spoyled."[11]

The most detailed observations of her children found in Anne's correspondence are her references to her oldest son Jack [John, born January 1669] and the two youngest, Fanny [Frances, born March 1681] and Clem [Clement, born February 1685]. Here Anne's comments reveal a tension between conflicting perspectives and expectations. On the one hand, the Dormer children are clearly depicted as unique individuals with impulses and desires of their own. At the same time, they are seen as carriers of hereditary traits derived from one or the other side of the family. Clem, her youngest, was especially dear to his mother because of his resemblance to her beloved sister. A delicate boy, "… I fancy him very like you, eyes and the rest …" as Anne wrote to Elizabeth.[12] The boy also reminded Anne of an older sibling at the same age. Clem had "a vast deal of witt" and was "just such an entertaining child as little Robin [Robert, born in 1676] was."[13]

Fanny, Anne's sole surviving daughter, was her declared favorite, partly because Fanny bore a strong resemblance to her older sister Nancy [Anne, born in July 1673], a much loved child who had died at eight years of age. In 1688 Anne wrote of seven-year-old Fanny: "my deare girle I bless God thrives, and is, I neede say no more, like my most beloved and never to be forgotten Nancy."[14] Musing on her fears that Fanny, like Nancy, might die young, Anne often repeated the consoling thought that "if this [daughter] lives she will be a comfort to me, and if shee dies shee will never knowe those sorrows I have found so bitter to me now … ."[15] A year later, Anne again described Fanny's disposition as "very like my beloved Nancy … if shee lives I shall greatly joy in her & if she dies shee will know no sorrow … ."[16]

In contrast to his siblings, Jack Dormer is depicted as a problem child whose undesirable traits (as the Cottrells believed) had been inherited directly from his father. Anne's family had never been fond of Robert Dormer: in their letters, Dormer is described as mean, self-centered, indolent, and mulishly obstinate. By 1688 the two sides of the family were barely on speaking terms. In the three-cornered exchanges between Anne, Sir Charles Cottrell, and the Trumbulls, all parties agreed that Jack embodied his father's worst flaws: he was variously described as stubborn, selfish, thoughtless, careless, ill-tempered, hard-hearted, and seemingly allergic to hard work.

---

[11] Dormer, Letters, fol. 157v (9 Aug 1686).

[12] Dormer, Letters, fol. 157v.

[13] Dormer, Letters, fol. 188v.

[14] Dormer, Letters, fol. 168r; see also fol. 204v.

[15] Dormer, Letters, fol. 168r.

[16] Dormer, Letters, fol. 204v.

Yet like all her relations, Anne assumed that birth order and gender would determine the future fate of each of her progeny. In a letter to her eldest son, Anne tried to soften the harsh realities of patriarchy: "You have one considerable advantage of all yr. Brothers in being born before ym [=them]. and so first loved, & by ye fav[ou]r of yr worthy Unkle, & deare Aunt, were early put into such a way as none of yr. Brothers can [ha]ve therfore if you goe on, & pursue as you may those advantages, you will every way find ye benefitt of itt … ." At the same time, Anne emphasized that with greater privilege came greater responsibility: "to whom much is given, much will be required, both in ys [=this] world, & in ye other & therfore deare Jack observe ye advices you dayly receive from yr. affectionate friends, who have no designe upon you but to make you considerable in ys. [=this] world, or happy in ye. next."[17]

Letters between Sir Charles Cottrell and the Trumbulls reveal a more pragmatic perspective. As his grandfather explained to Jack, the settlement which had resulted in his privileged role as designated heir had nothing to do with Jack himself: "if it had not beene for your Unckle Trumbull … you had beene left without any provision made for you; & must now have depended upon your Elder Brother for a dinner. Whereas by his [Trumbull's] meanes, Rousham is now yours, & he for your Aunts sake, & mine (for you were nothing to him, & never deserved any thing from him) made it his businesse to get an interest in your father, for no other end, but to get him to make a settlement for you, & your Brothers, wch with much difficulty at last he hapyly accomplished."[18] And in his communications with his daughter Elizabeth, Sir Charles characterized Dormer's motivation as an inflexible adherence to patriarchal rules of inheritance. The settlement in favor of Jack had "never been done at all but for his Uncle Trumbull's procurement, whereby [Jack] may see that without that the whole Estate had gone to his brother Robert; & at ye best his father would have had it sold & given equally amongst them all … since he sayd they were all but younger Brothers … ."[19]

But while Dormer had agreed to leave nearly the whole of his estates to Jack, Trumbull had failed to persuade his brother-in-law to make adequate provision for his wife Anne, his six younger sons, and his daughter, Frances. As the settlement stood, Jack's younger brothers would be even more impoverished as adults than they were as teens. Whereas each of them was to receive an allowance of 60 pounds per annum at age 16, at Dormer's death his younger sons were to inherit nothing but a capital sum of a thousand pounds apiece, yielding only 50 pounds per annum at current rates of interest. Anne had been assigned just enough capital to produce 400 pounds a year in income. As Sir Charles told Jack, this shameful neglect of the rest of the family had resulted from sheer indolence on Dormer's

---

[17]   Dormer, Letters, fol. 178r.

[18]   Sir Charles Cottrell, Letters to his daughter Lady Elizabeth Trumbull and his son-in-law Sir William Trumbull, 168–91, British Library, Additional MS 72516, fols. 1–155 (hereafter cited as Cottrell, Letters), fols. 34–5.

[19]   Cottrell, Letters, fols. 112–112v.

part: "Tis true it is not in such proportion to them, as it ought to have beene, but [your father] was so unwilling to give him selfe the trouble of looking into his estate that he knew not what he had, nor therefore what he might & ought to have done more for them … ."[20]

Once Jack became the official heir, the Cottrells increased their efforts to transform him into a tractable young man who would manage the Dormer estates prudently for the good of the family as a whole. As his grandfather wrote concerning Jack's prospects,

> nothing else can preserve him from the same ruine his bro[ther] is fallen into but the taking his friends advice, wch is to keepe safe company & live within his bounds, & not think his estate better then it is … [it] may soone come to nothing if he lay more upon it then it can beare as young heires commonly do, and as his father did turning a prodigall Youth into a miserable old age … .

Two years after the new will was signed, all attempts to civilize Jack appeared to have been in vain. Anne thought herself too soft-natured to have any effect on what amounted to a younger version of her husband. Assuring the Trumbulls that they made her "infinitely happy," Anne confessed "I never expect to be so in Jack, since his hard nature and wilfullness holds up to such a heigh[t]" She would no longer pretend to "do good upon him" herself, "unless perswading I believe him farr different from what he is will do somthing with him." Having struggled so long with her husband's "willfulness and hard nature," she would "never more engage in such another temper to dispute and convince … ." Other family members could carry on the struggle: "if he will not be what he ought I am resolved to give my self as little disquiett aboute him as is possible."

During the 1680s, Sir Charles Cottrell took each of his grandchildren to live with him for a time to acquire genteel manners in the household of an experienced courtier. Cottrell thought he had done well with the younger Dormer sons, but confessed he had not made a dent in Jack's old faults.[21] In 1685, when the Trumbulls were about to leave for France, Sir Charles suggested they bring Jack with them in their entourage. The Trumbulls, still childless, agreed to take over the burden of Jack's education. At age 16, Jack accompanied his aunt and uncle to their first diplomatic posting. He remained abroad with the Trumbulls for more than five years, first in Paris (1685–1686) then in Constantinople (1687–1690), until his return to England after the death of his father.

Anne declared that all authority over Jack was henceforth to reside in the Trumbulls, aided by their chaplain, Mr. Haley, who kept a close rein on Jack while serving as his intellectual and moral tutor. Everything Jack needed or desired—including love and money and his parents' blessing—was to be meted out at

---

[20] Sir Charles Cottrell, Letters to his daughter Lady Elizabeth Trumbull and his son-in-law Sir William Trumbull, 168–91, British Library, Additional MS 72516, fols. 1–155 (hereafter cited as Cottrell, Letters), fols. 34–5.

[21] Cottrell, Letters, fol. 15v.

second hand by his aunt and uncle. Anne instructed Elizabeth to tell Jack "we both send him our blessings with much kindness tho now neither of us can write to him."[22] The message was reinforced in later correspondence: "if there be any thing my deare sister, you would have me write to Jack as from my self I hope you will tell me … I always give him my blessing and love him like a Mother whose nature is too unhappily soft … ."[23] One letter addressed directly to Jack is an extended sermon rather than a proper letter, consisting of several pages of moral and religious advice.[24] In it, Anne stresses the vital importance to Jack of mastering his "passions" through self-discipline and hard work. These admonitions bear a striking resemblance to the advice Anne offered her husband in dialogues which she reported to her sister.[25]

Perhaps most shocking to modern sensibilities, Jack was to be told that his parents' love for him would be in direct proportion to his obedience to his aunt and uncle. As Anne told Elizabeth "we hope [he] makes it his busyness in all things to obey his unkle and you and to endeavour every way to deserve some part of the favour you both shew him, for upon his behaviour to you depends his fathers as well as my kindness."[26] Jack's supply of pocket money, too, was to be doled out in small amounts if and when he deserved it. Anne turned down her son's request for a regular allowance, partly because Jack's father was "so iron hearted to make a bargain that had he agreed to an allowance we should have had no reason to rejoyce in it … ." Moreover, Jack would have been liable "when he knew of something certaine … to spend it before it was due … ." Most important, "… you would have had less power over him then now that you give him I suppose pockett mony more or less as you find him deserve it … your venturing as far as you can to supply him with what he wants he will look upon as a kindness, which is lost when he can pretend to what he has as a bounty from his father."[27]

Family correspondence records many ups and downs in Jack's progress, as the Cottrells sat on the sidelines and watched anxiously for signs of improvement.[28] Backslidings were followed by Jack's repeated promises to try harder: he assured his grandfather "that upon his receiving ye sacrament, he has taken resolutions to do his duty more carefully in all respects … ." In 1687, Sir Charles wrote to the Trumbulls "I could not but laugh at the story of Jack's riding on the Resty Mule, wch was the fittest thing that could possibly [be] invented to make him know him selfe … ."[29] A year later, Sir Charles was sorry to hear that Jack refused to touch his violin; it would be a "great trouble" to Jack when he felt his father's anger,

---

[22] Dormer, Letters, fol. 156r.

[23] Dormer, Letters, fol. 175v.

[24] Dormer, Letters, fols. 178–179v.

[25] See for example Dormer, Letters, fols. 188v, 194–195v.

[26] Dormer, Letters, fol. 156r.

[27] Dormer, Letters, fols. 189r–v.

[28] For examples see Cottrell, Letters, fols. 26, 37v, and 38.

[29] Cottrell, Letters, fol. 48v.

"since he [Dormer] speaks often of it and expects to see him one of the best in England at that Instrument at his returne ... ."[30]

As Jack approached his twentieth year, the Trumbulls began to note real changes in their nephew, both physical and psychological. Anne was thrilled to learn of these signs that Jack was turning into a Cottrell: "I was transported with thy last which speaking how he grew tells me you think he will be as tall and you hope as good as our most deare and most worthy father [=Sir Charles Cottrell], oh how that hope rejoyces me and if amongst all, I can have one son like him, that is a blessing I would purchase at the price of all I have undergone in these years past ... ."[31] After his father's death in 1689, Jack did take on the role of the model son, having been persuaded by his grandfather to share some of his inherited wealth with his mother and his siblings. Although he never became a courtier (as his grandfather had hoped), in his career as a soldier he upheld the family honor.[32]

During the 1680s Jack's two youngest siblings, Fanny and Clem, were at home at Rousham with their parents. According to Anne, the two children brought her nothing but joy. Romping with them even served as a cure for Anne's bouts of "the vapours" or depression: "I take the Kings dropps and drink Chocalate and when my soul is sadd to death I run and play with the children ... ."[33] Fanny is described as "the cheerfullest little creature you ever saw ... ." Anne's father had given Fanny the task of cheering up her mother, almost as if Fanny were the parent and Anne the beloved and indulged daughter: "if I sitt pencive [=pensive] a little she'l come to me and cry you now you are with your Dull looks, my grand fa[ther] bid me make you cheerfull and I can gett never a bitt of cheerfullness out of you, come come I must have you play with me" and thus, Anne concluded, "the deare bratt will never leave me ... ."[34]

Encouraged by Fanny's quick intelligence, Anne devoted much time and labor to educating her daughter, who was "all I can wish her and so capable I grieve shee should loose a minute ... ."[35] There is no mention in the letters of any interaction between Fanny and her father. The picture created here is of an enclosed female world where mother and daughter cling to each other for comfort and protection. Fanny is cherished, tutored, and guarded in a way Anne might have wished for herself. Conscious of her own motherless childhood and its unhappy sequel, Anne repeatedly expressed the desire to make a better life for her daughter. Were Fanny stronger, Anne remarked, "I should have more hope to hatch her up which I will do al I can to do, and then submitt to my gracious Gods choice for me and her ... ."[36]

Clem [Clement], Anne's last-born, was three years old in 1688. He was still in the care of a maidservant, although his mother had begun to tutor him along

---

[30] Cottrell, Letters, fol. 79v.

[31] Dormer, Letters, fol. 199v.

[32] Cottrell, Letters, fol. 112v.

[33] Dormer, Letters, fol. 163r.

[34] Dormer, Letters, fol. 170v.

[35] Dormer, Letters, fol. 176v.

[36] Dormer, Letters, fol. 204v.

with Fanny. Even as a toddler, Clem was already a symbolic player in household politics. One day Clem bit his tongue, "and because it smarted he run to Maid Mary and fell a beating her … ." The incident had served Anne often since then "for a comparaison to shew him [Dormer] my case, for when he goes abroad and aboute and any thing crosses his Lordship then all the ill humore is to be vented upon me, and then I cry I [=aye] this is like Clem when he bitt his owne tongue he runs and beates his maid … ."[37]

On other occasions, Clem's status as a mere child gave him license to criticize his father, while Anne cheered him on from the sidelines. "Mr D was never fonder of any no nor ever studdied so much to please a child," Anne told her sister, "and he [Clem] has so many witty expressions that they help me often shew my Ld … many things betweene jeast and earnest I could not otherwayes represent to him." In one incident Clem complained of his father's meanness. Whenever Dormer cried "Clem I love thee" his son would reply, "do you … then what will you give me." Dormer would fetch something for Clem to look at for a while, but soon take it away again. In response, Clem expressed contempt for his father's miserliness: "truly … Ile love my good Mammy shee will give me things to be my owne, you shew me somthing now and then and so take it away from me againe but I don't desire my Mammy should gett such freakes, no body loves me that ever cozens [cheats] me." Anne confessed it made her laugh "to hear how the boy will pursue this theam, that no body loves that doth no[t] do somthing for him … ."[38]

These family scenarios dramatize some of the contradictions between traditional attitudes to childhood and more liberal approaches which were emerging at this time, notably the philosophy embodied in Locke's educational treatise, first composed as epistolary advice to the Clarke family during the 1680s.[39] Anne's letters depict her offspring as youthful participants in a household dynamic shaped by twenty-odd years of spousal abuse. The political struggle between Anne and Robert tends to engulf all other family relationships, including Anne's interactions with her sister, her father, the youngest as well as the oldest of her children. Jack appears to replicate Dormer's "hard-natured" character, while Clem serves as a model of Dormer's infantile irrationality, or stands in for his mother as critic of Dormer's egotism. In Fanny's future, Anne foresees the tragedy of her own life about to be repeated. At the same time, Dormer's patriarchal views served to reinforce the tangled web of hierarchical connections between family members. In preparation for adult life, children were defined by their elders as figures on a group trajectory rather than as autonomous individuals. In fulfilling what were then called "relative duties," sons and daughters never ceased to be regarded as children with respect to their parents, even when they attained their majority or (as in Anne's case) grew up to have children of their own.

---

[37]	Dormer, Letters, fol. 189r.

[38]	Dormer, Letter, fols. 188v –189r.

[39]	John Locke, *Some Thoughts Concerning Education* (London, 1693).

Chapter 8
"Obey and be attentive":
Gender and Household Instruction in
Shakespeare's *The Tempest*

Kathryn M. Moncrief

The Royal Shakespeare Company's 2006–2007 production of *The Tempest*, directed by Rupert Goold, featured Patrick Stewart as an imposing and angry Prospero, clad in animal skins, stranded in an inhospitable, snowy wasteland. The second scene, when the exiled Duke has decided, finally, to share with his daughter the mystery of her background and his own fallen fortunes, had a decidedly schoolmaster-student dynamic. Alone with her father inside their sparse, wooden shack home, Mariah Gale's teenaged Miranda sat in tense anticipation, knees together, back straight, hands clasped, her attention riveted on her father, speaking only after thrusting her hand into the air and waiting for permission to proceed, as a proper pupil might. As the scene progressed, she was a rapt listener, leaning in, absorbing and learning from his teaching, distressed by his story but hungry for more. Prospero relayed his tale with a mixture of obvious regret for his neglect of his former duties and insistence that Miranda understand what he was teaching her.

Throughout his interaction with his daughter, Stewart's Prospero, alternately tyrannical and gentle, insistently prompted Gale's charmingly naive Miranda to pay careful attention to what he had to tell her: "I pray thee mark me" (1.2.67), "Dost thou attend me?" (1.2.78), and "Dost thou hear?" (1.2.106), punctuate his story. Prospero's questions and admonitions—"Thou attend'st not!" (1.2.87)— were not, in the RSC production, as they are so often played, necessary prods to keep a drowsy Miranda awake but were instead energetic cues meant to reinforce an important lesson for the fully engaged girl. She was not, in this context, a child falling asleep throughout her father's long and tedious tale but rather a student in the midst of an important lesson. Miranda's respectful but energetically delivered responses, "O, good sir, I do" (1.2.88) and assurances that she is listening "most heedfully" (1.2.78), bore this out. Only at the end of the interaction did Prospero release Miranda from her lesson by quickly putting her to sleep.

This staging choice worked to foreground the pedagogical overtones implicit in the text, as well as the gendered nature and domestic location of the interaction.[1] That one of the first scenes in *The Tempest* (1611) emphasizes a moment of

---

[1]   See Allen Carey-Webb, who examines the pedagogical dimension of the play in relationship to the development of national identity and citizenship.

instruction involving a father/male schoolmaster tutoring his daughter/female pupil raises important questions about the practice and purpose of education in the household, especially the schooling of daughters, as well as its representation on stage. If, as the numerous published educational guides, parenting manuals, and catechisms suggest, education in the household was an ordinary, even common practice for girls, who were kept at home while their brothers left the home for formal schooling, how might staging it disrupt seemingly fixed practices and ideologies?

In her study of early modern domesticity, Wendy Wall writes, "Depicting the household in any manner had weighty consequences, for in English political treatises, conduct books, and sermons, the household was routinely touted as the foremost disciplinary site in the period" (1).

She continues, asking:

> But what if domesticity were already "estranged" in the early modern imagination? What if these scenes of domestic passion and panic simply foregrounded what everybody already, as some level, knew: that ordinary experience could be bizarre and disquieting? Might drama then implicitly unsettle ideologies resting on an ordered domesticity merely by revealing the disorienting nature of everyday practice? (2)

The opening educational scene in *The Tempest* is, on one hand, an unremarkable example of a father instructing and disciplining his daughter in a homely domestic setting, while at the same time, it is bizarre in location, the content of the lesson he seeks to impart, the additional members of his household (a magical sprite and a resentful island native), and the extraordinary methods he uses to maintain his order in the makeshift household. What, then, can be gained from examining the play through the lens household instruction? How does such a scene comment on the expectations for educating young women in the early modern period in England?

The Tempest displays an undeniable interest in the education of a daughter in the household; it is not alone among early modern plays in staging feminine instruction but examining it along with representative printed educational tracts and prescriptive texts that proliferated during the period helps to expose the ongoing dialogues surrounding the utility, necessity, and fears about girlhood education. This was a period of intense debate and heightened anxiety about the merits and ills—as well as the ultimate purpose—of educating girls.

Educational guides and books on parenting and childrearing, like other types of prescriptive literature, flourished in the early modern popular press and were part of the ongoing dialogue about women (and girls) during the period. While women's duties and roles were under scrutiny in a rapidly changing society, it comes as no surprise that educational literature, especially texts concerned with the training of girls, would participate in the same discourses.

The advent of humanism in England the first half of the sixteenth century, and the educational reforms it generated, continued to be influential well into the seventeenth century.[2] Humanist texts, like Juan Luis Vives's *Instruction of a Christen Woman* (1529) and *Plan of Study for Girls* (1523), Robert Ascham's *The Scholemaster* (1570) and Thomas Elyot's *Defense of Good Women* (1540), seem innovative in that they argue in favor of female education, including instruction in reading, writing, and languages. Hilda L. Smith observes, however, that the sweeping changes and educational reforms did little to alter the status of girls and women: "Demands for morality and chastity constrained women and narrowed their existence" (12). She concludes, "No humanist author placed women within the utilitarian core of humanist training and vocation. That women were intended as wives proved the single most important restriction on what they should learn and how they could use that learning" (13).[3] Early modern instructional texts were still part of a system of entrenched gender roles where feminine education focused on religious piety, domesticity, and women's subordinate place in the patriarchal system.

One of the most influential texts on childhood education, *Positions ... which are necessarie for the training up of children* (1581), by Richard Mulcaster, who was himself a schoolmaster, is particularly useful in understanding expectations for female education as it is typical of the genre. While Mulcaster, seemingly progressively, argues in favor of female education because "our countrey doth allow it, our duetie doth enforce it, their aptnesse calls for it, their excellencie commands it" (167) he is, at the same time, careful not to suggest radical change. The training of girls is a decidedly domestic affair, one that should be bounded by particular attention to custom, which does not include formal grammar school or university training: "I set not yong maidens to publike grammer scholes, a thing not used in my countrie, I send them not to universities, having no president thereof in my countrie, I allow them learning with distinction in degrees, with difference of their calling, with respect to their endes ..." (168). Mulcaster continues, detailing suitable areas of study and charging parents with the responsibility for their daughters' instruction:

> We see yong maidens be taught to read and write, and can do both with praise: we heare them sing and playe: and both passing well, we know they learne the best, and finest of our learned languages, to the admiration of al men... these qualities their parentes procure them, as either oportunitie of circumstance will serve, or their owne power wil extend unto. (168)

Reading, writing, singing, playing and skill with languages are of primary importance as is housewifery. Any supplementary knowledge, he concedes, which might include geometry, mathematics, physick, philosophy, drawing, logic and rhetoric, is necessary only for "such personages as be borne to be princes, or

---

[2]   Hilda L. Smith, 11.

[3]   See also Kate Aughterson, who seeks to dispel the myth that women benefited from humanist reforms; female education was still "firmly placed within a framework of marital subjection and the acquisitions of chaste, wifely virtues" (166).

matches to great peeres" (177). Mulcaster is aware of and reinforces the restrictions of both gender and class, noting that additional educational accomplishment would serve only those destined for ruling or aristocratic marriage.

Marriage, however, is the heart of the matter and the primary reason for providing girls with education. Women are to serve as worthy companions to their husbands and are, Mulcaster contends, "made for our comfort, the onely good to garnish our alonenesse, the nearest companions in our weale or wo" (169). To that end, a "youg maiden" is to be "trained in respect of marriage, obedience to her head" (174). Even more significantly, he asks, "Are they not seminary of our succession? ... Is it either nothing, or but some small thing, to have our childrens mothers well furnished in minde, well strengthened in bodie? Which desire by them to maintain our succession?" (168–9). Mulcaster's defense of female learning depends on the idea of succession and women's roles as "our childrens mothers." A woman's education is not, then, about her own intellectual fulfillment or for her private advantage but, in addition to adding to her husband's comfort, is necessary to benefit her children and the family's heirs.

Educational treatises that address women and domestic guides, including conduct books and marriage manuals are, unsurprisingly, remarkably similar in the ways they construct women and their purposes: women are to be modest, godly, and obedient to their husbands as they are ultimately bound for marriage, housekeeping and child-rearing.[4] The "main dutie" of a wife, notes Thomas Gataker in a marriage sermon, "is Submission; or Subjection" (7) to her husband to whom she should offer "Reverance, obedience, assistance" (11). In another sermon, *A Marriage Praier*, he concentrates on the importance of domestic skills: "Housewifely offices are no disgrace to any woman. It is a grace and a credit rather for a woman to be such ... . For this is the womans trade so to be: it is the end of her creation; it is that that she was made for" (18–19). A girl would have learned as part of her training, among other practical skills, cooking, brewing, sewing, needlework, gardening and small animal husbandry, childcare, and household management. While the husband was the head of the household, in day-to-day matters, the wife oversaw the maintenance and running of it.

Thomas Prichard's marriage guide, *The school of honest and vertuous lyfe: Profitable and necessary for all estates and degrees, to be trayned in: but (cheefly) for the pettie schollers, the yonger sorte, of both kindes, bee they men or women* (1579), in its title, plainly demonstrates the overlapping agendas of prescriptive and educational literature as it instructs both women and men, using specifically pedagogical language:

---

[4]   See Mendelson and Crawford, 89–92, and Kate Aughterson, 165–8. Both note the primacy of obedience and modesty in girls' education. See also Suzanne Hull's *Chaste, Silent and Obedient: English Books for Women 1475–1640* for her extended discussion of books for women in which she identifies the now familiar dictates of "chastity, silence and obedience" that dominate advice literature for women.

What a Wife ought to bee.
Here may you learne, that a Wife ought to be discrete, chaste, huswifely, shamefast, good, meeke, pacient, and sober, not in light contenance, nor garish apparrell with dyed or curled haire, painted nor pasted, but with a cumly gravitie and sad behaviour of a constant minde, true tongued, and of few words, with such obedience in all godlinesse to her Husband and head, as it beseemes a Christian to have unto Christ ... . (78–9)

What a husband ought to bee.
By all this yee may gather and learne that the man is the head, governour, ruler, and instructer (with gentil words and good example) the provyder, defender, and whole comforte of the woman, and oweth unto hym most fervent love and affection, all gentle behaviour, all faythfulness and helpe, all comforte and kindness, as to him selfe, his owne flesh and body ... . (81)

Both marriage partners are taught their appropriate roles, which are hierarchical and explicitly gendered. Directives for the wife stress her obedience and godliness while advice for the husband emphasizes his role as supreme governor and instructor in his household. Prescriptive and educational literature work in concert to form the girl for her primary roles in life (wife and mother), indoctrinating her into a system where gender roles were fixed and her duties unambiguous.

In *The Tempest*, Prospero's initial directions to his daughter, "Be collected" (1.2.13) and "Obey, and be attentive" (1.2.38), echo typical instructions for women found in domestic guides, where obedience routinely appears as an idealized feminine virtue as it does in *Counsel to the husband: To the wife instruction*, whose author urges "faithfull and dutifull obedience" (92). That Miranda has, in fact, been obedient to her father's wishes is evidenced by her strangely incurious response, "More to know/ Did never meddle with my thoughts" (1.2.21–2), as she allows him to choose what he will teach her. He continues her lesson, urging her, repeatedly, to remember while at the same time examining her for what she recollects of their past:

PROSPERO: Obey, and be attentive. Canst thou remember
A time before we came unto this cell?
I do not think thou canst, for then wast not
Out three years old.
MIRANDA: Certainly, sir, I can.
PROSPERO: By what? by any other house, or person?
Or any thing the image, tell me, that
Hath kept with thy remembrance.
MIRANDA: 'Tis far off;
And rather like a dream than an assurance
That my remembrance warrants. Had I not
Four, or five, women once that tended me?
PROSPERO: Thou hadst; and more Miranda. But how is it
That this lives in thy mind? What seest thou else
In the dark backward and abysm of time?

If thou rememb'rest aught ere thou came here,
How thou cams'st here thou mayst.
MIRANDA: But that I do not. (1.2.38–52)

Only when Miranda stumbles in her recollection does Prospero begin to allay what he has earlier acknowledged as her ignorance "of what thou art" (1.2.18) by revealing his title and her royal status. The ask-and-answer format of their dialogue, as well as the heavy emphasis on memory, works here like a catechism with a teacher instilling valuable lessons through structured interaction and required memorization and repetition.[5] Jeff Dolven notes the particular sixteenth century "preoccupation with *understanding*" (7), explicit parallels between educational tracts and printed catechisms, and the common use of memory exercises. A student's success "consists in accurate repetition, failure in anything short of it" (16). The same obsession with both repetition and understanding infuse Prospero's dialogue with his daughter.

The importance of memory, as well as the consequences of forgetting, are also apparent in Prospero's interaction with Ariel who, like another pupil, is ordered to "Speak" (1.2.260) and is then chided for being a "Dull thing" (1.2.285). The emphasis on what has been forgotten—"Dost thou forget" (1.2.250) and "Hast though forgot" (1.2.257)—is as frequent here as the insistence that Miranda remember. In this case, however, Ariel's failure to recall his lesson elicits remonstration and threats of punishment: "If thou more murmur'st, I will rend an oak/ And peg thee in his knotty entrails till/ Though howl'd away twelve winters" (1.2.294–6). Ariel's submissive reply, "Pardon, master" (1.2.296) highlights the hierarchical nature of the schoolmaster-pupil relationship and Prospero's supremacy in his own household.

In prescriptive guides of the period that detail the ordering and management of the household, families are frequently compared to commonwealths with each member—husband, wife, children, and servants—having rigidly proscribed duties and responsibilities. These extend not just to general behavioral and religious expectations, but also to the educational responsibilities of family members. For example, Dod and Cleaver's oft-reprinted *A Godly Form of Household Government* (1598) emphasizes the importance of the father's role as the head of the household and his responsibility for the education of his children: "The third dutie, which the chiefe governour must perform to all his family, is private instruction ..." (45). In practice, however, it was often the mother who supervised the education of her children at home.

Prospero, without a wife, fulfills the obligation to instruct his daughter. Lacking other options on his remote island (like hiring private tutors), but as a committed scholar in possession of books, he is in a position to educate his daughter himself. That he fashions himself as both ruler and schoolmaster-scholar

---

[5]   The catechismal method was commonly used for children of both sexes. See Hull, *Women According to Men*, 133–4.

dominates his speech. For him, a monarch without a country to rule, the roles of father, schoolmaster, and governor of his household collapse into one another. Throughout his story he repeatedly references his love of his books and his own devotion to study, as well as the fact that his singular obsession left the door open for his brother's usurpation:

> And Prospero the prime duke, being so reputed
> In dignity, and for the liberal arts
> Without parallel; those being all my study,
> The government I cast upon my brother,
> And to my state grew stranger, being transported
> And rapt in secret studies. (1.2.72–7)

And later,

> I, thus neglecting worldly ends, all dedicated
> To closeness and the bettering of my mind
> With that which, but by being so retir'd,
> O'ver-priz'd all popular rate ... . (1.2.88–91)

Prospero's lesson, his own indulgent absorption as a negative example, works as a cautionary tale about the consequences of too much study.

That Gonzalo saved the two things most precious to him—his daughter and volumes from his library—is, however, firm in Prospero's recollection: "Knowing I lov'd my books, he furnish'd me/ From mine own library with volumes that / I prize above my dukedom" (1.2.166–8). And, that he has used the books and his isolated environment, as a schoolmaster would, profitably to teach his daughter is important to him. He says:

> Sit still, and hear the last of our sea-sorrow;
> Here in this island we arriv'd, and here
> Have I, thy schoolmaster, made thee more profit
> Than other princess' can, that have more time
> For vainer hours, and tutors not so careful. (1.2.170–74)

Miranda has, apparently, been a devoted student as she has learned both the value of language and how to instruct. Later in the same scene she reminds an ungrateful Caliban of her own educational efforts:

> I pitied thee,
> Took pains to make thee speak, taught thee each hour
> One thing or other. When thou dist not, savage,
> Know thine own meaning, but wouldst gabble like
> A think most brutish, I endow'd thy purposes
> With words that made them known. (1.2.353–8)

Miranda operates here, as her father's substitute or, perhaps, in the role an older child in a household might take in tutoring a younger sibling or household dependent.

Like the prescriptive literature, *The Tempest* emphasizes the schoolmaster/ governor/father parallels and the necessity of maintaining order in the household through appropriate instruction and adherence to the duties associated with one's place in the hierarchy. Tellingly, however, Caliban's plans for a violent rebellion against Prospero's rule center on the destruction of his books, which Caliban recognizes as a source for Prospero's power and authority:

> Why, as I told thee, 'tis a custom with him
> I' th' afternoon to sleep. There thou mayst brain him,
> Having first seiz'd his books; or with a log
> Batter his skull, or paunch him with a stake,
> Or cut his wezard with thy knife. Remember
> First to possess his books; for without them
> He's but a sot, as I am; nor hath not
> One spirit to command; they all do hate him
> As rootedly as I. Burn but his books. (3.2.87–95)

While both Miranda and Ariel bend to Prospero's will, Caliban is openly disobedient, rejecting Prospero's teaching and his supremacy; his deepest wish is reduce his unwanted governor to his own status as a "sot," a goal he believes he will achieve by devastating both his body and his library. Caliban's refusal to learn, or to submit to Prospero's leadership, rehearses (at least temporarily) possibilities for subversion and revolt that Miranda and Ariel, both compliant students, fail to imagine. In Caliban's rejection of Prospero as his ruler, and his insistence on the destruction of Caliban's books, the connection between education and authority is most clear.

So what exactly does Miranda, who is (in contrast with disobedient Caliban) an assiduous student, learn? And what is the purpose of her instruction? Miranda's lessons are not confined to family history. Among her lessons are not only the story of her father's neglectful government and usurpation by an ambitious brother, but subtle warnings for a soon-to-be married girl as well: "Good wombs have borne bad sons" (1.2.120). Prospero, in his teaching, adheres to what Suzanne Hull recognizes, in a study of early modern prescriptions for raising daughters, as the primary duty of the father toward his daughter: "it was the father's responsibility to settle his daughter in an appropriate marriage and to see that she was brought up as a chaste and worthy candidate for that goal" (*Women According to Men*, 135). Like the educational treatises, the play shows marriage and childbearing as the primary objectives of a girl's education; Miranda is no exception as her education has been a gendered one, conforming to early modern constructions of and expectations for young womanhood.

Much of the action of the play is driven by the considerable energy Prospero devotes to arranging a match for his daughter; he has a suitor for her, the King's son, shipwrecked on the island by way of a magical sea-storm, and ensures that they will fall for one another. That her education is in service of a prosperous marriage becomes increasingly evident as the focus of the play quickly shifts from the past (Prospero's usurpation and Miranda's faint girlhood recollections) to the future (Prospero's restoration and Miranda's prosperous marriage). It is here that Prospero's claim to Miranda that, as her schoolmaster he has "made thee more profit/ Than other princess' can" (1.2.171–2) is most obvious.

Act I, scene 2 begins with Prospero's interaction and educational efforts with the three primary members of his island "household"—first Miranda, then Ariel, then Caliban—but culminates with the appearance of Ferdinand—the key to Prospero's grand (and profitable) plan for his daughter. Miranda expresses amazement at such an unexpected sight, "What, is't a spirit?" (1.2.410), and "I might call him/ A thing divine, for nothing natural/ I ever saw so noble" (1.2.418–20), but Prospero's aside is calculating: "It goes on, I see,/ As my soul prompts it" (1.2.420–21). With Ferdinand's entrance, the tone of the scene changes; the young prince declares Miranda a "goddess" (1.2.422) and desires her "good instruction" (1.2.425) before he inquires, "My prime request, … is … if you be maid, or no?" (1.2.426–8). Miranda is, again, her father's instructional surrogate and the courtship, as Prospero has intended, proceeds as he continues in manipulating their affections for each other.

The pedagogical implications of Prospero's relationship with Miranda, and revelations of the purpose of her instruction, surface again in his words of rebuke. In response to his harsh treatment of Ferdinand (designed by Prospero to elicit her tenderness for him), Miranda begs her father, "Make not too rash a trial of him" (1.2.468). His admonition of her: "What, I say,/ My foot my tutor?" (1.2.470) reveals again the hierarchical, gendered, and pedagogical nature of Prospero's relationship with his daughter. Her repeated appeals garner harsher words: "Silence! one word more/ Shall make me chide thee, if not hate thee" (1.2.476–7). She may operate as his approved substitute in educating Ferdinand but must not overstep in questioning her father's methods; doing so brands her a "foolish wench" (1.2.480). Neither is Ferdinand immune to Prospero's tests and lessons. He is ordered to "Come on, obey" (1.2.484) before being set on a course of exhausting physical labor.

As her brief courtship continues, Miranda's lessons in obedience are never far from her mind even as she becomes slightly disobedient in her pursuit of Ferdinand. She urges her suitor to rest as she knows her father's absorption in his books will allow respite, "My father/ Is hard at study; pray now rest yourself, / He's safe for these three hours" (3.1.19–21). When asked her name, she quickly gives it, but worries immediately that she has defied her father's command: "Miranda.—O my father, I have broke your hest to say so" (3.1.36–7). Warned by Prospero not to talk to Ferdinand, she vacillates between her own desire for him and father's instruction:

> How features are abroad
> I am skilless of; but by my modesty
> (The jewel in my dower), I would not wish
> Any companion in the world but you;
> Nor can imagination form a shape,
> Besides yourself, to like of. But I prattle
> Something too wildly, and my father's precepts
> I therein do forget. (3.1.52–9)

Realizing, perhaps, that forgetting her father's teaching is not a viable option, she struggles (not entirely successfully) with restraining herself. Prospero, hidden, but observing the pair, cannot conceal his delight at accomplishing his ends. His words are telling: "Heavens rain grace/ On that which breeds between 'em!" (3.1.75–6). His legacy (as a ruler and a father) depends on the success of the match he has facilitated; appropriate breeding is exactly what he intends. Prospero's instruction continues, though, even after the young couple has become engaged. On the verge of marriage as he tutors them on proper behavior, including the restraint of sexual passion until after the vows have been made official:

> If thou dost break her virgin-knot before
> All sanctimonious ceremonies may
> With full and holy rite be minist'red,
> No sweet aspersion shall the heavens let fall
> To make this contract grow; but barren hate,
> Sour-ey'd disdain, and discord shall bestrew
> The union of your bed with weeds so loathly
> That you shall hate it both. Therefore take heed,
> As Hymen's lamps shall light you. (4.1.13–23)

He is a careful father where his daughter's chastity is concerned, even in the final moments before their marriage is solemnized.

The play, like the abundant prescriptive and educational literature of the period, emphasizes that the ultimate end of a girl's education is her preparation for marriage and motherhood. Prospero works to regain his title, to put down the island insurrections, and take (mild) vengeance on his usurping brother, but chief among his concerns is matching Miranda with Ferdinand through whom he ensures his own future generation. Only after having secured her marriage does he declare the "revels ... ended" (4.1.148). His final goal, reclaiming his kingdom, follows swiftly upon Miranda's marriage in the single remaining scene in which Prospero, his own succession assured, resolves to "drown my book" (5.1.57).

Miranda does not question her father's plans for her future. She submits, willingly, to her father's teaching and to his marriage choice for her (he has succeeded in making Ferdinand her choice as well) and makes the transition from girl to wife. Prospero's success in preparing her in the duties of obedience and silence—indeed she says almost nothing during her wedding, marriage masque, or the final scene of the play—seems to mark her as thoroughly inscribed by a patriarchal value system in evidence in the play and in early English modern culture. She is last shown, however, engaged in game of chess, trading playful barbs with Ferdinand before she utters her famous final words in response to the assembled company:

> O wonder!
> How many goodly creatures are there here!
> How beauteous mankind is! O brave new world
> That has such people in't! (5.1.181–4)

Does this staged moment of delight and inquisitiveness show her as hopelessly naive, cripplingly hindered by her isolation and a gendered educational system that seeks only to keep her obedient? Or, does it show a keen and hungry mind and allow for the possibility of growth?

So, what do *The Tempest*'s domestic scenes suggest about gender and instruction in early modern England? The play raises questions about the purpose and effects of girlhood education and is perhaps best understood as engaging in the larger debate about women so much in evidence in the popular press. While Prospero's household, with its studious teacher–father and attentive student–daughter, shows some evidence of rehearsing potentially progressive educational strategies, the play, like the conservative educational tracts and prescriptive guides devoted to the construction of an obedient wife and well-ordered household, ultimately validates the early modern preoccupation with preparing daughters for married life. *The Tempest* is, at its heart, a marriage play in that it both endorses and celebrates the dominant cultural narrative of the father's responsibility for educating his daughter and for settling her, as Prospero does Miranda, in a prosperous and profitable marriage.

Works Cited

Primary Sources

B., Ste. *Counsel to the husband: To the wife instruction*. London: Felix Kyngston for Richard Boyle, 1608.

Cleaver, Robert and John Dod. *A codly [sic] form of householde governement: for the ordering of private families according to the direction of Gods word*. London: Thomas Creede for Thomas Man, 1598.

Gataker, Thomas. *Marriage duties briefly couched together* (sic). London: William Jones, 1624.

———. *A Marriage Praier , or Succinct Meditiations: Delivered in a Sermon on the Praier of Eleazer the Servant of Abraham*. London: John Haviland, 1624.

Mulcaster, Richard. *Positions wherin those primitive circumstances be examined, which are necessarie for the training up of children, either for skill in their booke, or health in their bodie*. London: 1581.

Pritchard, Thomas. *The school of honest and vertuous lyfe: Profitable and necessary for all estates and degrees, to be trayned in: but (cheefly) for the pettie schollers, the yonger sorte, of both kindes, bee they men or women*. London: 1579.

Shakespeare, William. *The Tempest. The Riverside Shakespeare*. Ed. G. Blakemore Evans. Boston: Houghton Mifflin, 1974.

Secondary Sources

Aughterson, Kate, ed. *Renaissance Woman: A Sourcebook*. London: Routledge, 1995.

Bushnell, Rebecca W. *A Culture of Teaching: Early Modern Humanism in Theory and Practice*. Ithaca: Cornell University Press, 1996.

Carey-Webb, Allen. "National and Colonial Education in Shakespeare's *The Tempest.*" *Early Modern Literary Studies* 5.1 (1999): 3.1–39.

Dolven, Jeff. *Scenes of Instruction in Renaissance Romance*. Chicago: University of Chicago Press, 2007.

Hull, Susanne W. *Chaste, Silent and Obedient: English Books for Women 1475–1640*. San Marino: Huntington Library, 1982.

———. *Women according to Men: The World of Tudor-Stuart Women*. Walnut Creek, CA: Alta Mira Press, 1996.

Mendelson, Sara and Patricia Crawford. *Women in Early Modern England*. Oxford: Clarendon Press, 1998.

Smith, Hilda L. "Humanist Education and the Renaissance Concept of Woman." *Women and Literature in Britain, 1500–1700*. Ed. Helen Wilcox. Cambridge: Cambridge University Press, 1996. 9–29.

Wall, Wendy. *Staging Domesticity: Household Work and English Identity in Early Modern Drama*. Cambridge University Press, 2004.

Chapter 9

Producing Girls on the English Stage: Performance as Pedagogy in Mary Ward's Convent Schools

Caroline Bicks

The past 20 years have witnessed a boom in early modern studies of gender and performance. Scholars have written extensively on boy-actors, male players, and adult actresses, and in doing so have transformed how we think about the production of gendered identities, and especially the transition from boyhood to manhood, in the period.[1] The girl, however, has remained an outlier to these studies and, as a result, comparably innovative theories of how girls—and specifically early modern girlhood—were imagined have not emerged. This critical lacuna exists for a few reasons: women did not appear on the English public stage until the Restoration; and the performing girl is difficult to find given the privileged attention by scholars of theater history to professional staged productions. While some excellent collections recently have exploded the narrow definitions of theatrical space and performance this traditional scholarship has underwritten, the early modern girl still remains an elusive subject, making only brief appearances in studies of the Jacobean and Stuart court masques.[2]

My goal in this essay is twofold: to bring a unique example of English girls on the early modern stage to light by exploring the student productions put on in the convent schools established by Mary Ward; and, in so doing, to contribute to and complicate current understandings of early modern English girls and girlhood. Ward was a Catholic Englishwoman who founded a religious institute abroad in 1611 modeled on the Society of Jesus. Schools for Catholic English girls were attached to each of her dozen foundations on the Continent; as part of the curriculum, Ward trained these girls in theatrical performance and public speaking,

---

[1] See, for example, *Enacting Gender on the English Renaissance Stage*, Viviana Comensoli and Anne Russell, eds (Chicago: University of Illinois Press, 1999); and Stephen Orgel, *Impersonations: the Perfomance of Gender in Shakespeare's England* (Cambridge: Cambridge University Press, 1996).

[2] See *Women Players in England, 1500–1660*, Pamela Allen Brown and Peter Parolin, eds (Aldershot: Ashgate, 2005); *Women and Dramatic Production, 1550–1700*, Alison Findlay and Stephanie Hodgson Wright, eds (London: Longman, 2000); and *A New History of Early English Drama*, John Cox and David Scott Kastan, eds (New York: Columbia University Press, 1997).

all the better to serve the ailing Catholic cause back home by becoming eloquent speakers of the true faith. To her critics, however, these performances trained girls in the art of unspeakable apostolic acts. Thomas Rant, agent of the English secular clergy in Rome, epitomized this point of view when he complained to the Pope in 1624 that Ward and her followers "lead a loose life. They run about all over England and associate with men ... and, on the Continent, *they train their pupils for just such a daring way of life by the production of plays*. In doing so, they are a threat to the women of England and a scandal to catholics" (emphasis mine).[3]

As Rant's complaint suggests, Ward's girl-actors complicate conventional readings of early modern girlhood as an uncontested space of presexual containment. If, as scholars have claimed, English daughters stood for the integrity of the patriarchal household, the state, and the English Church, then the potential exposure and transformation of the girl from modest daughter to daring apostle through performance and speech deconstructs this model in substantial ways.[4] In Rant's imagination, English girls have the potential to transform, via their stage-training, into females who are not contained within the bounds of acceptable behavior or attached to and owned by any one man.

Clare McManus offers us a glimpse of the girl-actor in her analysis of the 1617 performance of *Cupid's Banishment* before Queen Anne by the students of Ladies Hall at Deptford. McManus recognizes the value of this unique staging of the female voice and body for reconsidering the nature of female identity in the period, but she does not consider the implications of the masquers' status as girls in her analysis of gender and performance.[5] She alternates between calling them "young female performers," "early modern women" and "schoolgirls," a slippage that reflects the diversity that this female stage between childhood and marriage was pressured to encompass. My point here is not to criticize McManus's important work, but to highlight a larger problem that the early modern girl poses for scholars of the period: she is a shifty entity, difficult to locate and analyze, not only because "girl" denotes so many different ages, but also because of how

---

[3]   Translation from the Latin is in Henriette Peters, *Mary Ward: A World in Contemplation*, trans. Helen Butterworth (1991; Gracewing, 1994), 389.

[4]   See, for example, Peter Stallybrass's influential argument that the enclosed female body was an emblem for the state as "*hortus conclusus*, an enclosed garden walled off from enemies," and that it was consequently "the object of policing by fathers and husbands" ("Patriarchal Territories: The Body Enclosed," in *Rewriting the Renaissance*, Ferguson et al., eds [Chicago: Chicago University Press, 1986], 129).

[5]   Clare McManus, "Memorialising Anna of Denmark's Court: *Cupid's Banishment* at Greenwich Palace," in *Women and Culture at the Courts of the Stuart Queens*, Clare McManus, ed. (New York: Palgrave, 2003), 81–100. In her work on Stuart women on stage, Sophie Tomlinson similarly argues that female theatricality is a useful way into investigating the fashioning of female subjectivity. See her *Women on Stage in Stuart Drama* (Cambridge: Cambridge University Press, 2005).

we have been taught to think about her—as the woman/wife she will become.[6] Lawrence Stone's influential study of the family, for example, presumes a male subject in its discussion of children, and limits its discussion of girls to examples (like their encasement in "miniature adult clothes") that show them being molded according to an adult female ideal.[7] Such truncations or elisions of girlhood, it should be noted, are not the sole provenance of dated, male-centric scholarship; Catherine Driscoll argues that this model of human development especially informs the work of feminist scholars in that they "presume the primary importance of a feminist woman-subject."[8]

How, then, can we attend to early modern girls? One way, I want to suggest here, is by exploring moments in which they turn into spectacles—moments that scholars of early modern women and theater have analyzed in order to understand constructions of female identity. At the same time, my hope is to distinguish between the construction of girls and women, and, in the same vein, to examine girls as subjects who are not solely defined in relation to their fathers or future husbands. This last issue is especially important at this moment, I think, because it exposes another way in which the study of early modern women has been defined and, in certain ways, limited. Ward's performing schoolgirls, who ranged in age from six to eighteen, offer us a unique opportunity to think beyond these categories of male ownership and the traffic in women; for while these students provoked hostile responses that clearly grew out of an understanding of girls as the property and future property of men, they also were considered by some Catholic English subjects to be agents capable of healing and expanding a fragmented religious community through their performances. In these latter cases, they are not imagined in terms of their relationships to the men who controlled their bodies, but in terms of their ameliorative relationship to a larger ailing English Catholic community.

The multiple meanings that adhere in the early modern girl are especially legible in descriptions of Catholic schoolgirls and novices—young females potentially on the verge of entering a sisterhood. These girls threaten to remain in a perpetually in-between state of their gendered development, refusing to cross over from daughter

---

[6]   As Jennifer Higginbotham's research has revealed, "there was no dominant term for female children until the mid to late seventeenth century." See her "Fair Maids and Golden Girls: Early Modern Girlhood and the Production of Femininity" (unpublished diss., University of Pennsylvania, 2007), 19.

[7]   Stone, *The Family, Sex and Marriage in England 1500–1800* (1977; New York: Harper & Row, 1979), 116. Stone was influenced by the work of Philippe Ariès, who famously argued in his *Centuries of Childhood* that childhood, as distinct from adulthood, did not exist fully as a concept until the eighteenth century. Although this model has been refuted by a number of scholars, it remains remarkably tenacious, as Barbara Hanawalt notes. See her "The Child in the Middle Ages and the Renaissance," in *Beyond the Century of the Child: Cultural History and Developmental Psychology*, William Koops and Michael Zuckerman, eds (Philadephia: University of Pennsylvania Press, 2003), 21–42.

[8]   Catherine Driscoll, *Girls: Feminine Adolescence in Popular Culture and Cultural Theory* (New York: Columbia University Press, 2002), 165.

to wife, virgin to nonvirgin, girl to woman.[9] When Thomas Penson visited a convent in Antwerp in 1687, he encountered a young English novice standing at a grate. His description of this threshold moment brings the Catholic girl's liminality sharply into focus: "there soon appeared (as an angel of light) a delicate, proper, beautiful lady, all in white garments and barefaced, whose graceful presence was delightful to behold and yet struck an awful reverence, considering she was devout and religious."[10]

When the ideally contained virgin opens up and displays herself as both delightful and awful through performance, she potentially challenges ideological notions (modern and early modern) of what a girl is. After Penson's "angel" is feasted upon by his "greedy eye," he tells her that his English countrymen view her as being "buried alive ... within the confines of these walls." She counters his Protestant-inflected view with a response that refuses to conform to his image of what a girl wants: "Although for my part I may forsake this place when I please, being now but in the year of my noviceship, yet do assure you, Sir, ... I would not change conditions with any princess or noble lady in the world." In Penson's narrative, the novice threatens to remain on the threshold between girl and woman. She may leave the convent walls whenever she pleases; but she may choose never to leave at all.

In their recent study, *Girlhood: Redefining the Limits*, Jiwani et al. note that "girl" encompasses a host of often contradictory meanings: "the space of girlhood is one of contestation; marked by conflict, resistance, and change."[11] My analysis here of Ward's performing students is informed by this theoretical position as it considers multiple, sometimes competing ideas in its reconsideration of the early modern girl.

I

When Mary Ward left her parents in Yorkshire to join a convent of Saint Clares overseas in Saint-Omer in 1606, she was following the path of many English Catholic recusants' daughters. Five years later, she claimed to have had a divine revelation telling her to found a new order based on the Jesuit model. She left the Saint Clares and founded what would be the first of over a dozen houses on the Continent devoted to teaching Catholic English girls abroad and to saving Catholicism back home through missionary work. Although Ward's followers took vows, they refused enclosure. They needed to be able to move freely in order to accomplish their work. This direct violation of Tridentine decree left them vulnerable to a host of rhetorical attacks. They were commonly called bawds and

---

[9]   As Driscoll notes, "The virgin functions less as a liminal point between innocence and knowledge than between girl and woman" (140).

[10] *Touring the Low Countries: Accounts of British Travellers, 1660–1720*, Kees van Strien, ed. (Amsterdam: Amsterdam University Press, 1998), 59.

[11] Yasmin Jiwani, Candis Steenbergen, and Claudia Mitchell, *Girlhood: Redefining the Limits* (Black Rose Books, 2006).

"galloping nuns" because of their reputation for roving. Their refusal to follow Papal Law resulted in the Institute's suppression in 1631.[12]

Embedded in this recorded history of nonenclosure and public suppression is another much less visible pat of Ward's vision and of her Institute's operations: her training of English girls in the art of theatrical performance. In 1622, the Benedictine priest, Robert Sherwood, complained to the Pope that Ward's schoolgirls, "sent to them [Ward and her followers] to be educated, publicly produce immoral plays (*publice et non satis verecunde*), so that later they may consort with seculars or preach in churches in this bold manner (*hoc modo audacis*)."[13] By teaching girls the art of public speaking and performance, Ward was following the *Ratio Studiorum*, which outlines the pedagogical significance of theater within the Jesuit curriculum, and readily acknowledges the connection between student performance and religious zeal: "Young boys ... and their parents become marvelously inflamed, and also very much attached to our Society, when the boys are able to display on stage our labours."[14]

But Ward was teaching girls, not boys, to enflame their audiences. In the eyes of her English critics especially, her conflation of the schoolgirl with the actress/apostle implicated Ward in two ways: it exposed her (as Sherwood's complaint makes clear) as a bawd who forced English girls to perform immodest acts of public boldness; and it connected Ward to her Jesuit brethren and their infamous theatrical deceptions.[15] Anti-Catholic treatises regularly attacked the plays and spectacular exorcisms that Jesuits put on to incite audiences to conversion.[16] John Gee describes the Jesuits' "Theatricall and fabulous tricks"—the "Virginall, Monasticall, fantasticall. Sophisticall Contrivers and Actors" who "easily put on the person of St. Lucy, or the

---

[12]   The derogatory name "galloping nun" appears in a number of sources. See, for instance, "Sister Dorothea's Narrative," in Margaret Littlehales, *Mary Ward: Pilgrim and Mystic* (London: Burns & Oates, 2001), 251; and William Prynne, *Workes of darkenes brought to light* (London, 1645), 203. For an overview and analysis of the different religious factions working against Ward, see Laurence Lux-Sterritt, "An Analysis of the Controversy Caused by Mary Ward's Institute in the 1620s," *Recusant History* 25 (2001): 636–47.

[13]   Qtd. in Peters, *Mary Ward*, 342.

[14]   Qtd. in Robert Miola, "Jesuit Drama in Early Modern England," in *Theatre and Religion*, Richard Dutton, Alison Findlay, and Richard Wilson, eds (Manchester: Manchester University Press, 2003), 71–86, quotation on p. 72.

[15]   As Michael Zampelli, argues, "The animus of religious men toward the actress must be considered within a wider social context that also included a growing uneasiness with and hostility toward the more public activity of religious women intent on claiming their place in the apostolic mission of Roman Catholicism." See his "'The 'most honest and most devoted of women': An early modern defense of the professional actress," *Theatre Survey* 42 (2001): 8–23, quotation on p. 9.

[16]   As Swapan Chakravorty argues, "the stigma of the theatre attached itself especially to the Jesuit, who in Jacobean England had eclipsed the Machiavellian as the archetype of the evil thespian." See his *Society and Politics in the Plays of Thomas Middleton* (Oxford: Clarendon Press, 1996), 170.

Virgin Mary."[17] Ward had taken England's most precious commodities—its future wives and mothers—and turned them into virginal contrivers.

II

Ward made many direct appeals to the Pope for approval of her Institute. In one of them, she argued that in order to help "the sadly afflicted state of England" she and her companions needed to live a "mixed kind of life," one that allowed them to move freely between households, provinces, and countries.[18] She proposed this lifestyle so that "by this means we may more easily instruct virgins and young girls from their earliest years in piety, Christian morals and the liberal arts, that they may afterwards ... profitably embrace either the secular or the religious state." Ward conceived of her educational enterprise, one based in "the liberal arts," as instrumental to the promotion of the Institute's "mixed life."

We have scant evidence about the nature of the performances that were part of this education, but there are documented complaints against plays put on in the Liège school as well as a comedy performed in the Vienna school in 1628.[19] Laurence Lux-Sterritt additionally notes that, "In Munich, students were expected to perform a little celebratory play on special feasts and holy days, as well as for the clothing of postulants or to celebrate a visit by an important person." These performances, according to Lux-Sterritt's research, "gained the Institute's schools a certain renown and captured the interest of influential aristocratic and bourgeoisie families."[20]

It was their undetectable performances on English soil, however, that had Ward's opponents most concerned. By 1624 Ward already had made numerous trips back home to oversee the 30 known Jesuitesses of her Institute who were

---

[17]   John Gee, *New Shreds of the Old Snare* (London, 1624), 16–17.

[18]   "Memorial of Mary Ward," in Mary Chambers, *The Life of Mary Ward*, vol. 1, Henry James Coleridge, ed. (London: Burns and Oates, 1882), 376. Lowell Gallagher aptly describes this mixed life as "quasi-theatrical." See his "Mary Ward's 'Jesuitresses' and the Construction of a Typological Community," in *Maids and Mistresses, Cousins and Queens: Women's Alliances in Early Modern England*, Susan Frye and Karen Robertson, eds (Oxford: Oxford University Press, 1999), 199–217, quotation on p. 204.

[19]   See Peter Guilday, the *English Catholic Refugees on the Continent, 1558–1795* (London: Longmans and Green, 1914), 192; and Leo Hicks, *The Month*, "Mary Ward's Great Enterprise" (Part IV) 1928, vol. 2, 231–8, esp. p. 232. For recent examinations of Ward's pedagogical work with drama, see Sister Marion Norman, "A Woman for All Seasons: Mary Ward (1585–1645), Renaissance Pioneer of Women's Education," *Paedagogica Historica* 23 (1983): 125–43, esp. p. 135; and Rosemary A. DeJulio, "Women's Ways of Knowing and Learning: The Response of Mary Ward and Madeleine Sophie Barat to the *Ratio Studiorum*," in *The Jesuit Ratio Studiorum: 400th Anniversary Perspectives*, Vincent J. Dumenico, S.J., ed. (New York: Fordham University Press, 2000), 107–26, esp. p. 117.

[20]   Laurence Lux-Sterritt, *Redefining Female Religious Life: French Ursulines and English Ladies in Seventeenth-Century Catholicism* (Aldershot: Ashgate, 2005), 92.

at work in London.[21] The women helped Catholic priests in their underground operations, prepared the poor to receive sacraments, assisted with conversions, and accepted would-be students and members before sending them overseas to join one of Ward's houses.[22]

The underground nature of their activities necessitated a certain level of theatricality.[23] In a biography written by Ward's followers soon after her death in 1645, we learn that

> In England she went cloathed as became her birth for matter and manner, ... When it best suited with present occasions, she put on servants and meane womens cloathes; Our dearest mother employed herself & hers, sometimes disguised, sometimes in her owne Cloathes, using sometimes familiar conversation, other times authority.[24]

These quick changes in speech and costume translated easily into accusations of elusive and heretical activities. In his petition to the Pope, William Harrison, Archpriest of the English Catholic mission, wrote that

> These Jesuitresses have a habit of frequently going about cities and provinces of the kingdom, insinuating themselves into houses of noble Catholics, changing their habit often, ... Now publicly, now privately, now in noble dress, now in poor, now in cities, now in provinces, now many together, now alone, among men, seculars, and not seldom of bad morals.[25]

In Harrison's imagination, Ward and her followers are dangerously independent, changing locations as quickly as they change their habits and moving illegibly between public and private spaces.

Once inside a household, they could then move in on their prey: the innocent English girl. James Wadsworth, an anti-Catholic spy, reported of "the Jesuitrices, or wandring nuns" the following: that "Mistresse *Ward* is become mother Generall of no lesse that 200 *English* damsels, being most of them Ladies and Knights daughters, who live in their colledges at St. Omers, Leige and Colen, and from thence are for

---

[21] Littlehales, *Mary Ward*, 129.

[22] For an overview of this early history of the Institute, see Elizabeth Rapley, *The Dévotes: Women and Church in Seventeenth-Century France* (Montreal: McGill-Queen's University Press, 1990), 28–34.

[23] Miola argues that the Jesuits' theatrical training was in fact part of this larger survival tactic: "working in dangerous places such as England, Jesuit missionaries practiced impersonation to survive. ... the Jesuit way of proceeding necessarily required exercise of the theatrical imagination" ("Jesuit Drama," 73).

[24] Poyntz and Wigmore, *A Briefe Relation*, Bar Convent Archives (hereafter BCA), 14r–15v, 19v–20r.

[25] Harrison, "A Copy of the Information concerning the Jesuitresses," in Chambers, *The Life of Mary Ward*, vol. 2, 184.

England to convert their Country."[26] Ward, the bad mother, corrupts her stolen girls, ruining their futures for good. As John Bennett, agent of the English clergy in Rome, wrote of the Jesuitesses in 1622, they have "impeached the opinion which was held of the modesty and shamefacedness of our Country-women. ... [T]hey must dissolve, ... that they delude no more young women, to the hazard of their ruin."[27]

Within these hostile comments, the notion of girls as precious and malleable commodities in need of protection is clearly at work. By taking English daughters overseas, and teaching them how to perform, Ward threatened the reputation and "modesty" of all young Englishwomen. In 1624, John Gee complained in his *New Shreds of the Old Snare* that "*Priests & Jesuits* who entice the daughters of divers of our Gentry here in *England* to the Nunneries beyond the seas ... not onely transport them thither ... but also make use of those that are in the Cage already, that they may seeme to sing out the praises of the place where they are." The girls are forced to write laudatory letters by their "*Mother Abbesse* by the direction of an inspecting spirituall father," so that "other young Birds of that brood, remaining in *England*, may be drawn to flie to the same forain nests."[28] The mother abbess and Jesuit father threaten to replace the innocent English girl's proper gentrified parents. The caged girls sing and lure their young sisters overseas to join their reconfigured and corrupt new family.

Although Gee casts these performers as caged and coerced, the seductive dynamic he imagines between the girl-singer and her audience of young birds flying to join her raises the specter of the girls' latent power to perform independent acts of insinuation and conversion. By expressing concerns about girls corrupting other girls, then, such attacks betray conflicting notions about the agency of girls and the construction of girlhood itself. When does a girl shift from victim to victimizer—from acted upon to actor? Clearly she does not need to become a woman in order to enact this transformation, so how can one confine girlhood to any one predictable and recognizable model and set of behaviors?

III

Most of the references we have to Ward's theatrical work with girls exist in official Papal Archives and state letters drafted by men interested in suppressing her enterprise. In this last section, I want to try to recover another narrative about these dramatic activities by turning to other kinds of sources that document performances by the students who attended the Institute's English schools after Ward's death in 1645. Through these examples, it is possible to read the Institute's schoolgirls as agents of community building for England's Catholic citizens. Given the fragmentary nature of the evidence concerning the theatrical productions put

---

[26]   James Wadsworth, *The English Spanish Pilgrime. Or, a new discoverie of Spanish popery, and Jesuiticall stratagems* (London, 1629), 30–31. Folger copy HH212/9.

[27]   Letter of John Bennett, May 23, 1622, BCA, 1/1 30–31.

[28]   Gee, *New Shreds*, 113–14.

on at these schools, this last section is at times an imaginative reconstruction of the past, a reading backwards from eighteenth-, nineteenth-, and twentieth-century documents to the early days of the Institute's English foundations.

In a collection of essays on women players in early modern England, Alison Findlay locates examples of women participating in ceremonial performances reminiscent of the Old Religion. She cites one record from 1603 in Burnley in which "the women Children" participate in a rushbearing, a ceremonial decoration of the Church.[29] Scholars of Catholic recusancy especially have identified a number of alternative performances such as this one, and in so doing have provided valuable glimpses of early modern girls on a more broadly defined stage.[30] In the absence of any details of the plays put on in Ward's English foundations in London and York during the seventeenth and eighteenth centuries, this context is a valuable one for reconsidering the afterlife on English soil of Ward's performing schoolgirls.

The first English foundation of Ward's Institute was opened in Hammersmith in 1669 by Frances Bedingfield, one of Ward's followers. Although we have no records from that period that tell us what the girls were studying, there is a copy of the Rules for the Boarding School at Hammersmith in the York Bar Convent Archives that were drawn up by Bishop Petre in 1750. Through this we learn that music and dancing were taught to pensioners for an additional fee, but that "No children must be allowed ... to play Boys; no sort of plays or proverbs must be allowed of their own Composition, no Ballads kept or sung, but what the mistresses or Confessor has examined; Christenings weddings Burials are by no means to be represented by the pensioners," and "the reading of Play books or Romances" is prohibited.[31] While these rules obviously offer us no solid proof as to the status of theatrical productions in the English Institute schools, either in the seventeenth or eighteenth centuries, they do suggest some traces of dramatic activity. If "plays ... of their own Composition" were singled out as prohibited, then it is not unreasonable to imagine that other types of plays may have been allowed. Furthermore, the fact that the students were not allowed to play boys suggests that they were allowed to play girls.

The rule against reading play books is more perplexing. In a letter written from Ward in 1639, when she was in England, to one of her followers in Rome, she describes her "endeavor by prayer and private negotiation that we may have common schools in the great City of London." In the letter (written in lemon juice to avoid detection), Ward requests that her follower procure among other things "plays, all that is there, or can be had without notice or the least suspecting," to send to her in England.[32] The clandestine nature of her request for plays, together

---

[29]   Findlay, "Payments, Permits and Punishments: Women Performers and the Politics of Place," in *Women Players in England*, 45–67, quotation on p. 55.

[30]   See, for example, *Region, Religion and Patronage: Lancastrian Shakespeare*, Richard Dutton, Alison Findlay, and Richard Wilson, eds (Manchester: Manchester University Press, 2003).

[31]   Rules for the Boarding School at Hammersmith, BCA, 2A/37.

[32]   Qtd. in Chambers, *Life of Mary Ward*, vol. 2, 466–7.

with the later prohibition by the Bishop against reading play books, may tell us something about the perceived dangers (especially in London where they would have been more conspicuous to their enemies) of the Institute's theatrical activities.

Traces of the dramatic activities in England for which Ward's continental schools were known are found only in later accounts of the Institute's Bar Convent in York, established in 1686 by Ward's followers at the behest of a group of Catholic northern gentry. It is the longest-running extant convent in England. A memorandum book in the Bar Convent Archives documents the purchase of "hooks for the shepherdesses" and "a new black bag for the King's hair" in the early eighteenth century, presumably for Christmastime performances.[33] Henry Coleridge speculates that the schoolgirls at the convent would have performed the coming of the Magi at Kingtide for an audience of their relatives and for the Catholic nobility and gentry who had vacation homes in York that they occupied in the winter months.[34] Susan O'Brien's work on the Bar Convent traces how its school and the religious women who ran it were indeed central to the English Catholic community: "Strategically situated in York it became a clearing-house for news, an active centre within a Catholic network."[35]

The contexts that Coleridge and O'Brien provide offer an illuminating framework within which to reconsider girls as edifying agents of community building for England's disenfranchised Catholics, and not just as daughters and future wives. York, besides being a center of Catholic recusancy, was also a center of theatrical activity. As J.C.H. Aveling notes, "Apart from the ordinary shopkeepers tradesmen, the Catholic Community contained five small specialist groups—actors, schoolteachers, doctors, men in the building trade and artists."[36] Over 800 students studied at the Convent boarding school over the course of the eighteenth century, and their social backgrounds reflected this diversity. From school records, we know that the daughters of Thomas Keregan, an actor–manager who opened the New Theatre in Minster Yard in York, and Elizabeth Chalk, a London actress, attended the school from 1735–1739.[37] It is tempting to imagine that the Keregan girls' connections to York's first professional theater might have aided the students in their Kingtide performances. A review of a 1909 production of Rev. Robert Hugh Benson's *Nativity* by the Bar Convent students documents just such a connection between the theater and the school: the scenery "was managed by professional hands from the York Theatre."[38]

---

[33]   Anecdotes of the Bar Convent from the Year 1735, BCA, 3B/4.

[34]   Henry James Coleridge, *St. Mary's Convent, York* (London: Burns and Oates, 1887), 158–9.

[35]   O'Brien, "Women of the 'English Catholic Community': Nuns and Pupils at the Bar Convent, York, 1680–1790," offprint from *Monastic Studies* 1, BCA 5A/32: 269.

[36]   Aveling, *Catholic Recusancy in York, 1558–1791*, Catholic Record Society Publications, Monograph Series, vol. 2 (St. Albans, Hertfordshire, 1970), 145.

[37]   Ibid., 122.

[38]   The review, "A Christmas Mystery Play at St. Mary's Convent, York" is included in the 1908 Longmans and Green edition of *The Nativity: A Mystery Play by the Rev. R.H.*

It is worth pausing over descriptions of this production since they resonate with Coleridge's claims that the schoolgirls' performances in the early days of the Bar Convent provided an opportunity for English Catholics to gather together. The production "was acted six times altogether, to full houses, upon a temporary stage in the school-room of St. Mary's Convent, by the girls of the school, whose ages ran from six to eighteen."[39] One reviewer waxed poetic over the spiritually edifying effects of the girls on stage: "that the destined end of the performance was attained, namely the deepening of the spiritual sense in the beholders of the sacred mystery commemorated, was evidenced by the fact that many present, and those not exclusively of the gentler sex, were observed to be moved even to tears." In the audience were "a large number of guests, including the Lord Bishop of Olenus, a considerable number of the clergy, Lady Beaumont and her two daughters, and many other friends." Here, the spirits of male and female audience members alike are enriched, and all are moved to tears by the girls' performance.

Moving back in time to the nineteenth century, Coleridge provides us with another description of the girls in performance in which they similarly serve to unite and uplift their audience. He cites a published notice of the Institute's bicentennial celebration, attended by clerical guests and secular friends, written by one of its members:

> What with recitations, and tableaux, and a concert—in which their music shone to great advantage—and the performance of a Calderonic drama, in very good verse indeed, and with beautiful songs interspersed, the young ladies certainly did a great deal to help to make their visitors wish that, if possible, the centenary might come more than once in their lives.[40]

Here, the girls perform in a variety of venues: singing as well as acting. At no point are they read as stepping beyond the bounds of acceptable female behavior; instead, they leave their visitors wanting more.

As early as 1690, the students of the Bar Convent participated in an annual processional in honor of St. Michael, protector of the Convent. Coleridge describes the procession that took place during the bicentennial celebration as "ordered in accordance with the old tradition of the House—the youngest child in the school walking first, carrying the picture of St. Michael."[41] A first-hand account of this processional appears in the Bar Convent School Magazine from 1931. Here, "an Onlooker" describes how

> a procession of white-veiled schoolgirls came slowly from a passage to my left. Ranged in order of height, it ended with a small child, flanked by two others

---

Benson that I consulted at the York Minster Archives. The reviewer also notes that "the bambino was supplied by a well-known firm in London."

[39]   Preface to *The Nativity*.

[40]   Coleridge, 375.

[41]   Ibid., 376.

bearing lighted candles. This child bore a picture ... [In the chapel] the children stood in a semi-circle just outside the sanctuary, the smallest in their midst; the gold, flower-decked altar shone with brilliantly reflected light from the dome, while young voices sang on the quaint impressive music in an atmosphere of radiant joy that I shall not easily forget.

Although written in the twentieth century, this description, along with the others I have touched on here, offers us a glimpse into how the Institute's schoolgirls might have served to impress and uplift an early modern Catholic audience through their performances of spectacular religious rituals as well as scripted plays.

But can we find any evidence that a seventeenth-century audience would have viewed the performing girl as just such an ameliorative agent? By turning to representations of Ward's own girlhood, I believe we can. Some of Ward's followers on the Continent commissioned a group of 50 oil paintings, made from the time just before Ward's death in 1645 to the end of the eighteenth century, and commemorating the Life of Mary Ward from childhood forward. In this series, it is possible to see how her girlhood was constructed and displayed by her followers to produce a spiritual foundation for the Institute via a pictorial narrative about Ward's early development. The first of the series shows Mary as a mere toddler, speaking her first word: Jesus (Fig. 9.1). The child supports herself on a chair while the surprised onlookers show their obvious surprise at her religious precocity. The image is a speaking picture, a performance with the young Ward as the central player and we, along with the women in the painting, her awestruck audience.

The fourth painting in the series offers up another kind of moving picture as the ten-year-old Mary is shown first—to the left—in her parents' burning house in Mulwith, then in the middle being led out of the house by her father (Fig. 9.2). The painting depicts a story from Ward's early history in which Mary had gathered her younger sisters to her when she noticed the house burning. Rather than leaving the house, she sat them down to pray to the Virgin for help. As with the first painting, the picture displays Mary in the midst of an inspirational religious performance: her girlhood is produced as a model upon which the singing, acting, and processing girls of Ward's English Institute would be based—girls who potentially healed ailing Catholic communities when they performed on English soil.

Mary later wrote of the event:

[We] went into a lower room of the house. There stood a trunk or coffer filled filled with linen damask, which I had heard some say my mother laid apart for me. This coffer, with the help of my sisters, I drew into the chimney of the same room, and then we set ourselves to pray the Mother of God that she would not permit the house to be burnt.[42]

---

[42] *Till God Will: Mary Ward Through her Writings*, M. Emmanuel Orchard, ed. (London: Darton, Longman and Todd, 1985), 7.

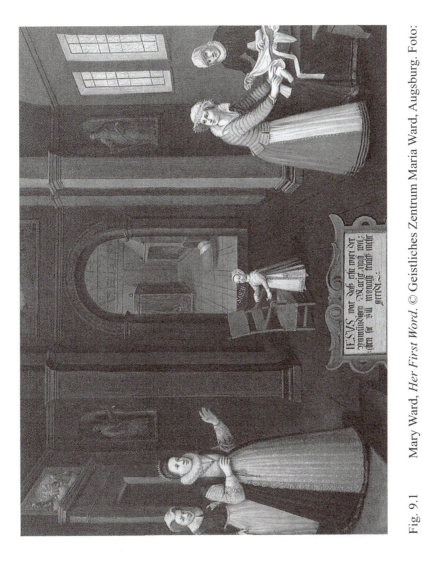

Fig. 9.1   Mary Ward, *Her First Word.* © Geistliches Zentrum Maria Ward, Augsburg. Foto: Tanner, Nesselwang.

Here Ward takes the trunk her mother gave her, surely a kind of hope chest, and turns it from a symbol of her future as a married woman to a prop in her hagiographic drama; the mother of God replaces her earthly mother and womanly model. Through this memorial reconstruction, Ward explicitly figures herself as occupying and owning the liminal space between childhood and adulthood. Like Penson's speaking angel, and Ward's performing students, Mary dramatizes her early modern girlhood as a fluid and negotiable site—a stage upon which all kinds of girls might be produced.

Fig. 9.2   Mary Ward, *Fire in Mulwith*. © Geistliches Zentrum Maria Ward, Augsburg. Foto: Tanner, Nesselwang.

PART 3
Transitional Stages:
Growing Up and Growing Old

Chapter 10
Boys to Men:
Codpieces and Masculinity in
Sixteenth-Century Europe

Carole Collier Frick

Childhood has long been seen as a discrete part of life, partitioned off from adulthood by a scrim of parental concern and protection. We tend to think of childhood as a time of innocence and play, so-called "rosy childhood," a stage of life in which the child is shielded by parents and family from the harsh realities of adulthood. This notion of the inherent innocence of the first years of a child's life, however, is a relatively recent idea unknown in the medieval and Renaissance periods, according to Philippe Ariès, who located its emergence first in the early seventeenth century in Europe.[1] Even though Ariès believed that medieval children lived very dissimilar lives to their early modern successors and has been criticized in subsequent scholarship for his assertion that parents were not as invested in their children emotionally due to the vicissitudes of the day, I will argue that perhaps their parents were similarly invested emotionally in their children's lives, but that fundamental beliefs about childhood led their parents not to separate children from their own adult experiences in the same way that parents began to do in the early modern period.[2]

Ariès has written that in the long medieval era, the seven ages of human life was an accepted concept, originating in sixth century Byzantium by Fulgentius's reading of the *Aeneid.* The first stage was characterized as from birth to the age of seven,

---

[1]   Philippe Ariès, *Centuries of Childhood. A Social History of Family Life* (New York: Alfred A. Knopf, 1962), 109.

[2]   For the subsequent scholarly critique of Ariès's conclusions of the benign neglect of children by their parents in the medieval period due in part to high infant mortality, see, for example, David Herlihy, *Medieval Households* (Cambridge: Harvard University Press, 1985); Barbara Hanawalt, *The Ties That Bound: Peasant Families in Medieval England* (New York and Oxford: Oxford University Press, 1986); Shulamith Shahar, *Childhood in the Middle Ages* (London and New York: Routledge, 1990); Pierre Riché and Danièle Alexandre-Bidon, *L'enfance au Moyen Age* (Paris: Editions du Seuil. Bibliothèque Nationale de France, 1994); R.C. Finucane, *The Rescue of the Innocents. Endangered Children in Medieval Miracles* (New York: St. Martin's Press, 1997); Louis Haas, *The Renaissance Man and His Children: Childbirth and Early Childhood in Florence, 1300–1600* (New York: St. Martin's Press, 1998); Sally Crawford, *Childhood in Anglo-Saxon England* (Gloucestershire: Sutton Publishing Ltd., 1999); and Nicholas Orme, *Medieval Children* (New Haven and London: Yale University Press, 2001).

these children being termed "infants." This was followed by the second period of life, from age 7 to 14, called *pueritia* (boyhood), and it is this age that will primarily concern us here.[3] As Ariès noted, each stage of life had its appropriate dressing conventions, in which "infants" went from wearing little collared robes as they began to walk, and then transitioned at around the age of seven to more specifically gendered costume.[4] However, in the tumultuous sixteenth century in Europe, the sartorial markers between *pueritia* and *adolescens* at 14 became blurred with the introduction of the codpiece on young boys. The necessity arose to present an uninterrupted display of overt masculinity in formal dress. In Fig. 10.1, we see the codpiece as part of Ranuccio Farnese's formal portrait. Here, Pope Paul III's grandson is pictured as a serious boy (or is he already a man?) about midway through his *pueritia*, about the age of 11 or 12.[5]

In this chapter, I want to explore the codpiece for young boys and to inquire as to its meaning. Here, I will discuss this aspect of the changing styles of the time, especially in the clothing of boys beginning early in their *pueritia* and into early *adolescens*. In their ensembles the codpiece played an important role. In this century of tumultuous change, it seemed to be crucially important to those adults who commissioned the images of these male children so costumed to demonstrate familial stability with this socially constructed image of masculinity. What was its meaning at the time? Here, I will argue that the picture of familial continuity and strength that portraits of nubile females had accomplished for the families of the upper ranks in the fifteenth century, portraits of young males of the same stratum of society shown in codpieces did for the sixteenth. When the necessity for displaying such stabilizing outward signs of masculinity waned in around 1580, the codpiece disappeared for all males of the upper classes beneath new styles of garments, fashioned to address new societal concerns.

Notions of Childhood

Evidence of a basic continuity between childhood and adulthood came from accepted cultural notions of human nature (including those of young children) as being tainted by original sin. David Herlihy wrote that St. Augustine's conclusions regarding children were that "evil establishes its dominion over the growing child." In fact, Augustine believed that "the innocence of children is in the helplessness of their bodies, rather than any quality of soul."[6] In the same vein, Cardinal

---

[3]   This was followed by the third age, "*adolescence*," which could go on until the age of 21, but could last until the age of 35, according to some writers. The fourth age, "*youth*," followed this, and did not end until 45 or 50. The fifth age was "*senectitude*" or "*gravity*," and lastly the sixth, "*old age*," which ended in "*senies*" and death. See Ariès, *Centuries*, 18–22.

[4]   Ariès, *Centuries*, 50–53.

[5]   The artist Antonio Moro painted Ranuccio's younger brother Alessandro in 1550. This painting is in Parma, National Gallery. Alessandro wears the same type of padded *braghetta*.

[6]   David Herlihy, *Medieval*, 27.

Fig. 10.1   Titian, *Portrait of Ranuccio Farnese*, 1542. Board of Trustees, National Gallery of Art, Washington, DC.

Bellarmini opined from Rome in 1620, that infants were in the same category as animals and the insane, being deprived of reason.[7] Children were therefore not normally sheltered from sexual matters among their elders, and social practices concerning infants and sexuality routinely included casual genital stimulation by family members and servants close to the child.

Like adults, children were thought to be tempted by worldly vices such as games of chance, playing cards, and to be able to be seduced into dancing, drinking, and sexuality. Look closely at Fig. 10.2, Bruegel's painting entitled *Children's Games* from 1560. Boys are shown smoking pipes, gambling and drinking, brandishing large sticks, swimming in the nude, blowing up pigs' bladders, and generally engaging in violent physicality with others. In fact, in sixteenth-century Europe, the boundary of innocence that we entertain today between childhood and adulthood was not recognized.

In the Christian tradition, the training of children to eschew inherent worldly desire was therefore considered a vital parental duty toward their offspring.[8] At school age, around six or seven for boys, children went to be trained to read and write. However, their school books, such as the popular *Colloquia* from 1538 written by Humanist master Juan Luis Vives (dedicated to the 11-year old Prince Philip of Spain), consisted of 25 lively and humorous Latin dialogues full of bawdy Rabelaisian jokes about bodily functions, playing cards and dice, schoolmasters who smell worse than goats, schools that "abound in dirt and filth," along with dancing and consorting with girls. The very first dialogue in fact has a maid waking up two boys in her charge with: "May Jesus Christ wake you from your dreams of vice. Boys, are you ever going to wake up today?"[9]

In learning their Latin grammar and then rhetoric, boys were guided through the personal correspondence of Cicero as examples of excellence in composition. His *Epistulae ad familiares*, written as an adult, were replete with the realistic concerns of adulthood: a worthless son-in-law, frustrations with political affairs, and personal sorrows, triumphs, and disasters. Young boys memorized these earthy topics written in elegant Ciceronian Latin in order to be able to use his Latin phrases as adults.[10] Epic Roman poetry also made up an integral part of the curriculum, especially Vergil's *Aeneid*, full of the lusts and violence of the pagan

---

[7]   "… sono servi naturalmente coloro, che sono senza ratione, come le bestie, ovvero son privi dell'uso di essa, come i fanciulli, e i pazzi." *Dell'Uffizio del Principe Christiano. Libri Tre composti dall 'Illustrissimo, e Reverendissimo Sig. Card. Roberto Bellarmini della Compagnia di Giesu Volgarizzati dal Sig. Marcello Cervini*, in *Siena Appresso Ercole, e Agamemnone Gori*, 1620, 30, quoted by Roberta Orsi Landini, "L'abbigliamento infantile fra Cinque e Seicento," in *Il vestito e la sua immagine*, Jeanine Guérin dalla Mese, ed., *Atti del convegno in omaggio a Cesare Vecellio nel quarto centenario della morte*. Belluno 20–22 settembre 2001, 143.

[8]   Herlihy, *Medieval*, 28.

[9]   Paul F. Grendler, *Schooling in Renaissance Italy. Literacy and Learning, 1300–1600* (Baltimore: Johns Hopkins University Press, 1989), 199–200.

[10]   Grendler, *Schooling*, 219–22.

Fig. 10.2   Pieter Bruegel, *Children's Games*, 1560. Kunsthistorisches Museum, Vienna.
Photo credit: Erich Lessing/Art Resource, NY.

warrior past. Grendler writes that it was thought that "poetic descriptions of evil" would "invoke horror in the reader" and thereby engender virtuous behavior in children.[11] Finally, the comedic plays of Terence (populated with errant soldiers, nobles and courtesans, father-son conflicts, social parasites, and crafty servants), along with the poetry of Horace and Ovid, rounded out the very adult literature that boys were exposed to as schoolboys. This included Ovid's explicitly sexual *Ars amatoria* and the 21-verse letters of the *Heroides*, a sort of female soap opera of betrayal, longing, desertion, and passion. It would not be until the seventeenth century that schools would begin to expurgate texts for children, making them what would come to be seen as more "appropriate" for the young.[12]

Certainly, the realm of clothing reflected this view of childhood as well. Children were outfitted like their parents, and for seemingly logical reasons. Not only for boys but girls as well, dressing practices, as demonstrated in the artwork of the period, formally outfitted children as little adults. The costume of young boys in the sixteenth century was especially different from what would replace it later (sailor suits with short pants, for example). This included the wearing of codpieces (Fig. 10.3), seen in the outfits of sixteenth-century male toddlers as young as the age of four. Francois Bunel's *Retrospective portrait of Henri IV as a child*, c. 1563, shows a codpiece on Henry IV of France at around this age.

Clothing as History

Art historians have long been interested in the clothing depicted in paintings from the Renaissance period as a tool to accurately date significant works of art. What does this say? Could it point to the fact that clothing, grounded in material culture and reflective of social and political currents, speaks louder than any other visual marker of its time? And if this is true, then what does that imply? That clothes are outward manifestations of social concerns? That clothing can act as a buttress for the individual (and a threatened culture, as archaeologist Michelle Marcus has argued) against disturbing events; people wearing defensive clothing in uncertain and threatening times (such as our latest taste for camouflage prints and clothes sewn inside out, with seams exposed; thick platform shoes, flat, wide boots, and protective, upturned collars on coats)?[13] Historians of the material culture of Europe during the Renaissance now realize that not only the time period and mode of constructing the garment can be read by "reading" the clothes, but that thinking about costume is much more than the study of beautiful silks or the identification of innovations in sleeves. Clothing practices are also vital physical signs of the concerns of the time and place in which they originate, and can be eloquent in their language.

---

[11]   Grendler, *Schooling*, 236–7.

[12]   Ariès, *Centuries*, 108–9.

[13]   Michelle Marcus has written on clothing as social defense in ancient Persia. See Michelle I. Marcus, "Incorporating the Body: Adornment, Gender, and Social Identity in Ancient Iran," *Cambridge Archaeological Journal*, vol. 3, no. 2 (1993): 157–78.

In general we could say that the way which the majority of people clothed themselves before our current age of commercial capitalism, was local, contingent upon the limitations of the material culture in which they lived. Dependent upon the availability of wool or linen, silk or cotton, ornaments or a specific dyestuff, the clothing practices in a particular region and within a certain social stratum were always tied to the physical and economic environment of which they were a part. The wider choices open for the fashionable costume of the wealthy elite however, freed them from these mundane considerations. Clothing instead became a powerful visual designator of the more abstract political and social concerns and attitudes of their wearers, indicative of changing cultural mores and compelling contemporary events. Especially in this period of flux, that is, the age of the High Renaissance (1500–1600), we can read the vicissitudes of the times in the new ways in which bodies were dressed, and in the way in which fashions were adopted and then depicted in paintings commissioned by those caught up in the shifts of European power.

Earlier, in a less self-conscious fifteenth-century Italy, clothing in the sovereign communes of Italy had been recognizable by distinctly regional features, but overall had had an unarticulated silhouette characterized by multiple layers of thin garments congenial to the Mediterranean climate.[14] In the city spaces of the north, however, urban masculine dress began to reflect the Humanist valued "*vita activa*" over the "*vita contemplativa*." Especially among young urban *cognoscenti*, the modest robe of the fourteenth century gave way to a newly revealing style of dress for young men of action, consisting of a shortened tunic and soled hose. In the sixteenth century for men, the upper-body vest (or doublet) called the *farsetto* gave way to the longer and stiffer quilted *giubbone*. Lined and soled hose (*calze-brache, calze-solate*) became breeches and then widened into pumpkin-shaped pantaloons. As doublets and tunics grew ever shorter, the codpiece emerged initially as a necessary modest addition to complete the male costume, and the way in which elite males dressed changed dramatically.

---

[14] In fifteenth-century Italy, female dress consisted of the *camicia* (undershirt), the *gamurra* or *cotta* (basic long dress), the *cioppa* (sleeved overdress) or *giornea* (sleeveless overdress), and then, for the street, the *mantello*, or cloak. Men wore the *camicia* as well, over which came the *farsetto* (quilted doublet) and *calze* (hose), covered by the tunic (which could be sleeved or sleeveless, and went by many names, including the *giubbia, villano, cotta, cioppa, giornea,* or *lucco*. Over this, in cold weather or for traveling, men wore a cloak, which also had many variations, the *cottardita, mantello, robba,* or *sacco*. Children wore small versions of their parents' styles, often with a little apron (*grembiule*). See my *Dressing Renaissance Florence. Families, Fortunes and Fine Clothing* (Baltimore: Johns Hopkins University Press, 2002), 159–64.

Dressing Children

At birth, dressing practices for babies in the sixteenth century remained what they had been for centuries. Babies were tightly swaddled with wide bands of soft, washable linen; each limb carefully wrapped, as newborn bodies were considered malleable like wax, and therefore needing the corrective strictures of tight encasement in bands of cloth. At six months of age, all babies went from swaddling to long little undershirts (*camicie*) fashioned of linen or wool, which could have collar and sleeves, sometimes decorated with lace.

The first real garment for a child of either sex was a long, loose, collared dress (in sixteenth-century Italy called an *ungheresca* or *ungherina*), which was added as the overgarment for the child.[15] Tiberio Titi's, *Ferdinand II de' Medici at 22 months* (1612) shows the long dress on a 22-month-old boy. Laced in the front, with long sleeves attached at the shoulders with more laces, Roberta Orsi Landini writes that this design was of Islamic origin and did not change with fashion, due to its inherent practicality for babies. For the clothing of male babies, in between the *camicia* (long undershirt) and the *ungheresca* (loose dress), a *giubbone*, or long doublet which covered the chest, was added to the costume, along with long socks (*calze*). At about eight months, there are records of male babies also having little white satin shoes (*scarpettine*).[16]

Some gender differentiation was therefore already present by the first year of life for children's dress, even though the male elements of dress were concealed at this stage in a male child's costume beneath the *ungheresca*. Until the child was about a year and a half, his or her *ungheresca* had long leading straps sewn into the shoulder seams that hung down on each side of their back, so that an adult could steady them as they began to learn to walk. The hair of both male and female toddlers was also left long by their families, and therefore the visual appearance of toddlers outwardly was the same.

After the age of two, however, the long, loose *ungheresca* disappeared for boys, and only little girls continued to wear it. Male toddlers, instead of appearing in the "feminine" clothing of the one-piece *ungheresca*, were transitioned into two distinctly "masculine" garments, the *giubbone* (long doublet) and a *casacca* (overtunic), with shoes in the Spanish cut (*scarpe "a taglialla spagnola"*), as well as lined full-length stockings. This necessitated the addition of the codpiece (*braghetta*) for the toddlers of the upper classes (just like their elders), to cover the functional opening in the stockings, which were attached at the waist to the *giubbone*. The male children of the working classes however, were not so covered, the opening in the *calze* remaining in view. We therefore have the codpiece appearing in the children of the upper classes as young as the age of two.

---

[15]   Roberta Orsi Landini, "L'abbigliamento," 147.

[16]   Landini, "L'abbigliamento," 148.

The Codpiece Appears

Codpieces began as simple triangular flaps, one point at the bottom, two to each side at the top, laced with "points" (or *aiguillettes*) to the hose and doublet, to cover the male genital area at the fork of the tights, when tunics become short and then shorter, after 1450.[17] In Fig. 10.3, a drawing made from Janet Arnold's of the 1562 grave remains of Cosimo I and Eleonora, the rather complex design of this garment feature can be seen. The codpiece of their son Don Garzia, who died at the age of 15, consisted of a small folded pouch slashed to allow crimson satin pulled through. Although it was decorated with slashing, its design was modestly utilitarian.

The *braghetta* then became part of boyhood costume, and was included in the clothing display of boys linked to elite males, either as sons or nephews, as here in Fig. 10.4, Moroni's ambiguous *Portrait of a Man and Boy*, from around 1545. Is the man his father? His uncle? Their relationship is not clear. But what *is* clear is that the boy's codpiece has been sewn on top of his breeches, as an integral part of the basic design of his well-tailored outfit.

The codpiece soon transcended its modest beginnings to emerge as a commanding feature built into the dress of soldiers, sovereigns, their sons, their court dwarfs, and later, even into the costume of northern peasant men (as can be seen in the paintings of Bruegel).[18] We also see the *braghetta* on youths employed by nobles at court, as pages to the older men in Fig. 10.5, Bronzino's painting of the young Lodovico Capponi, a page at the Medici court. He wears a white satin codpiece which draws attention to itself in this rather melancholic rendering of the young man. His physical display corresponds to a certain Mannerist insouciance that gives an impression of physically nonchalant potency. This is the performance of the masculine, even at a young age. But what was the message?

Marjorie Garber has noted that in Shakespeare's *The Merry Wives of Windsor* (among other plays), there was an ongoing pun on the use of the word "page," especially in the names of characters who were cross-dressed, bringing about intentional gender disorder. She argues that eventually the term "page" became "a code word for a male homosexual love object."[19] A deeply somber *St. Louis King of France with a Page* by El Greco, painted around 1585, depicts the sainted

---

[17] The word "cod" in English slang referred to the scrotum. Jeffery C. Persels has noted that the *aiguillettes* tying the codpiece to the hose became the subject of much eroticism at the time, as their loosening came to be symbolic of the prelude to sex. See Jeffery C. Persels, "Bragueta Humanistica, or Humanism's Codpiece," *Sixteenth Century Journal*, vol. 28, no. 1 (Spring 1997), p. 81, n.9.

[18] See Lawrence Gowing, *Paintings in the Louvre* (New York: Stewart, Tabori and Chang, 1987), 244–5 for a formal mid-sixteenth century court image of *Cardinal de Grandvelle's Dwarf* (with sword, staff, and large hunting dog) by Antonio Moro, wearing a deep blue-and-gold striped doublet with peplum and matching codpiece, along with a full-length cape and hat of the same fabric.

[19] Marjorie Garber, "Fetish Envy," *October*, vol. 54 (Autumn 1990), 52–3.

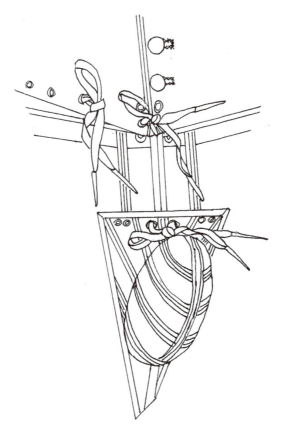

Fig. 10.3   Drawing of a simple sixteenth-century codpiece. Author's copy of Janet Arnold drawing of Don Garzia's codpiece from the 1562 Medici graves goods.

king crowned and in sixteenth-century plate armor fitted around a codpiece. His young page, perhaps eight to ten years of age, peers around the side of Louis's body from the back, gazing down directly at the codpiece. Allegedly, the painter's own son, Jorge Manuel, modeled for this picture, and we cannot see his full court costume. However, the fascination he displays with Louis's codpiece is arresting.[20] Will Fisher has recently argued that the codpiece was of two basic types; one emphasizing the scrotum, signaling the ability to reproduce oneself, and the other resembling an erect penis, to demonstrate the ability to dominate women by penetration sexually.[21] He asserts that both were concerned with the display

---

[20]   See Gowing, *Paintings*, 280–81, for the El Greco image that came into the collection of the Louvre in 1903.

[21]   Will Fisher, *Materializing Gender*, 68–9.

Fig. 10.4   Giovanni Battista Moroni, *Portrait of a Man and a Boy*, c. 1545–
1550. Photograph © 2010, Museum of Fine Arts, Boston.

Fig. 10.5   Agnolo Bronzino, *Portrait of Ludovico Capponi*, c. 1550–1555.
                 © The Frick Collection.

of masculine power. But the question then remains, what did this have to do with prepubescent boys, and why is his page so attenuated to it?

This new, virile display began after initial New World contact in 1492 and the period of the Italian Wars beginning in 1494. It then developed during the 1519 ascendance of Charles V, Holy Roman Emperor and King of Spain, and continued into the reign of his son and heir, Philip II. During this period, styles of dress became more international, yet simultaneously more homogeneous in flavor, reflective of the need of his subjects to recognize the hegemony of this new international power that threatened all local sovereignty.[22] Codpieces, along with other elements of masculine display such as short hair, beard, goatee, and moustache, became *de rigueur* in male dress (the *"capi maschili"*) after 1530 for State portraits.[23] The tripartite sociopolitical upheaval of the sixteenth century— namely Europe's first encounters with "primitive" New World males, the invasion of the Italic peninsula by foreign troops, and the overt threat posed to any extant ruler by the engorgement of the Holy Roman Empire under Habsburg heir Charles V—changed dressing practices for elite European men and their kinsmen. Not only did they have to demonstrate loyalty to the Empire through their formal clothing (especially in the besieged northern Italian cities of Milan, Genoa, and Florence), but the display of overt masculinity became essential. For European nobles, their sartorial attachment to the new Emperor became a critical issue of personal honor and a matter of basic social survival.[24]

Military styles, first worn by the German Landsknecht, then Swiss Reisläufer, became ubiquitous in early sixteenth-century fashion. In Moroni's *Portrait of a Soldier* from the 1550s, the ensemble of the elite squad of important men of Spanish-dominated Europe was in general composed of the quilted *giubbone* with close-fitting sleeves of various styles, and the short *calzoni* or *brache* (breeches puffy and slashed, or the slimmer paned trunk hose), and a prominently displayed *braghetta*, or codpiece. The ensemble was often was topped with a *cappa* (short cloak), jauntily worn. The fierce color combination of black and red was favored, according to Grazietta Buttazzi, in this period of conflict.[25]

---

[22]   At first, it was French fashion that was cited as corrupting the honest costume of the past, but soon Spanish styles dominated and were also roundly condemned. This was not, of course, the first time that foreign influences had been seen negatively. In the early fourteenth century, the Florentine chronicler Villani had scolded, in his *Cronica*, that "outrages remained ... they wanted striped cloth and foreign cloth ... sending as far as Flanders and Brabant for it ... ." Giovanni Villani (d. 1348). *Cronica*, 8 vols. (Florence, 1832), bk. 9, ch. 150, 226–7.

[23]   See Jane Bridgeman, "'A guisa di fiume ...'. I 'ritratti' di Cesare Vecellio e la storia del vestire," in *Il vestito e la sua immagine*, 81–2.

[24]   See Yves Castan, "Politics and Private Life," in *A History of Private Life*, Philippe Ariès and Georges Duby, gen. eds, vol. 3, "Passions of the Renaissance," Roger Chartier, ed. (Cambridge, MA and London: Belknap Press of Harvard University Press, 1989), 21–42.

[25]   Grazietta Buttazzi, "Le pompe et superflue vesti de huomini et donne," in *Alessandro Bonvicino Il Moretto* (exhibition catalogue from Comune di Brescia). Bologna: Nuova Alfa Editorial, 1988, 253.

J.R. Hale noted that the images of foot soldiers wearing codpieces and generally dressed in clear defiance of contemporary sumptuary legislation, would eventually replace the image of the aristocratic knight in the graphic art of the Renaissance.[26] The prolific output of engravings depicting soldiers, their camp followers and entire supply trains by artists of every rank, testifies to the popularity of such images in the public imagination, and would account for the fascination with not only the codpiece, but slashed and beribboned styles as well.[27] Early on, Stephen Grancsay had firmly connected the codpiece with armor design, noting that as the costume for foot soldiers became more fitted in the early sixteenth century, the codpiece became necessary for protection. Foot soldiers wore the custom-made velvet jacket (*brigandine*) with small overlapping metal plates that were fastened to the facing of the garment for protection in battle. These short armored jackets, worn with thick, padded hose, necessitated the addition of the codpiece at the fork of the legs.[28]

The military wear adopted by the elite for State dress included the sleeveless *giornea* (tabard), shorter *colletto* (half-tabard), the *giubbone* (which eventually took the "peasecod belly" shape of the breast-plate of military armor called the cuirass), the *berretta* (beret), and the flat *scarpe punta quadrata* (square-toed shoes) like those worn by mercenary soldiers.[29]

At this time, artists painting for court commissions were called upon to record the garments and styles that were adapted into high fashion for the clothing of the elite. The artistic innovation of the full-length portrait, unknown in fifteenth-century Italy, presented the challenge of portraying masculinity in all its physicality, which had not been dealt with before visually in art.[30] The full-length image of the young Ferdinand II of the Tyrol by German court painter Jakob Seisenegger (from 1542) is thought to have influenced Titian's early full-length portrait of Charles V with hound. The challenge of how to depict a now necessarily vigorous masculinity thus had to be addressed for the first time in portraiture. The appearance of these

---

[26]   J.R. Hale, "The Soldier in Germanic Graphic Art of the Renaissance," *Journal of Interdisciplinary History*, vol. 17, no. 1, "The Evidence of Art: Images and Meaning in History" (Summer 1986), 86, 102–5.

[27]   Keith Moxey's *Peasants, Warriors, and Wives: Popular Imagery in the Reformation* (Chicago and London: The University of Chicago Press, 1989), provides a valuable overview of such images from the graphic arts of the sixteenth century.

[28]   Stephen V. Grancsay, "The Interrelationships of Costume and Armor," *The Metropolitan Museum of Art Bulletin*, new series, vol. 8, no. 6 (Feb. 1950), 184, 186–8.

[29]   They were called *scarpe "alla francese"* at first, a sign that all foreign fashions had previously been attributed to the French. See Grazietta Buttazzi, "Un paio di pianelle cinquecentesche delle Civiche Raccolto di Arte Applicata di Milano," in *Il costume nel 'età del Rinascimento*, Dora Liscia Bemporad, ed. (Florence: Edifir, 1988), 341.

[30]   Janet Cox-Rearick. Catalogue of *Splendors of the Renaissance: Princely Attire in Italy*. Reconstructions of Historic Costumes from King Studio, Italy, by Fausto Fornasari. (New York: Art Gallery of the Graduate Center. The City University of New York, March 10–April 24, 2004), 9.

"State Portraits" of a nobleman or military commander wearing the "*capi maschili*" including the codpiece, gave rise to an entirely new way to visualize potency. But what did it actually show?

Reading the Codpiece

We think we already know what the codpieces meant, that it was a simple "masculine display." As here worn almost casually (and yet not), in Fig. 10.6, Moroni's 1565 portrait of Antonio Navagero of Venice, the codpiece seems to be simply a masculine display. It seems to say, "I'm not afraid of you. I'm not intimidated, and, in fact, you should beware of me, because this phallus (the symbolic penis) is impressive. Demonstrably, I am bigger than all of you."[31] But, I will argue, the message was not as straightforward as all that. Recently, Will Fisher has discussed sixteenth-century beliefs of the mutability of sex along a physical continuum, citing well-documented contemporary medical cases where physical exertion, an emotional trauma, or even the habit of cross-dressing, were thought to bring about a change of sex; a girl becoming a boy, a young man becoming a young woman.[32] He argues, following Jones and Stallybrass, that the belief in the ability of clothing to "deeply make" a person's identity could have contributed to the popularity of the codpiece. Such an obviously masculine dressing feature could engender masculinity; could fix the mutability of sex, stabilize it, and, in fact, increase its potency.[33] The codpiece became the guarantor of masculinity in a century that was threatened by new international challenges and also had basic concerns about the nature of sexuality. Valeria Finucci has addressed this cultural dis-ease with the very definition of masculinity and femininity as well.[34]

Taking an anthropological approach, more than a decade ago, Grace Vicary had argued that the sartorial expansion of the codpiece was due to the mid-sixteenth-century epidemic of syphilis (the "pox"). The treatment associated with the disease

---

[31]   See Judith Butler, *Bodies that Matter: On the Discursive Limits of "Sex"* (New York: Routledge, 1993).

[32]   Fisher, *Materializing Gender in Early Modern English Literature and Culture* (Cambridge: Cambridge University Press, 2006), 6–12.

[33]   Fisher, *Materializing Gender*, 59–67. His discussion of the seventeenth-century display of one of Henry VIII's red-lined codpieces in the Tower of London is interesting for the belief in the sexual potency that it was thought to still contain (71–4). For medieval concerns with stabilizing gender through outward dress, see Rita Copeland's discussion of Quintilian's concerns in his *Institutio oratoria* that gender identity must be held in acceptable modes of dress, style being defined as the "part of rhetoric that can be seen … whether as dress on the body or as the bodily exterior itself" in "The Pardoner's body and the disciplining of rhetoric," in *Framing Medieval Bodies*, Sarah Kay and Miri Rubin, eds (Manchester and New York: Manchester University Press, 1994), 145–7.

[34]   See Valeria Finucci, *The Manly Masquerade: Masculinity, Paternity, and Castration in the Italian Renaissance* (Durham, NC: Duke University Press, 2003).

Fig. 10.6   Giovanni Battista Moroni, *Portrait of Antonio Navagero*, 1565.
              Pinacoteca di Brera, Milan. Photo credit: Photoservice Electa
              Mondadori/Art Resource, NY.

required the application of mercury ointments and bandages which could have been accommodated by the increased dimensions of the new shape of this dress feature, which she characterized as a "roomy box."[35] Codpieces therefore, she asserts, would not have been seen as symbols of virility, as Leo Steinberg had argued earlier, but rather a sign of being infected with syphilis.[36] This theory explaining the changes in codpiece design however, while compelling, would not explain the appearance of what I call "display" *braghette* on children, who could not have reasonably been thought to be similarly infected, even if their fathers happened to be. The notion that a *pater familias* with the disease would then replicate a codpiece of the same padded and enlarged design on his own son or nephew does not seem likely.

Taking another look at Navagero's outfit more closely, we can begin to read the codpiece. In Moroni's depiction, his ermine-trimmed dark cloak falls casually open, revealing an almost prim red wool doublet, snugly buttoned all the way down to the peplum at his waist, which then gives way to an astonishingly revealing display of this Venetian patrician's manhood, in a clearly articulated large red codpiece and tights. Peter Humfrey tells us that Navagero is here represented as governor of Bergamo in this picture; a patrician podestà.[37] But Humfrey's discussion of this image curiously lacks any mention of Navagero's display. Was it such a given in sixteenth-century costume that it merited no discussion? Those who study human bodies historically have written that bodies are systematically encoded by the culture of which they are a part. Miri Rubin and Sarah Kay call the body "a privileged site, vehicle and metaphor of political struggle" in the medieval period.[38] The display of bodies is a long way from being just simply natural. Navagero's posture, leaning back slightly on a table, with the hint of a knowing smile demonstrating his ease in command, accompanies the phallic display. This is not just "natural." One's eye is drawn to what is presented, and I believe that here this demonstrates an overt masculine challenge to any viewer.

Jeffery Persels linked such aggressive masculinity to the new Renaissance adoption of the *vita activa*, which emphasized the importance of rhetoric in the *studia humanitatis*, in opposition to the introspective "effeminacy" of scholasticism with its *vita contemplativa*. In Rabelais's 1532 *Pantagruel*, the comically masculine character of Panurge dons a huge codpiece to do battle with the scholastic Thaumaste, challenging him to a dual of bodily signs, rather than verbal debate. Panurge's codpiece is three feet long and squared, while Thaumaste wears the long gown of academe. In a triumph of masculinity, Panurge reduces

---

[35] Grace Q. Vicary, "Visual Art as Social Data: The Renaissance Codpiece," *Cultural Anthropology*, vol. 4, no. 1 (Feb. 1989), 8.

[36] Vicary, "Visual Art," 19. As evidence, she points to the possibility that Charles V, Holy Roman Emperor, Henry VIII of England, and Francis I of France had all contracted syphilis. See also Leo Steinberg, *The Sexuality of Christ in Renaissance Art and Modern Oblivion* (New York: Pantheon, 1983).

[37] See Moroni book for Humfrey's commentary on painting.

[38] *Framing Medieval Bodies*, introduction by Sarah Kay and Miri Rubin, 5.

the academic to loss of all bodily control, whereupon he retires in confusion and defeat, Panurge's exaggerated phallus winning the day.[39]

Clothed bodies are extensions of bodily encodings, and can even foreground ideas that have been initially inscribed onto the body, by fragmenting it into pieces, into disconnected parts, into almost separate entities, in order to produce a human spectacle that is capable of thwarting any corporeal coherence. Fisher, in fact, terms the codpiece a prosthetic, both for its detachable nature and also for its "standing-in" for the penis as phallic display. In the plays of Shakespeare, even female characters, such as Lucetta and Julia in *Two Gentlemen of Verona*, tentatively consider donning this ultimate male object as part of their disguise.[40] Others have seen the codpiece as a fetish object compensating for a basic anxiety about sexuality.[41] But still, the question remains, why display a cod "piece" on a young boy?

Performing the Codpiece

Feminist theorist Judith Butler has written extensively on the body as performance, as the societal expression of sex or gender. She argues that the body, especially as presented wearing formal costume, is not the "natural" body of an integral ego, but rather is a fantasized production of cultural meaning. She reminds us that the phallus is the symbol of the penis, not the penis itself.[42] I would argue that the display codpiece is an example of such a fantasized production, the spectacular codpiece becoming the dominant feature of a man's ensemble for the viewer's delectation. Gudrun Ekstrand has written on the remarkable large puffy codpieces of the two extant Sture family suits from 1567, "bubbling forth" from between their paned breeches (*pluderhose*).[43] They were clearly the most flamboyant decorative feature of the entire costume. In postmodern times, Deleuze and Guattari have written on the importance of the concept of the fragmented body as a means to de-privilege the Freudian emphasis on the phallus.[44] However, in the costume from the sixteenth century, it is precisely this fragment of the body, this body part, which has been constructed purposely in the symbolic order. By framing the phallus sartorially with the codpiece, high Renaissance costume created a

---

[39]   Persels, "Bragueta," 79–84.

[40]   Fisher, *Materializing Gender*, 23–33, 65.

[41]   See Garber, "Fetish Envy," *October*, vol. 54 (Autumn 1990): 45–56, where she argues that the codpiece acts as a sort of "theater of display," similarly to the difference between the detachable phallus and the penis itself. The codpiece then becomes a detachable fetish in her reading; a style that "puts the goods in the shopwindow," and in so doing, belies a masculine anxiety about sexuality.

[42]   Butler, *Bodies*, 81.

[43]   Gudrun Ekstrand, "The Sture Suits from 1567 at Uppsala Cathedral, Sweden," in *Il costume*, 296–8.

[44]   Gilles Deleuze and Felix Guattari, *Anti-Oedipus: Capitalism and Schizophrenia* (Minneapolis: University of Minnesota Press, 1983).

mechanism by which to exhibit and even flaunt an unnatural masculinity which could then serve to visually combat perceived threats to its hegemony.

Certain male bodies, including specific young boys, were selected to serve as the vehicles and metaphors for the political struggle upon which their very survival depended. Far from simply demonstrating male virility, I believe that the codpiece betrayed a new sense of masculine unease, as European males were caught between a need to show an aggressive physicality in the face of serious threat (from within and outside of Europe); sartorially becoming "civic" soldiers on the forefront of the attack to their sovereignty, and at the same time, displaying a self-awareness of a rapidly developing vulnerability to forces out of their control. This psychological dichotomy revealed itself in the bizarre style of what I have termed the "presentation" codpiece, worn for public display. Sanchez Coelho's 1573 *Portrait of the Archduke Albert VII* shows a boy as an authority in training, almost dwarfed by his large hunting dog. But he confidently sports his elongated quilted doublet, round paned trunk hose, and at the center of his body, the *braghetta*, which has been pushed forward tautly for visual inspection.

In this world of the unexpected and undoubtedly shocking discovery of an entirely heretofore unknown continent in the Western hemisphere (where New World males were basically unclothed), Finucci points out in her book *The Manly Masquerade* that Paracelsus was moved to muse as to whether or not the aboriginal populations of the Americas were in fact even human.[45] Images of these "savages" illustrated books such as Theodor de Bry's *America*, from 1592. These images show nearly naked native men, one featuring them pouring molten gold into the mouth of a Conquistador dressed in the *capi maschili* of an elite sixteenth-century male. His powerless codpiece is barely visible in between the panes of his pumpkin-shaped trunk hose.[46] As if to point to the evidence that European males were certainly human, elite men then (following Steinberg's argument), made prominent the display of the phallus to certify their own superiority; their most evident sign of humanity. And, to ensure an unbroken line of the transmission of power between generations, their sons and nephews needed this sartorial bravado as well. But this was only necessary for about 75 years during this psychic crisis.

In the sixteenth century then, clothing practices were altered dramatically along with the social reality of the Italian upper classes, and all was revealed, or *was* it?[47] Codpieces did become huge, padded, brightly colored, puffed, lined,

---

[45]   Finucci, *Manly Masquerade*, 73.

[46]   See image from Stephen Greenblatt's *Marvelous Possessions: The Wonder of the New World* (Chicago: University of Chicago Press, 1991), Fig. 4.

[47]   The fanciest dress of the males had not been generally depicted in Quattrocento art in northern Italy (unlike the Cinquecento), because the merchant elite who commissioned formal portraits of themselves (in those communes without a noble court) were too self-conscious in their desire to demonstrate a certain "republican" mien to be revealing of actual dress practices in their portraits. This does not mean that they did not dress elaborately off canvas. In fact, see the decorative arts of *majolica*, *cassoni*, and *deschi da parto* (among others) for male costume display.

and slashed, as in Fig. 10.7, on Guidobaldo della Rovere, painted by Bronzino in 1532. The images they commissioned of themselves, their sons, their nephews, and pages at court, allowed viewers a visual access to their bodies that had never been available before. Newly exposed and highlighted bodies were spotlighted in a way that was unprecedented.

Think about the active young males of the previous century. What were we privileged to see of their bodies? Can we visualize Lorenzo de' Medici's physicality as a teenager? Or his younger brother Giuliano's? Such exposure and full articulation of bodily parts seems unthinkable. What about the bodies of other powerful males of the previous century? Cesare Borgia? The young Michelangelo? And then look at della Rovere. Look at what we see of him. Bold, assertive, and yet visually quite vulnerable. His very armor has been carefully constructed to fit around the large red padded *braghetta*. Slashed patterns cover his formal armor. Inside comes outside. Outside and inside are conflated. Not only slashed fabric, but also styles of breeches, the paned trunk hose that are all but shredded, allowing eyes in places where they had never been allowed before. In Fig. 10.8, Prospero Alessandri, as painted by Moroni in around 1560, has just the tip of his codpiece peeking out. Alessandri's motto displayed on the right reads "between fear and hope." This out–in confusion, I would argue, is not accidental, not casual, but rather a deliberately tentative simultaneity of presentation and withdrawal, of sartorial offering and withholding; the very image of conflict. Besides the phallic display, the slashing also accentuates the duality of protection and availability, creating disunity, disorder, sending signals of sartorial chaos, complication. Although for some 75 years, the *braghetta* expanded and morphed into a position of centrality in male portraits, by the early seventeenth century, this display had disappeared, once again hidden into the folds of newly encompassing doublets.

Conclusions

In the first decades of the sixteenth century, display *braghette* had been first seen in the dress of mercenaries, hired to fight for Church and Empire. This style of codpiece then became fashionable in the dress of the elites for whom they toiled. As childhood was not considered a world apart from the adult milieu, children were not treated as innocents, but rather were exposed to everything their parents were. Therefore, when sartorial practices changed and codpieces began to be worn regularly by men of a certain class, it was natural to include them as a feature in

---

The women however, were dressed by their families in magnificent costume, "sacred dolls," as Richard Trexler memorably termed them, to show off the wealth of their line. Ghirlandaio's almost life-size full-length portraits of the women of the Tornabuoni family in Santa Maria Novella were perfect vehicles for vestimentary display. But sumptuary legislation did still intervene regularly to temper dress, some 300 laws being passed in 48 separate Italian municipalities between 1200 and 1500. See Catherine Kovesi Killerby, *Sumptuary Law in Italy 1200–1500* (Oxford: Clarendon Press, 2002), table on pp. 28–9.

Fig. 10.7   Agnolo Bronzino, *Portrait of Guidobaldo della Rovere*, 1532. Palazzo Pitti, Florence. Photo credit: Scala/Ministero per I Beni e le Attività culturali/Art Resource, NY.

Fig. 10.8   Giovanni Battista Moroni, *Portrait of Prospero Alessandri*,
              c. 1560. Sammlungen des Fürsten von und zu Liechtenstein,
              Vaduz-Wien.

the dress of their male offspring. Children were essentially dressed as if they were already the adults they were destined to become, and so this new dressing feature of the codpiece was also added to the costume of those male children of the elite.[48]

With the advent of the codpiece, male costume became increasingly sexualized. In fact, Finucci has termed the sixteenth century the "erotic" century, evidenced in part by its literary production on sexual themes emblematized by such works as Machiavelli's *La mandragola*, Tasso's *Gerusalemme liberata*, and Ariosto's *Orlando furioso*.[49] Social practices in dress came into alignment with this cultural trend. Even little boys could, and did, wear the codpiece. Eventually, codpieces were worn on all levels of society and appeared on males of all social classes and of all ages, in artwork by artists as diverse as Bronzino, Titian, Moroni, Holbein, Clouet, and Bruegel, among others.

By the dawn of the seventeenth century, however, the development of stabilized absolutist states in Europe was further along; the ruling classes more securely intermarried. In the next decades, the *braghetta* would disappear entirely from male dressing practices in Europe; overt phallic display no longer needed for their very survival. European masculinity was no longer threatened *en masse*; boys no longer needed to be presented as virile males-in-training. Codpieces instead now appeared on male dancers performing at court in fantasy productions for the idle elite. The turbulent transition from late medieval to early modern Europe had been weathered, patched over sartorially, and boys would find new definitions awaiting them which did not include outward displays of their impending manhood.

---

[48]   If a boy was from a peasant family, he was dressed as his father was as well.

[49]   Finucci, *Manly Masquerade*, 30–33.

Chapter 11
Marvell, Boys, Girls, and Men: Should We Worry?

Diane Purkiss

Thomas Fairfax was the architect of the Parliamentarian victory in the Civil Wars; it was he who created and controlled the crucial New Model Army infantry. Often portrayed as somehow rather a simple soul, it was his very simplicity which helped him as a commander. Yet in June 1650, he abruptly resigned his command, refusing to lead an army into Scotland. We also know from a poem he wrote that he was horrified by the execution of Charles I the previous year. He settled into a retirement, an idyllic retirement, a Virgilian dream: writing, building a new house, book-collecting, making a garden. Andrew Marvell stayed at his home Appleton House from late 1650 until 1652, and he was tutor to Fairfax's daughter, Maria.

If, then, we want to talk about men and boys, education, and girls, and gardens, we cannot do better than to begin with this man tutoring, instructing this daughter of this father, this girl who in various guises keeps bursting into a poem that is supposed to celebrate her father. We might in fact begin with the simple question: why is a poem celebrating Fairfax, architect of the New Model infantry, practically bursting with young women? Moreover, as we shall see, the poem's dialectical arrangement of a young girl contrasted with a man of action is repeated, endlessly repeated, in Marvell's other poems: Marvell's elegy on Cromwell ends distracted by Cromwell's young daughter from Cromwell himself, while Marvell's little T.C. and his complaining nymph engage with the civil war and the political turmoil of the age by their difference from these scenes. "Young Love," too, is haunted by the young girl.

The repeated references to young girls raise an obvious question for a twenty-first century reader, one we should not shirk. Should we worry about the plethora of young girls here? That is, should we leap to the conclusion that there is sexuality here, that these girls, some of whom are overtly eroticized, generically and lyrically, are objects of desire? Patient exploration will show that they are indeed the destinations of desire, but in a complex rather than in a simple way. What is desired is not the conquest of a young girl, not her induction into sexuality, but a particular and cultural marked moment before the genesis of masculinity can begin. Earlier critics identified this preoccupation with girls as a return to what they termed the "green world," but they overlooked the gendered and sexualized connotations of the word "green" that required the signifier of a prepubescent girl to exemplify them.[1]

In order to understand the young girl, it is helpful to begin with Maria Fairfax and Appleton House because not even the most anxious or suspicious critic is likely to believe that she is an erotic figure. Indeed, Maria is an *an*erotic figure, displacing the anxiously depicted lesbian eroticism of the nuns whose place has been taken by the Fairfaxes.[2] Maria Fairfax appears in the poem just as the estate or country house celebration of retirement almost threatens to stop the poem completely:

> But now away my Hooks, my Quills,
> And Angles, idle Utensils.
> The *young Maria* walks to night:
> Hide trifling Youth thy Pleasures slight.
> 'Twere shame that such judicious Eyes
> Should with such Toyes a Man surprize;
> *She* that already is the *Law*
> Of all her *Sex*, her *Ages Aw.*

In the word "surprize" there is a glancing allusion to virgin goddesses—Artemis, Athene—whose leisure is surprised by an unlucky mortal, but in those legends it is men who surprise the goddess and not vice versa. In "Appleton House" virgin sternness becomes a surprise to men, whose contamination by "pleasures" unspecified is condemned by them. Marvell is thinking among other things of the moral allegorization of the myth of Diana and Actaeon, where Actaeon's dogs represent his own passions, which tear him to pieces. The poet's fishing becomes a brutal disruption of Edenic stasis. Maria's stasis in singular girlhood also halts the garden, halts nature itself, turning it to a vast hush. She is also the maker of the garden since "'tis she that to these gardens gave/ The wondrous beauties that they have." This is because the gardens not only reflect but express her qualities. Maria, as her name suggests, is both connected to and contrasted with the nuns who precede her, who represent her protective virginity and its creation of a *hortus conclusus* space, but who cannot make it fecund and productive.[3]

---

[1]   Donald Friedman, *Marvell's Pastoral Art* (London: Routledge & Kegan Paul, 1970); or the excerpt of that argument published as "Knowledge and the World of Change: Marvell's 'The Garden,'" in *Modern Critical Views: Andrew Marvell*, Harold Bloom, ed. (New York: Chelsea House, 1989), 77–100.

[2]   'Each Night among us to your side/ Appoint a fresh and Virgin Bride;/ Whom if *Our Lord* at midnight find,/ Yet Neither should be left behind./ Where you may lye as chast in Bed,/ As Pearls together billeted./ All Night embracing Arm in Arm,/ Like Chrystal pure with Cotton warm.' The emphasis on chastity is undercut by the sensuous imagery. Marvell, Upon Appleton House, XXIV. All quotations from Marvell's poems will be taken from *The Poems of Andrew Marvell*, Nigel Smith, ed. (London: Longman, 2003).

[3]   John Rogers, "The Enclosure of Virginity: The Poetics of Sexual Abstinence in the English Revolution." Richard Burt, John Michael Archer, eds, viii, 340 pp.; *Enclosure*

Maria's virginal seclusion also makes her an apt image of her father's retirement, his private life, in opposition to celebrations of his public role. Here Marvell is thinking not only of Evander in the *Aeneid*, but also of the various stoical *contemptus mundi* poems of Elizabethan and Jacobean retirement, and even of Shakespeare's late romances, in which the father finds rest from politics or labor only in a natural space with a daughter. While Fairfax himself in his own poems celebrates ruins as metaphors for an absolute retirement, Marvell sees Appleton House as something that has to be snatched from ruin(s). This idea is given corporeal form in the poem, when Isabella Thwaites is snatched by William Fairfax in the poem's dramatic staging of the capture of virginity by the active male. That trope of setting the girl in motion in order to rescue her also has a cognate in Thomas Fairfax's own experience during the war, where his own child was threatened by the conflict which she now symbolically closes out. He writes:

> my daughter, not above five years old, being carried before her Maid, endured
> all this retreat a Horseback, but Nature not being able to hold out any longer, she
> fell into frequent swoonings, and in appearance was ready to expire her last.'[4]

This is Maria, now the goddess-like bringer of stasis and repose. When Marvell writes that "the gardener had the soldier's place" and of the nursery as a magazine, the stoves as winter quarters, and so forth, he is contrasting the arts of the garden with the arts of war by drawing attention to the oddity of the comparison, and so emphasizing the arts of peace by the inclusion of a girl nearly destroyed by war. The metaphorical Maria's future fecundity is represented by the plethora of meanings she generates. So fecund an image is Maria that she also represents the Fairfaxes' legitimate occupation of the land by all-but-literally tying them in with its history in the image of Maria as the mistletoe growing on the Fairfax oak and the druid image that accompanies it. Maria is precisely the longed-for garden space of a femininity conflated with the garden itself.

But why is the green girl such an apt metaphor for the green world? This same trope—the conflation of the girl with nature itself—animates "Young Love", based as it is on the Anacreontic Greek lyric that solicits the love of a very young girl. But Marvell adapts that pretext to make the girl even younger than she is in the original. While the Anacreontic poem registers the girl as unripe grain and grapes, Marvell describes her as blossoms that are "too green." Green signifies blossoms that are not yet ripe even as blossoms, blossoms that have not yet begun to become fruit, let alone to ripen. By addressing the girl as "infant," too, Marvell makes her as young as possible. The word derives from Latin *infans*, which means a child too young to speak:

Acts: Sexuality, Property, and Culture in Early Modern England (Ithaca: Cornell University Press), 229–50.

    [4]   *Short Memorials of Thomas Lord Fairfax, Written by Himself*, 1699, 86.

> Come, little Infant, Love me now,
> While thine unsuspected years
> Clear thine aged Fathers brow
> From cold Jealousie and Fears.[5]

The poem's reading has been marked by recent controversy. It has been suggested by Derek Hirst and Steven Zwicker that the poem is homoerotic because in Stanza IV the poet writes that

> Love as much the snowy Lamb
> Or the wanton Kid does prize,
> As the lusty Bull or Ram,
> For his morning Sacrifice.

At this particular moment, certainly, Marvell is making a distinction between childlike eroticism and adult lust around the masculine. But the metaphor is complex and difficult to gloss accurately. Hirst and Zwicker say this: "For Marvell to disclose amatory desire as the eroticization of the child marks sexual liminality as an integer in a more private and daring engagement—one that yields to and yet would annihilate the authority of fathers."[6] This is in fact the exact opposite of the truth when we look back at Stanza III:

> Common beauties stay fifteen
> Such as yours should swifter move
> Whose fair blossoms are too green
> Yet for lust, but not for love

Here it is clear that Marvell is out to disclose not the eroticization of the child but the pleasure of a child who is enjoyed precisely because she is not eroticized, or even because she has a magical power not to be eroticized however much she is urged or chided forward. "Our sportings are as free/ As the nurse's with the child," writes Marvell, now constructing a female–female presexual state of sensuous play to contrast with the worrying animal masculinity of the bulls and rams. The kid is wanton not because it is sexual, but because its lack of sexuality leaves it freer to explore its own senses. Such young bodies have the power associated with Maria Fairfax, the power to draw the old back into their own "green world" of unregulated pleasure.

---

[5]   Smith connects the poem with *Greek Anthology V*, 124, citing J.B. Leishman, *The Art of Marvell's Poetry*, with a preface by John Butt (London: Hutchinson, 1966), 167, in which "young loves (*neoi Erotes*) are shotting their arrows," but in this poem youth as target is a girl whose grapes are not yet ripe; Marvell makes the girl younger, not yet bearing fruit at all. Smith also cites Carew's "The Second Rapture," but that signifies the girl as mature through metaphor while registering her age as 13.

[6]   "Andrew Marvell and the Toils of Patriarchy: Fatherhood, Longing, and the Body Politic," *ELH* 66, no. 3 (Fall 1999): 629–54. See also the more recent "Eros and Abuse: Imagining Andrew Marvell," *ELH* 74, no. 2 (Summer 2007): 371–95.

I shall continue to gloss this by exploring the idea of the "green girl" much more fully in Marvell's work. Central to it is the idea of a sensual pleasure that precedes and therefore holds at bay a troubling, even transgressive eroticism, an idea even more evident in relation to another poem, "The Picture of Little T.C. in a Prospect of Flowers." T.C. is a green girl too: "in the green grass she loves to lie/ And there with her fair aspect tames/ The wilder flowers, and gives them names:/ But only with the roses plays;/ And them does tell/ What colour does become them, and what smell." Again the girl, lost in her own "golden age" of childhood—yes, that idea is present here, early though it might seem—and the flowers, especially the brief-flowering roses, are engaged in seductive play. At the beginning of her own life, the girl can act like Milton's Eve, and name the flowers; indeed, infant play has become a kind of Eden here. The girl is the principal metaphor for an Edenic moment which extends to embrace a goddess-like purity, since "wanton Love will one day fear/ And under her command severe/ See his bow broke and ensigns torn." She is linked with the artificial prolongation of that moment by the underlying Persephone myth, which is evoked in the violets that are one of Persephone's chief symbols. She is asked to use her almost supernatural power to command nature in order to "procure/ That violets may a longer age endure." Violets are especially linked with the deaths of girls and with transience, which is why Laertes wishes that from Ophelia's fair and unpolluted flesh violets might spring. This will be an alteration in state for Ophelia, who was called a "green girl" by her father earlier in the play when she interpreted Hamlet's overtures romantically rather than seeing their sexual menace. Persephone represents the violation of a young girl, herself a flower.

As well as Persephone, the goddess Flora is vital here. In Ovid's *Fasti* and in Renaissance iconography she is an ambiguous figure.[7] In the myth the nymph Chloris, whose name means green, is ravished by Zephyrus, the West Wind, and is reborn as Flora, goddess of flowers. Hence Flora represents not so much fertility but in particular the moment in spring when the greenness of new growth (Chloris) breaks into multicolored flowers. The Romans themselves understood this not only as April breeding lilacs out of the dead land, but also in terms of the greensick young girl becoming the displayed object of desire, flowers. Plain green becomes gaudy or bedizened. This is why the Floralia, the Roman festival of the goddess Flora, was also a festival associated with prostitutes, a tradition reflected in her representation in Venetian art. Ovid's Flora is also associated with a kind of

---

[7] See Ovid *Fasti V*, 183ff, where flora is hailed as "mother of flowers." The many colors of her garden are powerfully emphasized: "In the fields that are my dower, I have a fruitful garden, fanned by the breeze and watered by a spring of running water. This garden my husband filled with noble flowers and said, 'Goddess, be queen of flowers.' Oft did I wish to count the colours in the beds, but could not; the number was past counting" (J.G. Frazer's translation). A reasonable summary of the evidence on Flora can be found in Maggie Kilgour, "Eve and Flora" *Paradise Lost* 5.15–16. *Milton Quarterly* 38:1 (2004): 1–17. For *Flora meretrix*, see Ann B. Shteir, "Flora primavera or Flora meretrix? Iconography, Gender, and Science," *Studies in Eighteenth Century Culture* 36.1 (2007) 147–68.

redistribution of grazing rights to the plebs, at odds with the privacy Marvell wants for his garden-girls. To go from Chloris to Flora is for Marvell to fall.

This narrative comes in part from the classics. In classical mythology, the conflation of young girls with flowers always implied a sexual threat; Persephone, for instance, called "a fairer flower by gloomy Dis" by Milton, is one of many young girls who are picking flowers when they are themselves plucked. Catullus writes in his formal epithalamion, or wedding song, "Just as a flower that grows in a garden close, apart/ Unbeknown to sheep .../ Many boys have longed for it and many girls:/ But when its bloom is gone, nipped off by a fingernail,/ Never boy has longed for it and never girl/ A maid too while untouched is dear to her family/ But when she loses her flower/ Then no-one wants her."[8] So while cavalier poets urged girls to gather their rosebuds, Marvell reversed the image, insisting that girls should try to prolong rather than to shorten the moments of deferral and delay. Be green for as long as possible, he urges. Avoid flowers.

In contemplating Marvell's green girls, we can think not only of Maria in Appleton House, who is an object of happy contemplation because she is stalled in greenness, but also of T.C., and of the Nymph Complaining, and of Marvell's claim in "The Garden" that "Apollo courted Daphne so/ Only that she might Laurel grow/ And Pan did after Syrinx speed/ Not as a nymph but as a reed." These women represent a kind of ultimate conflation of girl and garden that brings out the linkages between girls and flowers, but also refuses them. Laurels and reeds remain green and never break into colour—they remain Chloris and are never Flora. Why? Wasn't this counterproductive? Counter-Reformation, even? When Marvell writes—self-conscious, paradoxical—of the happiness of a garden without a partner, or of "vegetable love" generated by the lady's almost-everlasting "no", what is going on?

Of course, all seduction poetry depends on a lady's no to set it in motion. It can only exist in the space of that no, just as the escapades of Apollo and Pan are made possible and visible by the resistance of nymphs they pursue. As well, the laurel and the reed are symbols of poetry itself. Marvell is linking poetry and poetic fame to the "no" of a woman who will remain forever a girl. And the same thing, or something similar, happens in *The Nymph Complaining for the Death of her Faun*, in which the faun's death allows it to be arrested at a presexual moment before it can become "lilies without, roses within." The very moment of arrest is captured and hence doubly arrested in a work of art: "First my unhappy statue shall/ Be cut in marble, and withal,/ Let it be weeping too: but there .../ There at my feet shalt

---

8   Catullus LXII: Vt flos in saeptis secretus nascitur hortis,/ ignotus pecori, nullo conuolsus aratro,/ quem mulcent aurae, firmat sol, educat imber;/ multi illum pueri, multae optauere puellae:/ idem cum tenui carptus defloruit ungui,/ nulli ilium pueri, nullae optauere puellae:/ sic uirgo, dum intacta manet, dum cara suis est;/ cum castum amisit polluto corpore florem,/ nec pueris iucunda manet, nec cara puellis. *The Poems of Catullus: A Bilingual Edition*, trans. Peter Green, University of California Press (August 2005), translation mine.

thou be laid,/ Of purest alabaster made:/ For I would have thine image be/ white as I can, though not as thee."[9]

The last line confesses, however, to the inadequacy of art as a means for preserving the moment of cessation of movement; the statue can't keep the fawn perfectly white, can't stop the moment of decline from perfect whiteness, just as the poem can't seem to preserve either nymph or fawn at the moment of pastoral bliss when both are at one with a cleansed world.

Why lilies and why roses? The fawn is conflated with both. In John Gerard's *Herball*, the white lily is the madonna lily, lilium candidum, that—signficantly—flowers before the red rose.[10] So the lily is about an earlier period of life. As well, lilies famously last only a day or two in flower, so it's about a moment that can easily be lost, a moment subject to the ruinous hand of time. This is the kind of thing Shakespeare has in mind when he talks of Elizabeth I as "a virgin/ A most unspotted lily." Gerard also says that it's called Juno's rose, because it "as it is reported came up of her milke that fell upon the ground. But the Poets feign, that Hercules, who Jupiter had by Alcimena, was put to Juno's breasts whilest she was asleepe; and after the sucking there fell away an abundance of milk and that one part was spilt in the heavens, and the other upon the earth; and that of this sprang the Lily." In Gerard, then, it's a story where the lily signifies the infancy and nourishment of a hypermasculine hero. But the milk also signifies not nourishing the hero since it spills because Juno snatches her breast away as soon as she wakes and realizes what is happening. So the lily is about infancy, but it's also about loss of the mother. This is the symbolic key to the situation.

Roses, on the other hand, immediately suggest the English monarchy to Gerard, who says they should be placed first in gardens because they symbolize it. But he also associates it with a particular form of pastoral, Anacreontic pastoral, which for the Renaissance means a poetry about the naughty boyish games of a baby Cupid who "doth wrap his head round with garlands of rose."[11] So the rose here is a symbol of a kind of eroticism of the child, cleansed of anything actually erotic. What we have here is a kind of psychic pattern, a repeating figure in Marvell's symbolic universe, the figure of a young girl or feminized young boy who stands at the brink of an adult world understood as perilous and who is celebrated for not having yet crossed the line into that world.

It is an error, I think, to see these figures as tainted by what William Kerrigan has termed "nympholepsy"; rather they seem to signify a phase in the life of

---

[9] Victoria Silver discusses the connections between regicidal fantasy and the figure of the young girl in "The Obscure Script of Regicide: Ambivalence and Little Girls in Marvell's Pastorals," *ELH* 68, no. 1 (Spring 2001): 29–55.

[10] *The Herball, or, Generall Historie of Plantes*, 1597, 42.

[11] "Renaissance Anacreontics," Janet Levarie, *Comparative Literature*, vol. 25, no. 3 (Summer 1973), 221–39.

masculinity which is associatively linked with childhood.[12] Renaissance writers understood masculinity as in some sense born from a childhood located in the feminine world, even as sculpted painfully from a girlish self accustomed to feminine pleasures. The reason for this was very simple. Male childhood experience was split in two by an event marked by breeching, the putting on of doublet and hose. This could sometimes be merely a symbolic moment, but it was also the name for the time when a far more radical change occurred; better-off boys were handed over to the care of tutors or to school, while other boys were given over to a master to be trained as apprentices. Before breeching, boys inhabited a female world, signified by the long gowns they wore. It was ruled by the mother and by female servants. After breeching, these servants were often dismissed completely, and male attendants installed. This was the beginning of masculinity, which had to be born painfully from a cozy feminine world, and maintained by learning and beatings. It meant parting with the mother and entering a world in which for people of Marvell and Fairfax's class, a different language—Latin—was spoken.

School was an all-male world in which behavior was enforced by severe beatings. Renaissance boys were at school all day and many were at all-male boarding schools. What they learned was seen as incomprehensible to their mothers and sisters; Latin language study, it has been suggested, was a kind of puberty rite from which masculinity was made.[13] But since it was hard and alien, early childhood may have been seen as a kind of lost Eden, and it would be aptly represented as a little girl, or as a markedly feminized little boy—Cupid, for example—because it was associated with femininity, because sisters didn't have to leave it behind.

What Marvell then does is to make a further association, a symbolic retelling of this childhood trauma, between leaving home to go to war and leaving femininity to go to school, and further between leaving the old royal regime behind for the republic and this traumatic breech in childhood. But Marvell is also worried by the notion that retirement is somehow feminine—precisely because it's so desired, it becomes troubling to him. I want to suggest that in Marvell's constant reversion

---

[12]	William Kerrigan, "Marvell and Nymphets" *Greyfriar* 27 (1986), 3–21. The idea that strong feelings about little girls must be sexual also deforms the otherwise attentive readings of Crewe, in Jonathan Crewe, "The Garden State: Marvell's poetics of enclosure" in *Enclosure Acts: Sexuality, Property, and Culture in Early Modern England*, Richard Burt, John Michael Archer, eds (Cornell University Press, 1994), and Jonathan Goldberg, *Voice Terminal Echo: Postmodernism and English Renaissance Texts* (London and New York: Methuen), 1986, 14–32. When this passage was complete, I was delighted to come across Catherine Robson, *Men in Wonderland: The Lost Girlhood of the Victorian Gentleman* (Princeton: Princeton University Press, 2001), which makes a similar argument about Victorian masculinity.

[13]	On this theme in general and its reflections in the Latin study texts of the day, see my *Literature, Gender and Politics during the English Civil War* (Cambridge: Cambridge University Press, 2005), Introduction, 5ff, and on Latin language see Walter Ong, "Latin Language Study as a Renaissance Puberty Rite," *Studies in Philology* 56, 1959, 103–24.

to the figure of a little girl—in a garden—as a sign of all that is private, enclosed, retired, safe from the public world of war and politics and the state, we have nothing less than a retreat from masculine pain into a child's world of feminine pleasure, a retreat that is also and sometimes explicitly a retreat from adult sexuality. There is a longing here for precisely that safety, that maternity which masculinity must disavow. And it is coupled with an anxiety about the fragility of psychic defenses, because these feminine worlds of childhood are always being menaced or even broached by masculinity in the form of education, or in the form of the poet and poems themselves, signs of education. We can see especially in *The Nymph Complaining* a representation of a kind of atrocity story extremely common during the war; the fawn's death is caused by a trooper, and many critics have remarked that the nymph is in a maternal relation to him. Ripping a fetus from its mother's living womb was the *ne plus ultra* of atrocity stories. It began to circulate in the Thirty Years' War, and—especially—the Ulster Rising, both conflicts where Protestants could link it with icons and hence with witchcraft. One account of it makes it very clear what is at stake:

> they [Irish rebels] being blood-thirsty salvages..not deserving the title of humanity without any more words beat out his brains, then they laid hold on his wife being big with child, & ravished her, then ripped open her womb, and like so many Neros undauntedly viewed natures bed of conception, afterward took her and her Infant and sacrificed in fire their wounded bodies to appease their Immaculate Souls, which being done, they pillaged the house, taking what they thought good, and when they had done, they set the house on fire.

This horrible story may or may not be true: stories like this had propaganda value far in excess of any simple truth. The Irish rebels literally cut off the Protestant heir destined to inherit land ordained his by providence. What is odd about the story is that the baby is treated like a relic or icon, transgressively broken up. When Cheapside Cross was torn down, the iconoclasts assailed it by tearing the figure of the infant Jesus from the arms of its mother and smashing it on the ground, like Lady Macbeth herself. Iconoclasm fantasizes about itself, its own heart of darkness. This Erichthonian crime is doubly linked with patrilinearity and the replication of the father in the body of the infant, both because the icon is a threat to that identity, being a false and deceptive replication, and because in the same way relics were not true synecdoches, but offered, necromantically, to control those to whom they appeared to offer power.

As well as this *specific* trope, there was a more general kind of atrocity story in circulation in which the war was seen as a threat to the father's identity understood through a baby. The Leveller Richard Overton offered a description of his wife, Mary, dragged through the London streets on a hurdle while clutching her six-month-old baby in her arms. The royalist Richard Atkyns told the story of his wife who tried to follow him:

> She adventur'd without a pass, which proved very unhappy, for at Nettlebed, a party of Sir Jacob Ashley's Souldiers ... took her prisoner, and carried her on to Reading, where the waters being then overhigh, she took a great fright. ... When she came to London, she found her house full of souldiers, and could not be admitted there ... seeing her goods carried away before her face ... she fell ill and miscarried (as I understood) of three children, and was very near her death.[14]

In all these stories, the enemy is witchlike in its callous disregard for both paternal lineage and maternal security. The body of the mother, reconfigured as a sign of civil peace and safety, is violated by the removal of her child. The child becomes a fetish of the war's dead, just like the faun in Marvell's poem. And yet there's also a sense in which this is a figuration of that more primal separation from the realm of the mother which is viewed as essential, but also as an harbinger of war. Yet if we hear the tone of the poem correctly, there's an effect of enormous and tragic distance; grief and horror can only appear in the heavily mediated and disguised form of an overtly simple pastoral, voiced by a little girl whose own simplicity prevents her from understanding the complex emotions to which her own speech alludes. It's a figuration not just of innocence but of inexperience. And the poem at once longs for the nymph to be a refuge and presents her as ultimately vulnerable. Longings for femininity in a masculine world—longings to inhabit a feminine space—can only be ignoble and embarrassing.

Cromwell, on the other hand, is constantly and enviously signified being born again as a force of masculinity from within that feminized world. In a very dark allusion to Homer's portrayal of Hector's doomed son, Astyanax, Marvell depicts Cromwell holding his baby daughter Elizabeth, and makes an explicit contrast, as Homer does, between the warlike male body, the softness of the baby, and the softness of the maternal breast:

> Her when an infant, taken with her Charms,
> He oft would flourish in his mighty Arms;
> And, lest their force the tender burthen wrong,
> Slacken the vigour of his Muscles strong;
> Then to the Mothers brest her softly move,
> Which while she drain'd of Milk she fill'd with Love. (31–6)[15]

This is not merely an image of paternal affection, or family values. In showing Cromwell capable of tenderness, Marvell implicitly refutes the notion that his Herculean qualities are inimical to the weak and the helpless. In particular, Cromwell's restraint in deliberately weakening his muscles, deliberately softening his body, figures him not merely as protector of the vulnerable, but as in control

---

[14]   *The Vindication of Richard Atkyns*, 1669, 45.

[15]   For Hector and Astyanax, see Homer, *Iliad*, 6, 460ff. Astyanax recoils from Hector's male body and clings to the full breast of his nurse.

of his body and its acts; this is a Hercules without the *furens*. It's an image of his relations with the feminized state. Here, rather than possessing, penetrating, and exploiting femininity, Cromwell protects it, as a good father of the household. Because the lactating breast here is imagined not as part of Elizabeth Cromwell, but as a kind of entity in itself, it too is subtly linked to Cromwell, so that his hard muscles, available though still relaxed, are counterpointed by a source of feminine nurturance of which he is the guarantor. Here is the godly *paterfamilias*, capable of an almost feminine nurturance, but innately—and literally—the Protector. Here, too, is a subtly Christological figure to set against Charles's powerful adoption of that image.[16]

Like Maria Fairfax in "Upon Appleton House," Elizabeth offers a way out for the burden of masculinity, a burden of violence and excess and blood. Without being in the least a radical or feminist figure, the daughter can contain masculinity without weakening or diluting it. And yet even for Cromwell the figuration of the father is not an unproblematic and uncontradictory resolution of the longing for Edenic girlhood and the social need to be a man. The haunting of the tender figuration of Cromwell and Elizabeth by the equally tender but more ominous figures of Hector and Astyanax, however, means that the entire image is bracketed by a consciousness that heroes are those who face death. Here, the order of deaths is reversed, however; in Homer, the child dies as a result of the father's death, but here the father dies as a result of the child's death. So important is Elizabeth's death that Cromwell's own could easily be read as an anticlimax; a more interesting possibility is that Marvell has chosen to represent Cromwell's own death through the death of a woman–child. Implicitly, this gives Cromwell the vulnerability of the very state–family that he as *paterfamilias* must protect. Of course, when Hector dies the fall of Troy is assured, so there is an obvious sense in which Cromwell's death *is* the death of the state; this is signified not only by the chaos in nature wrought by his demise, the storm, but by the inversion of the events in the Hector story. The death of a child leads to the death of her original, her father; why then should not his death lead to the death of his original, nature? Here Marvell simply evokes the standard metaphoric apparatus for the death of a king.

Having carefully established the traces of softness and femininity in Cromwell, Marvell can now turn to his military successes. Cromwell is celebrated less as a victor than as the man who gave meaning to the empty signifiers of war by filling them with religion. Having talked of "inward Mail" and cities conquered by a prayer, Marvell at last allows himself the image of Cromwell as a hard body:

---

[16]   On the significance of breasts and breastfeeding in early modern culture, see among others Kathryn Schwartz, "Missing the Breast," in *The Body in Parts: Fantasies of Corporeality in Early Modern Europe*, David Hillman and Carla Mazzio, eds (New York and London: Routledge, 1997), 147–210, and my *The Witch in History* (London: Routledge, 1996), Chapter 5.

Hence, though in battle none so brave or Fierce,
Yet him the adverse steel could never pierce. (195–6)

Instead, Cromwell's heart is pierced by pity for the foes he kills:

Pity it seem'd to hurt him more that felt
Each wound himself which he to others dealt. (197–8)

In elegantly compressed form, these lines engage with and refute the notion that a hard and armored body makes for a hard heart. Marvell insists that Cromwell is invulnerable, unassailable, but also insists that he can be assailed, though only by emotions of empathy.

One of the attractions of Cromwell for the nation was that he offered an apparently secure masculinity, one less likely to collapse miserably into femininity, one able to resist the longing to be a little girl at mother's knee. That pre-civilized childhood state was the only one in which man could walk "without a mate" and escape the burdens of violence and eroticism. Yet precisely because it was so ideal, it also represented a stasis which the active male was obliged to resist. It was only after many years of civil war had made the violence of masculinity seem repugnant that a stoical withdrawal into the feminine Golden Age of the garden of childhood could be imagined without disgrace.

Chapter 12
Martyrs and Minors:
Allegories of Childhood in Cervantes

Emilie L. Bergmann

Francisquisto:	Even if they give me two tops I won't be a Moor!
Juanico:	What a childish thing to say!
Francisquito:	See here, Do you think I'm kidding?
Juanico:	We're dealing with serious matters as if we were grown men, and you're talking about tops?
Francisquito:	Must I always be in tears? By my faith, brother, take care of yourself, so that the torments of Mohammed don't destroy you.[1]

The author of *Don Quixote* spent five years as a captive in Algiers, from 1575 to 1580; his courage was legendary among his fellow captives. One of the first works he wrote after his rescue was the play *El trato* (or *Los tratos*) *de Argel* (Life in Algiers), which gave Spanish audiences a shocking view of captivity in an environment that Cervantes called "Purgatorio en la vida/ Infierno puesto en el mundo" (*Trato* I. 5–6) (Living purgatory; hell on earth). Miguel shared the first two years of captivity with his brother Rodrigo, and when sufficient funds were raised by their mother to ransom one of them, Miguel insisted that his brother be liberated first (Garcés 45). Cervantes was finally rescued by a Trinitarian monk, Fray Juan Gil, whom he honored in *El trato de Argel* by bestowing his name on the bearer of the fictional captives' ransom. In *El trato de Argel*, a young child, Francisco, exemplifies steadfast faith, while his brother Juan cannot resist the temptations of nourishing food and a comfortable life. Juan takes his master's name and adopts luxurious Muslim dress, outward signs of his rejection of Christianity, including his Christian family.

---

[1]   *Los baños de Argel* (The Dungeons of Algiers) "Francisquito: ¡Aunque me den/ dos trompos no seré moro! Juanico: ¡Qué niñería! Francisquito: Pues bien:/ ¿piensas que estoy burlando? Juanico: Estamos cosas tratando/ como si fuésemos hombres,/ ¿y es bien que el trompo nombres? Francisquito: ¿He de estar siempre llorando?/ Mi fe, hermano, tened cuenta/ con vos, y mirad no os hunda/ de Mahoma la tormenta" (II. 248–9). Translations of the three plays discussed are my own.

Thirty years later, Cervantes revisited the trauma of captivity in *Los baños de Argel* (The dungeons of Algiers). He added diminutives to the two brothers' names, thus enhancing their childishness. And yet, childish playfulness in *Los baños* paradoxically enables Francisquito to choose martyrdom over apostasy. As Ellen M. Anderson has observed, "these bleak alternatives are embraced by the child playfully ... the two boy-captives in this play can choose to respond to the fate chosen for them by their owner by temporarily adopting Moslem clothing without endangering their identities" (48). While their father is initially alarmed to see them in Muslim costume, they assure him that this does not indicate a loss of faith. Francisquito, according to Anderson, "is given *gracia* (both grace and a graceful sense of humor)" (49), the lightness of heart attributed to some martyrs.[2] His ability to play distinguishes him from his counterpart Francisco in *El trato de Argel*. Francisco's "playful sense of identity allows him to contemplate, and momentarily to absorb, the role of the other without losing his identity—in theological terms, his immortal soul" (Anderson 49).[3]

My focus will be on the heroic boys in three of Cervantes's theatrical works: *El cerco de Numancia* (The Siege of Numantia), written in the mid-1580s; *El trato de Argel*, written around 1581–1583; and *Los baños de Argel*, published in 1615; with brief references to the *Novelas ejemplares* (exemplary novels) whose female protagonists' early lives are significant, *La gitanilla* (The Little Gypsy Girl), *La española inglesa* (The English Spanish Girl), and *La ilustre fregona* (The Illustrious Kitchen-Maid), and one in which a young illegitimate child serves as catalyst for his parents' reunion and marriage, *La fuerza de la sangre* (The Power of Blood).

Los baños de Argel is unique in its depiction of a relatively complex child character who displays humor, defiance, and steadfast faith. *El trato* and *Los baños* are among the handful of Cervantes's works that include young children rather than adolescents such as Leonora, who at the age of 13 or 14 becomes the wife of the 68-year-old Carrizales in *El celoso extremeño*; the eponymous 14- to 17-year-old *pícaros* Rinconete and Cortadillo; or the adolescent shepherd Andrés in *Don Quixote* Part I, Chapter 4, whom Quixote fails to rescue from the brutality of his master, Juan Haldudo. The boy who accompanies Maese Pedro (Master Peter) and narrates the scenes performed in his puppet show appears to be a younger child, since he is referred to only as "muchacho" and "niño."[4] Both are responsible for adult tasks, and both are castigated for falling short of adult standards.

---

[2]   A popular example is St. Lawrence's legendary quip to his tormentors while being executed by burning on a grill, "I am done on this side! Turn me over and eat!"

[3]   The playful confrontation with the other, including impersonation of others, is typical of the most engaging female characters in *Don Quixote* and is an important aspect of Cervantes's posthumously published *Persiles y Sigismunda*.

[4]   The term "mozo/a" can refer to a youth or an adult servant, but the usage of "muchacho" and "niño" together denotes preadolescence.

In light of the very limited appearance of young children in early modern Spanish literature, their scarcity in Cervantes's writing should come as no surprise. The significant exception in early modern Spanish literature appears to be the picaresque; Cervantes's ambivalence toward the genre has long been a critical focus (Guillén, González Echevarría). It is telling that the protagonists of Cervantes's version of picaresque are adolescents in *Rinconete y Cortadillo* and canines in *El coloquio de los perros* (*The Dogs' Colloquy*). Narrative subjectivity in the picaresque is split between the articulation of memory by the adult narrator and the inarticulable experience of the vulnerable child. Despite common critical reference to the *pícaro* as both narrator and protagonist, for example in the anonymous *Lazarillo de Tormes* and Mateo Alemán's *Guzmán de Alfarache*; the protagonists are designated by the diminutives "Lazarillo" and "Guzmanillo," while the adult narrators Lázaro and Guzmán shape recollected actions, thoughts, and dialogue with the rhetorical devices of pathos, irony, satire, and moralizing.[5] The *pícaro* is triply marginalized: by society as poor and young, and by the selective memory of the adult narrator, who uses the child's experience for the adult purpose of justifying the person he has become. Claudio Guillén calls the *pícaro* a "half-outsider" (80); his literary status as a child character is as ambiguous as his precarious social status as an adult.

Infancy and early childhood are distanced in *La ilustre fregona* and *La gitanilla* by reunion with parents and reintegration into an elite social milieu in the narrative present after years of separation from them. The suspiciously refined kitchen maid Costanza is reunited with the high-ranking father who raped her mother (a widow of the highest nobility) in *La ilustre fregona*, while both mother and father recover the daughter who was stolen from her crib as an infant in *La gitanilla*. Now 15, she has learned to sing and dance among her Roma surrogate family, but has kept her "virtue" intact. By attributing to these young women's lineage the moral qualities that distinguish them from the low-caste innkeepers and tricksters among whom they spent their childhoods, these two *novelle* link the idealization of "blood" to idealizing romance plots, those regarded by Ruth El Saffar as typical of Cervantes's later *Novelas ejemplares*. The matrimonial denouements of these *novelle* hinge on the presence of the parents not only for their consent but also to certify the daughters' noble lineage and thus their suitability as spouses. Because of the emphasis on the marriage plot, adolescents abound in early modern Spanish literature, but young children are rare.

As the dialogue from *Los baños de Argel* illustrates, child characters in Cervantes's early theater and in his later narrative works have a dual role as emblems and active defenders of Spanish Catholic cultural identity.

---

[5] Dunn, for example, explains the lack of "interiority" in *Lazarillo de Tormes* in terms of adult criteria, arguing that the narrator's references to pain and fear belong to comic genres (171). Because of their foundational status, the seven relatively brief *tratados* of the *Lazarillo* are among the most contested among Hispanists. For an overview of approaches to the picaresque see the MLA *Approaches to Teaching the Picaresque*, edited by Anne J. Cruz.

Liminal figures poised between nonexistence and adulthood (from an early modern perspective), Cervantes's child characters, like the "niño" who narrates the action staged in Master Peter's puppet show, also bridge literary genres: epic, hagiography, theater, novel, romance. But these children retain their distinct Iberian or Catholic cultural identities in open or clandestine defiance of the distinctly opposing cultural identities of Rome, Islam, or Protestant England. In the Algiers plays and *La española inglesa*, the child characters exemplify religious and national identity; in *Numancia*, a young child prefigures the glorious future of Spain, which by Cervantes's time commanded, albeit precariously, an empire whose extent would have been unimaginable to the Roman conquerors of *Hispania Tarraconensis*. While the children's roles limit the range and depth of psychological characterization, they exercise moral autonomy. Although the child characters have little experience, knowledge, or physical strength they must succeed in making the most daunting of choices. The vulnerability of these emblematic figures reinforces the audience's wonder at their youthful wisdom and courage, but in *Los baños de Argel*, Cervantes also introduces a distinctly modern sense of destabilized identity.[6]

The scarcity of Cervantes's child characters and the adult burdens placed on their shoulders might appear to support Philippe Ariès's highly influential thesis that childhood as a cultural concept is a relatively recent invention. Despite Ariès's disclaimer that "this is not to suggest that children were neglected, forsaken or despised. The idea of childhood is not to be confused with affection for children" (128), his thesis led historians of the family to argue that high rates of infant and maternal mortality and economic and social conditions such as primogeniture rendered the early modern family an emotional desert.[7] Historians Shulamith Shahar, David Herlihy, and Linda Pollock and literary scholar Margaret L. King, among others, have argued against this characterization. What is most evident from recent historical studies of childhood and the family, for example in David Kertzer and Marzio Barbagli's 2001 collection of historical studies, *Life in Early Modern Times, 1500–1789*, and the studies collected in James Casey's *La familia en la España mediterránea (siglos XV–XIX)*, is the diversity of legal and social aspects of family life in early modern European culture.

Donald D. Miller observes how Cervantes uses comedy and satire to deconstruct Renaissance ideologies of the family in *Don Quixote*, in which the central family groups display "aspects of psychological and social dysfunction";

---

[6]   George Mariscal discusses this aspect of early modern Spanish culture and Cervantes's work in the first two chapters of *Contradictory Subjects*.

[7]   For example, despite cautioning readers against "a reductionist position that there is a simple and direct correlation between the level of mortality and the amount and degree of affect at any given moment in history (55)," Lawrence Stone concludes: "About all that can be said with confidence on the matter of emotional relationships" in the early modern family "is that there was a general psychological atmosphere of distance, manipulation and deference … . It was a structure held together not be affective bonds but by mutual economic interests" (88).

only the sketchiest of Cervantine family portraits matches the guidelines of conduct manuals (76). Questions about the relationships between early modern literary representations of the family and historical reality are particularly challenging for Hispanists, since the social sciences were proscribed areas of research during the Franco dictatorship (1939–1975).[8] Spanish social and economic history is different enough from that of Northern Europe that conclusions regarding the latter cannot be applied simply or directly to Spanish family relationships of the same period.

The apparent flatness of child characters in Cervantes's theater and fiction is particularly surprising in light of the multidimensionality of his female characters, but a partial explanation may be found in his literary models. In *Don Quixote* (1605; 1615) and in his Christian romance *Los trabajos de Persiles y Sigismunda*, published posthumously in 1616, Cervantes expanded upon female characters from influential works of the sixteenth century: the heroic, autonomous Bradamante, who goes to battle in male armor; Angelica, who defies a host of Christian men and chooses as her lover the Saracen Medoro, in Ariosto's *Orlando furioso* (1532), and the amazon-like shepherdess Felismena in Jorge de Montemayor's pastoral novel *Los siete libros de la Diana* (1559). Equally compelling preadolescent characters were rare if not nonexistent, except in hagiography or the picaresque. The most memorable female characters in *Don Quixote* are Dorotea, who disguises herself first as an adolescent boy and then as Princesa Micomicona not only to save her honor but to improve her social status through marriage; Marcela, who affirms her right to live as she pleases without returning the love of her male admirers; and Ana Félix, who dresses as a corsair to captain a pirate ship and rescue her lover Don Gregorio from the Turks (*DQ* II. 63).[9] Nearing the end of Quixote's journey, Cervantes thus returns to the traumatic scene of his captivity in Algiers, which María Antonia Garcés considers a major source of his creativity throughout his literary career.

If the child characters in the theatrical works written soon after his rescue are born of Cervantes's terrifying experience of captivity, they also reflect his well-documented courage and his four attempts at escape (Garcés 38–60).[10] Cervantes actively encouraged and helped to plan the escape of five young renegades,

---

[8]   For recent historical studies on early modern women in Spain and Spanish America, see Morant, vol. 2; on literature and history, the collections edited by Agustín Redondo and by Helen Nader; and the monographic studies of marriage and family relationships by Armon, O'Connor, Poska, Sears, Strother, and Vollendorf.

[9]   Cervantes's questioning of traditional representations of love, courtship, and marriage, and the alternatives he suggests in his fiction have been explored by Ruth El Saffar, Anne J. Cruz ("Psyche and Gender"), María Antonia Garcés, Robert Ter Horst, and Diana de Armas Wilson, among others. Several essays appeared in *Quixotic Desire*.

[10]   Garcés draws upon Antonio de Sosa's *Topografía e historia general de Argel*, formerly attributed to its editor, Diego de Haedo; Cervantes's "Información de Argel," and Jean Canavaggio, *Cervantes. Entre vida y creación*. Alcalá de Henares: Biblioteca de Estudios Cervantinos, 2000.

Christians who had converted to Islam (Garcés 58). The child characters in the Algiers plays had historical counterparts: "Of 978 cases of renegades studied by the historians [Bartolomé and Lucile Bénassar], half were under the age of 15 when seized by Barbary corsairs, and a quarter were between 15 and 19 years old" (Garcés 58).

The triumph of national and religious orthodoxy in these plays depends upon the moral fortitude of children faced with horrific punishments, torture, and death. Bariato, the sole survivor of the Roman siege of the defiant Iberian town of Numantia, throws himself from a parapet rather than be taken captive and paraded through the streets of Rome as evidence of imperial conquest.[11] The first of the four acts of *Numancia* closes with a prophecy by a personification of the River Duero (played by a young boy), that Spain would someday conquer the Numantians' oppressors (Act I, lines 469–72).[12] Immediately after Bariato's suicide in Act IV, "Fama" foretells how Numantia's heroism will echo through the ages. Since these prophecies had been fulfilled by the sixteenth century, it is tempting to regard the child Bariato as father to Spain's imperial manhood, far outstripping the predecessor, Rome. However, while it is commonplace to regard the child on the threshold, always in the process of becoming more adult-like, the child characters in *Numancia* and *Los baños de Argel* show their maturity by choosing martyrdom, thus the course of their lives is completed in childhood.

Pathos is a powerfully dramatic effect of the presence of children as well as mothers on stage in *Numancia* and the Algiers plays (Canavaggio 350–52; Friedman 67–9). The audience of *El cerco de Numancia* is called upon to witness the active stoicism of proto-Castilian (Celtiberian) mothers who sacrifice their nurturing and protective roles to defy the Roman conquerors. To dramatize the suffering inflicted on the inhabitants of Numantia by the Roman siege, a child asks his mother why they don't sell their belongings to buy bread; she responds that there is no bread, and he can suck only blood from her emaciated breasts (Act III, lines 576–95). Once the Numantians have made their decision, the mothers pursue their children through the streets, murdering them before committing suicide themselves. Canavaggio argues against comparing the violence of this scene with Neo-Senecan tragedy, popular on the sixteenth-century Spanish stage before Lope de Vega transformed the genre (350). Indeed, while Cervantes seems to escalate the horrific infanticide of *Medea* from an individual to a citywide level, there is an important difference: the meaning conferred on the infanticide by the sole survivor Bariato's decision to join the slaughtered children in death. Bariato's leap from the tower culminates the horror of mass suicide, but it also seals a foundational act,

---

[11]   Roman historical accounts, including those of Appian and Livy, recount the Numantians' astonishing resistance to Roman rule, from 153 to 133 BC. Most of Numantia's inhabitants resorted to suicide only after a second, eight-month siege under the command of Scipio Africanus.

[12]   De Armas notes that this prophecy includes references to two Spanish threats to the authority of the papacy (50).

confirming dramatically that Cervantes's late sixteenth-century audience belongs to a Castilian cultural tradition of preferring death to dishonor.

Fred de Armas has written about the similarities between this dramatization and Raphael's depiction of suffering at all levels of society in his Vatican fresco *The Fire in the Borgo* (1508), part of the decoration of the Stanza del' Incendio (50–55). Here, as in *Numancia*, the suffering is shared by the youngest members of the community, but the fire will be extinguished by the Pope making the sign of the cross in the background and the naked, vulnerable children will be rescued by their mothers. The destruction of Numancia in Cervantes's play is complete, but the tragedy is framed by the sixteenth-century perspective of the play's prophecy of a Castilian empire that will dwarf Rome's. This ideological framework is complicated in *Numancia* by the relationship between Imperial Rome and Castilian cultural identity, inflected by historical distance and sixteenth-century Spanish concerns with the ethics of conquest and colonization.[13]

In the final scenes of *El trato de Argel* the young Francisco witnesses the arrival of the ship bearing Fray Juan Gil with the slaves' ransom. As Bariato exemplifies proto-national autonomy in defiance of the Roman Empire, Francisco's steadfast devotion to the Virgin Mary as Intercessor exemplifies the Spanish ideal of Christian faith. Unlike Bariato and the martyred boy captive Francisquito in the later play *Los baños de Argel*, Francisco survives to witness the earthly reward of his faith.

The cruelty of commerce in human beings is depicted with emotional intensity in *El trato de Argel*, Act II, as merchants heartlessly separate two young children, Francisco and his brother Juan, from their father and pregnant mother, referring to the children as "perritos" (pups). Young Francisco has not yet lost all of his milk teeth, a detail that intensifies the pathos of the scene: when a prospective buyer tries to open his mouth to check his health as if he were a horse, Francisco is afraid that the Muslim merchant is about to pull one of his teeth. He cries out "¡No me la saque, señor;/ que ella misma se cairá!" (II. 183–4) ("Don't pull it out, sir; it will fall out on its own!"). To the merchant's question, "Si te compro, ¿serás bueno?" (*Trato* II. 192) (If I buy you, will you be good?) Francisco responds with mock-innocence that suggests future defiance: "Aunque vos no me compréis,/ seré bueno" (*Trato* II. 193–4) (Even if you don't buy me, I'll be good). His brother Juan, torn from his mother before she could dispel his fear that she was abandoning him, despaired and renounced his Christian faith, while Francisco listened to her reminders to pray to the Virgin Mary, attributing to her the power to "limar tu cadena/ y volver tu libertad" (*Trato* II. 243–4) (wear away [literally, file] your chain and return your freedom to you). In *Los baños de Argel*, there is no maternal figure; only an elderly father, called "Viejo" (old man) in the play. Instead of the nurturing feminine, the crucifixion that awaits Francisquito is invoked when he asks his father to replace a cross his Muslim masters have torn from his rosary (*Baños* II. 457–60). The two boys are dressed in Muslim clothing, but Francisquito

---

[13]   See Willard King's reading of *Numancia*.

assures his father that he still identifies himself by his Christian name, denying the name his master has imposed on him. In *El trato de Argel*, Act III, Francisco is horrified that his younger brother Juan has rejected his Christian name and adopted the name of his Muslim master, "Solimán." For the sake of physical comforts, Juan has abandoned his blood relation and his Christian faith: "Adiós, porque es gran pecado/ hablar tanto con cristianos" (*Trato* III. 350–51) (Farewell, for it is a great sin/ to speak at such length with Christians).

Both plays foreground the sexual vulnerability of young boys. In *El trato de Argel*, a prospective buyer remarks, "Enamorado me ha/ el donaire del garzón" (II. 273–4) (I'm smitten with the lad's charm).[14] Francisco reiterates the attribution of sexual corruption to the Algerian elites: "¡Oh tierna edad, cuán presto eres vencida,/ siendo en esta Sodoma recuestada ..." (III. 355–7) (Oh tender age, how quickly you are conquered in this decadent Sodom [literally, supine]), and the protagonist Aurelio elaborates further with a plea to the audience for alms to liberate Christian captives:

> ¡Oh, cuán bien la limosna es empleada
> en rescatar muchachos, que en sus pechos
> no está la santa fe bien ar[r]aigada!
> ¡Oh, si de hoy más, en caridad deshechos
> se viesen los cristianos corazones,
> y fuesen en el dar no tan estrechos,
> para sacar de grillos y prisiones
> al cristiano cativo, especialmente
> a los niños de flacas intenciones! (*Trato* III. 358–66)
> (Oh, how well alms are employed in rescuing young boys, in whose breasts holy faith is not yet firmly rooted! Oh, if only from now on, Christian hearts were softened by charity, to give generously to rescue from irons and prison cells the Christian captives, especially young children, weak of will.)

The propagandistic urgency of this passage draws upon sexual anxieties. The "sodomitic" desires and practices of the captors will be adopted by young renegades along with their religion. French, Portuguese, and Spanish Christian observers demonized the Muslim world for its distinct sexual mores, among which polygamy and divorce were permitted. They described the competition among wealthy and powerful corsairs to show off their most lavishly dressed "garzones" (Garcés 112–13).[15] Once converted to Islam, renegades became known for their extreme cruelty toward Christians, a display of allegiance to their new faith. As Garcés has noted, apostasy was common among young captives, although captive priests, including Teresa de Jesús's confessor Fray Jerónimo Gracián de la Madre de Dios, conducted clandestine masses for slaves and renegades who practiced their

---

[14]   The Gallicism "garzón" carried homoerotic connotations; see Garcés, 112–13.

[15]   In response to scholarly speculation regarding Cervantes's sexual experiences in Algiers, Garcés argues that the 32-year-old maimed, battered soldier was no "garzón" and there was testimony to the absence of "vice or scandalous behavior" during those years (115).

religion in secret (Garcés 210). Cervantes's child characters in the Algiers plays have important roles beyond that of mere poster children for charity. Isolated from family and community, these boys risk losing their Spanish Catholic identities. Each one will exercise his free will to choose between an easy but immoral life, or, as a Christian, suffering and possibly death.

Cervantes's depiction of young captives' victimization by the temptations offered by decadent Muslim rulers parallels in some ways the hagiographic narrative of the child martyr, St. Pelagius (Pelayo). Mark D. Jordan remarks that 13-year-old Pelagius of Córdoba, martyred in 925 or 926, became younger, more eloquent, and more desirable in successive narrations of his resistance to the "Sodomitic vices" of the caliph of Córdoba, 'Abd ar-Rahman III (10). Three texts narrate Pelagius's martyrdom: a text written before 967 by an otherwise unknown cleric, Raguel; a poem by Hroswitha of Gandersheim, and a Mozarabic liturgy, probably written after 967. The liturgical praise of Pelagius brought attention to homoerotic desire, literally singing the praises of an "ephebe," as Jordan terms him, whose physical beauty increased with his spiritual purification as he prepared himself for martyrdom. Jordan remarks, "[a]s it begins to act out its own worship of the boy-saint, the Christian community seems as much bothered by his beauty as was the caliph" (27–8). In the hagiographic narratives, Pelagius rejects the Caliph's verbal and physical attempts at seduction with "the contemptuous question, 'Do you think me like one of yours, an effeminate (*effeminatum*)?'" (Jordan 13). The hagiographic accounts include an odd gesture for a young man intent upon protecting his virtue: he rips off the rich garments the Caliph has given him. "Instead of concealing what the king wants, he presents it aggressively" (Jordan 16). The hagiographic narratives of Pelagius's martyrdom are sufficient justification for Jordan's erotic readings. When the gesture of the future martyr's casting off of borrowed finery is repeated on stage by Francisquito in *Los baños de Argel*, it is worth noting that the term "desnudarse" in a stage direction denoted removal of the outer garments rather than stripping to the skin. The young boy's body is at least partially displayed, however, for the eyes of his frustrated master the Cadí, but the gesture is also framed as a step on the *Via crucis*: an imitation of Christ stripped of his garments. Like Christ, Francisquito will be tied to a column and whipped.

The Cadí imposes his eroticizing gaze in the slave-market scene in *Los baños de Argel*, in which he asks if there are any boys ("¿Hay muchachos?") and remarks that Spanish boys are extraordinarily beautiful ("de belleza extraña"). Once he has purchased the two boys, the Cadí takes the first step toward initiating them into Algerian court culture with an attempt at religious instruction. Francisquito wins the skirmish, armed with more numerous and powerful prayers. First, he responds with "Ave María" and "Gracia plena," and then jokes, "¿Ya os turbáis?/ Pues si es que aquesto os indina,/ ¿qué hará cuando me oyáis/ decir la *Salve Regina*?/ Para vuestras confusiones,/ todas las cuatro oraciones/ sé, y sé bien que son escudos a tus alfanjes agudos/ y a tus torpes invenciones" (1092–1100) (Does that upset you? Well, if you're indignant about that, what will you do when you hear me recite the *Salve Regina*? To confound you, I can recite all four prayers, and I know that they are shields to your sharp scimitars and your clumsy fabrications). After this scene in which the Caliph's power to reward or punish is mocked by Francisquito's bold affirmations of faith, he discards the top that he and his brother had spun earlier—now he "puts away childish things"—but he also throws off the luxurious Muslim garments his master has forced him to wear: "que es bien que vaya ligero/ quien se atreve a esta carrera" (II. 1114–15).

Significantly, the scenes of seduction in *El trato de Argel* and the later *Los baños de Argel* are those in which the adult male protagonists resist the overtures of their masters' adulterous wives, much as Joseph rejected Potiphar's wife. Both the moral risks and the potential rewards of giving in to these women pale beside the dangers of slavery for the younger male characters. In Act III of *El trato de Argel*, Juan's name change foretells what would happen to the adult Pedro, who imagines that he can remain a secret Christian while dressing as a Muslim and enjoying the benefits promised him by his owner's wife. Francisco's dismay at his younger brother's conversion dramatizes the arguments the character Sayavedra (an alter ego of Cervantes) uses to dissuade Pedro from abandoning the outward manifestations of Christianity along with the worst burdens of captivity.

In *Los baños de Argel*, Francisquito and his brother have a final exchange: "Francisquito: No le temes? Juanico: No le temo" (F: Are you afraid of [the Cadí]? J: No, I'm not afraid). When Francisquito is tortured to death by his captors while tied to a column, his father compares his son's martyrdom to Christ's crucifixion. In addition to the pathos of the suffering or death of a child, these roles also give the child characters an autonomy denied them by the concept of children as incomplete adults. Steven Rupp identifies the function of the child characters in the Algiers plays as examples of spiritual (as opposed to military) heroism. Thus, as martyrs and witnesses to suffering and martyrdom, children participate in adult matters of life, death, and religious belief, although Francisquito never lets the audience of *Los baños de Argel* forget that he is a young child who has just learned to read and still knows how to play.

The peril in which a child is placed in the exemplary novel *La fuerza de la sangre* is more problematic, serving to resolve a problem of family honor rather than national or religious interests. *La fuerza de la sangre* is probably the most difficult of the exemplary novels to present to contemporary students, because the "happy ending" consists in a young woman, Leocadia, marrying the man who raped her. In early modern Spanish fiction and theater, it was necessary to erase the stain on the family honor through matrimony or through revenge, murdering the rapist, or both victim and rapist (often depicted as a seducer who falsely promises marriage). *La fuerza de la sangre*, however, blurs the distinction between harmonious matrimony and aggression by displacing violence from the perpetrator to the innocent child born of a violent act. Leocadia's four-year-old son Luisico becomes the catalyst for his unmarried parents' reunion when he is trampled by a horse outside the home of his paternal grandparents. María Zerari includes him among passive, silent (literally *infans*, nonspeaking) child characters, "phantoms" who serve as strategic or thematic plot devices (154–6). At four years, Luisico is just old enough to resemble his father and be valued by his grandparents but it is troubling that the plot's happy resolution depends upon child endangerment.

Infants and very young children are plot devices connected with paternity in much of early modern literature. Preciosa, the protagonist of *La gitanilla* is reunited with her parents, and in *La ilustre fregona* the repentant father of Costanza, the so-called kitchen maid, finds his daughter just at the age when she can marry with parental consent. Preciosa has grown up in among gypsies, whose moral code is described with such repetitive, exaggerated opprobrium by Cervantes that it must be read as ironic, particularly the insistence that thievery is passed down from generation to generation. Costanza has spent her first 15 years among boisterous travelers at an inn, but both young women's ability to keep their purity among thieves and gamblers confirms their noble lineage.

The captivity of a young girl in Protestant England tests her Catholic faith in *La española inglesa*. The "English Spanish girl" Isabel, whose name in Spanish is equivalent to that of the English queen Elizabeth I, is captured during the siege of Cadiz by an English mariner who happens to be a secret Catholic. The narrative is grounded in historical events, but the protection of the child character's religious faith and her chastity depends upon a series of fortunate coincidences and the secret identity of her adult protectors during her childhood.[16]

The heroic Christianity of the boys in Cervantes's *Numancia* and Algiers plays and the purity of the young girls in his exemplary novels have visual counterparts in paintings of the Holy Family, child saints, and the Immaculate Conception by Bartolomé Estéban Murillo (1617–1682). In post-Tridentine Spain the cult of the Virgin Mary's conception without sin was promoted vigorously, and Murillo received numerous commissions to paint this image for religious institutions. The painter was known for his intense personal faith and his work with the Confraternity of Charity in caring for the poor. Peter Cherry notes that Murillo's success was "partly due to the strong devotional feelings that his paintings aroused" (10), and explains children's "important affective role in Murillo's religious narratives; in particular they act as vehicles for colloquy with the viewer" (13), comparable to the roles of the young captives in the Algiers plays.

Claudio Guillén rightly pointed out that the comparison between the literary representation of the *pícaro* and "Murillo's paintings of young ragamuffins" is "insufficient" (75). Similarly, Peter Cherry distinguishes the two traditions and emphasizes the autonomy of the urchins in Murillo's genre paintings, in contrast to the servitude of the *pícaro* (23). Although Murillo's secular images of children were "theoretically condemned to a lowly status for their excessive naturalism" (Cherry 24), and are now considered excessively sentimental, Cherry praises the "naturalism" of his depiction of children in both religious and secular paintings.

---

[16] Carroll Johnson's historical study of this *novella* is essential. See also Fuchs, *Passing for Spain*.

The comparison is more often made between Velázquez and Cervantes for their innovations in artistic realism and their profoundly philosophical and psychological approach to representation of the human. The autonomy of Murillo's street urchins and the theatrical expressivity of his representations of the sacred embodied in the young can illuminate the study of child characters in Cervantes's early plays as well as the adolescent girls in his exemplary novels. Although his child characters are few, the spiritual heroism of the young captives and the moral autonomy of even the youngest of these characters, so often ignored, is at the center of Cervantes's work.

Works Cited

Anderson, Ellen. "Playing at Moslem and Christian: The Construction of Gender and the Representation of Faith in Cervantes's Captivity Plays." *Cervantes* 13 (1993): 37–59.

Ariès, Philippe. *Centuries of Childhood*. Trans. Robert Baldick. New York: Random House, 1962.

Armon, Shifra. *Picking Wedlock: Women and the Courtship Novel in Spain.* Lanham, MD: Rowman and Littlefield, 2002.

Bénassar, Bartolomé, and Lucile Benassar. *Les chrétiens d'Allah: l'histoire extraordinaire des rénegats XVIe et XVIIe siècles*. Paris: Perrin, 1989.

Brooke, Xanthe, and Peter Cherry. *Murillo: Scenes of Childhood*. London: Merrell, 2001.

Canavaggio, Jean. *Cervantès, un théâtre à naitre*. Presses Universitaires de France, 1977.

Casey, James; Francisco Chacón; Enrique Gacto; Isabel Moll; Primitivo J. Pla; Antoni Simón; Bernard Vincent. *La familia en la españa mediterránea (siglos XV–XIX)*. Barcelona: Editorial Crítica, 1987.

Cervantes Saavedra, Miguel de. *Comedia famosa de El trato de Argel*. Cervantes Virtual (online resource) Digitized Version of *Obras completas de Miguel de Cervantes Saavedra. Comedias y entremeses*. Rudolph Schevill, ed., Madrid, Gráficas Reunidas, 1920. 7–102, http://www.cervantesvirtual.com/FichaObra.html?Ref=8703.

———. *Comedia famosa de los baños de Argel*. Cervantes Virtual (online resource) Digitized Version of *Obras completas de Miguel de Cervantes Saavedra. Comedias y entremeses*. Ed. Rudolph Schevill. Madrid, Gráficas Reunidas, 1920. 235–352, http://www.cervantesvirtual.com/FichaObra.html?Ref=8678.

———. *El ingenioso hidalgo don Quijote de la Mancha*. Ed. Luis Murillo. 2 vols. Madrid: Castalia, 1978.

———. *Novelas ejemplares*. Ed. Harry Sieber. 2 vols. Madrid: Cátedra, 1981.

———. *Los trabajos de Persiles y Sigismunda*. Ed. Juan Bautista Avalle-Arce. Madrid: Castalia, 1969.

Cruz, Anne J., ed. *Approaches to Teaching the Picaresque*. NY: MLA, forthcoming.

———. "Psyche and Gender in Cervantes." *The Cambridge Companion to Cervantes*. Ed. Anthony J. Cascardi. Cambridge: Cambridge University Press, 2002. 186–205.

De Armas, Frederick A. *Cervantes, Raphael and the Classics*. Cambridge: Cambridge University Press, 1998.

Dunn, Peter N. *Spanish Picaresque Fiction: A New Literary History*. Ithaca, NY: Cornell University Press, 1993.

El Saffar, Ruth. *Beyond Fiction: The Recovery of the Feminine in the Novels of Cervantes*. Berkeley: University of California Press, 1984.

El Saffar, Ruth, and Diana de Armas Wilson, eds. *Quixotic Desire: Psychoanalytic Perspectives on Cervantes*. Ithaca, NY: Cornell University Press, 1993.

Friedman, Edward H. *The Unifying Concept: Approaches to the Structure of Cervantes's "Comedias."* York, SC: Spanish Literature Publications, 1981.

Fuchs, Barbara. *Passing for Spain: Cervantes and the Fictions of Identity.* Champaign-Urbana: University of Illinois Press, 2003.

Garcés, María Antonia. *Cervantes in Algiers. A Captive's Tale.* Nashville, TN: Vanderbilt University Press, 2005.

González Echevarría, Roberto. "The Life and Adventures of Cipión: Cervantes and the Picaresque." *Celestina's Brood: Continuities of the Baroque in Spanish and Spanish-American Literatures.* Durham: Duke University Press, 1993. 45–65.

Guillén, Claudio. *Literature as System.* Princeton: Princeton University Press, 1971.

Hegyi, Ottmar. *Cervantes and the Turks: Historical Reality versus Literary Fiction in "La gran sultana" and "El amante liberal."* Newark, DE: Juan de la Cuesta, 1992.

Herlihy, David. *Medieval Households.* Cambridge, MA: Harvard University Press, 1985.

Johnson, Carroll. "*La española inglesa* and the Practice of Literary Production." *Viator: Medieval and Renaissance Studies* 19 (1988): 377–416.

Jordan, Mark D. *The Invention of Sodomy in Christian Theology*, Chicago, 1997.

———. "Saint Pelagius, Ephebe and Martyr." *Queer Iberia: Sexualities, Cultures, and Crossings from the Middle Ages to the Renaissance.* Ed. Josiah Blackmore and Gregory Hutcheson. Durham and London: Duke University Press, 1999. 23–47.

Kertzer, David I. and Marzio Barbagli. *Family Life in Early Modern Times, 1500–1789.* New Haven: Yale University Press, 2001.

King, Margaret L. *The Death of the Child Valerio Marcello.* Chicago: University of Chicago Press, 1994.

King, Willard. "Cervantes's *Numancia* and Imperial Spain." *MLN* 94:2 (1979): 200–221.

Mariscal, George. *Contradictory Subjects: Quevedo, Cervantes, and Seventeenth-Century Spanish Culture.* Ithaca, NY: Cornell University Press, 1991.

Martín, Adrienne. "Images of Deviance in Cervantes's Algiers." *Cervantes* 15 (1995): 5–15.

Miller, Donald D. "Dysfunction, Discord, and Wedded Bliss: Baroque Families in *Don Quijote*." *The Ties That Bind: Questioning Family Dynamics and Family Discourse in Hispanic Literature.* Ed. Sara E. Cooper. Lanham, MD: University Press of America, 2004. 63–78.

Morant, Isabel, ed. *Historia de las mujeres en España y América Latina.* 2 vols. Madrid: Cátedra, 2005.

Nader, Helen, ed. *Power and Gender in Renaissance Spain: Eight Women of the Mendoza Family, 1450–1650.* Champaign-Urbana: University of Illinois Press, 2004.

O'Connor. Thomas A. *Love in the "Corral": Conjugal Spirituality and Anti-Theatrical Polemic in Early Modern Spain.* New York: Peter Lang, 2000.

Pacheco, Francisco. *Arte de la pintura* [1638]. Ed. F.J. Sánchez Cantón. 2 vols. Valencia, 1956.

Pollock, Linda. *Forgotten Children: Parent-Child Relations from 1500 to 1900.* Cambridge: Cambridge University Press, 1983.

Poska, Allyson M. *Women and Authority in Early Modern Spain: The Peasants of Galicia.* Oxford: Oxford University Press, 2005.

Redondo, Augustin, ed. *Autour des parentés en Espagne aux XVIᵉ et XVIIᵉ Siècles: Histoire, Mythe et Littérature.* Paris: Sorbonne, 1987.

———. *Figures de l'enfance.* Paris: Sorbonne, 1997.

———. *La formation de l'enfant en Espagne aux XVIᵉ et XVIIᵉ Siècles.* Paris: Sorbonne, 1996.

Rupp, Stephen. "Remembering 1541: Crusade and Captivity in the Algiers Plays of Cervantes." *Revista de Estudios Hispánicos* 32 (1998): 313–35.

Sears, Theresa Ann. *A marriage of convenience: ideal and ideology in the Novelas ejemplares.* NY: Peter Lang, 1993.

Shahar, Shulamith. *Childhood in the Middle Ages.* New York: Routledge, 1990.

Stone, Lawrence. *The Family, Sex and Marriage in England 1500–1800.* New York: Harper and Row, 1979.

Strother, Darci L. *Family Matters: A Study of On- and Off-Stage Marriage and Family Relations in Seventeenth-Century Spain.* New York: Peter Lang, 1999.

Ter Horst, Robert. "The Sexual Economy of Miguel de Cervantes." *Bodies and Biases: Sexualities in Hispanic Cuiltures and Literature.* Ed. David William Foster and Roberto Reis. Minneapolis: University of Minnesota Press, 1996.

Vollendorf, Lisa. *The Lives of Women: A New History of Inquisitorial Spain.* Nashville, TN: Vanderbilt University Press, 2005.

Wilson, Diana de Armas. *Allegories of Love: Cervantes's "Persiles and Sigismunda."* Princeton: Princeton University Press, 1991.

Zerari, María. "L'enfant en question: autour de la nouvelle, de Miguel de Cervantès à Luis de Guevara." In Redondo, ed. *Figures de l'enfance.* 149–66.

Chapter 13

Portraiture and Royal Family Ties: Kings, Queens, Princes, and Princesses in Caroline England

Julia Marciari Alexander

Professor Kevin Sharpe proclaimed in his monumental Personal Rule of Charles I that "[Anthony] Van Dyck's portraits of the king and his family were … the highest documents of [the king's] authority to rule."[1] Cultural historians corroborate this view, and art historians specifically have consistently interpreted the paintings produced for Charles I as integral, visual agents in the fashioning of the personal rule.[2] It would be hard to argue otherwise, given the numerous, spectacular portraits of the king and his family that were painted by the Flemish artist Anthony Van Dyck between 1630 and 1640. In political, cultural, and art historical studies, these works have been amply examined and put forth as emblems of the two styles of monarchy—the political and the personal—that the physical person of Charles I was understood to embody.[3]

While the portraits of the king and his queen, Henrietta Maria, have been studied with an eye to unraveling their meanings individually and collectively, little attention has been paid to the specific ways in which the portraits of Charles I's family and children (Figs. 13.1–5) functioned within what Sharpe

---

[1]   The two most substantial, recent studies of Charles I and his reign are: Charles Carlton, *Charles I, the Personal Monarch* (Routledge: London & New York, 1983; second edition, 1995) and Kevin Sharpe, *The Personal Rule of Charles I* (New Haven and London: Yale University Press, 1992). Sharpe, 181.

[2]   For a summary of the interpretative and historiographical material of all Van Dyck's portraits analyzed in this paper, see Oliver Millar, "Van Dyck in England," Part IV of *Van Dyck: A Complete Catalogue of the Paintings*, by Susan J. Barnes, Nora de Poorter, Oliver Millar, and Horst Vey (New Haven and London: Paul Mellon Centre for Studies in British Art by Yale University Press, 2004), 419–642. Also, see Kevin Sharpe, *The Personal Rule*, esp. Chapter IV, "Portraits of Power: Personalities and Factions," 131–208 and Chapter V "The Reformation of the Court and Administration," esp. pp. 222–35.

[3]   In defining the characteristics of the "personal rule" (the 12 years following the 1628 assassination of his notorious favorite, George Villiers, 1st Duke of Buckingham), historians have focused on the ways that Charles I and his court literally and metaphorically understood and interpreted the physical and metaphorical "body" of the king; for the theoretical explication of the king's two bodies see Ernst Hartwig Kantorowicz, *The King's Two Bodies: A Study in Mediaeval Political Theology* (Princeton: Princeton University Press, 1957).

correctly posits as the visual program that fashioned Charles's personal rule. Furthermore, these portraits are also products of and participants in a significant shift that occurred between 1600 and 1650 in the perceptions of childhood and family life. Through an examination of a small number of portraits by Anthony Van Dyck of Charles I's family and children, this essay serves as a position paper rather than a full-scale examination of the topic at hand; it aims to tease out the questions we should be asking of these portraits and to provide an explication of some of the ways in which, when provided with more careful study of the documents that will allow us to understand the nature and facts of royal childhood at the Caroline court, these portraits could fulfill Sharpe's assertion that they, like the single and double portraits of their parents, were "the highest documents of [Charles I's] authority to rule."

On arriving at Charles I's court—for the second time—in 1632, Van Dyck immediately began a series of portraits of the king and his family, the largest and most physically imposing of which is a portrait of Charles and his family as it would have been that year.[4] This portrait [Fig. 13.1] is clearly meant as a formal recording of the appearance of the king and his growing brood of heirs, and one commentator has recently dubbed this picture as "a taut synthesis" of the king's family image.[5] According to a contemporary inventory, Van Dyck's painting, which originally measured nearly 10 feet high and 8.5 feet wide, was hung at the south or west end of the Long or "Matted" Gallery "towards the Orchard,"[6] which was above the long "Stone" gallery.[7] These galleries were part of the King's

---

[4]   It represents the first recorded payment by the king to the Flemish painter, whose fame had been cemented through earlier stays in Italy, England, and the Netherlands—on 8 August the king authorized a payment of £100 for "One great peece of O[u]r royall selfe, Consort, and children." See Millar 2004, 459.

[5]   Jerry Brotton, *The Sale of the Late King's Goods: Charles I and His Art Collection* (Basingstoke and Oxford: Macmillan, 2006), 159. Brotton's assessment/synthesis of the making and meaning of Charles's art collection and its dispersal is aimed at a broad crossover audience and has been criticized by art historians for playing fast and loose with the facts (again these remarks have largely been made to the author of this paper in conversation rather than in print). Perhaps this is due to the fact that, as is required for crossover books, Brotton combines fact with speculation about the personal motives of Charles's collecting; for example, Brotton, in the phrase cited here about the *Great Piece*, asserts a psychological "personalization" of the king's engagement with Van Dyck's picture by stating that Charles found the painting "a taut synthesis that Charles found irresistible," although we have no physical evidence of his reaction to the work other than his continued patronage of the artist and its prominent placement in Whitehall Palace.

[6]   Millar 2004, 459.

[7]   Incidentally, after the Restoration, having been bought back into the Royal Collection by Charles II, the painting was placed once again in the same location, most likely as a reminder both of Charles II's family lineage but also as a visual relic, as was the Holbein Mural, of his father's reign and presence in the palace—again, as a symbol of the King's two bodies—indeed, of the two bodies of both himself and his father.

Fig. 13.1   Anthony Van Dyck, *Charles I and Henrietta Maria with their two eldest children*, 1632. The Royal Collection. © 2011 Her Majesty Queen Elizabeth II/The Bridgeman Art Library.

Apartments, connected to the Privy Chamber, and they formed a series of spaces that were at once quasi-public, where the courtiers could see and meet with the king. Although she had apartments at Whitehall, the queen's official residences were at Somerset House down river, and the children's household was located at St. James's Palace.

Van Dyck clearly devised his image to hang in the spot in which it was placed upon completion. The landscape just behind and to the left of the king depicts almost exactly what one would have been able to see from the windows adjacent to where the painting hung: the river and the buildings at Westminster (notably the Parliament House and Westminster Hall).[8] By integrating what would have been a "real" vista into his "performed" image, he creates an image that fuses both the actual and the metaphorical; in other words, the "Great Piece" (whose size, placement, and subject matter were indeed "Great" in its fullest sense) confirms that the painting itself was meant to be indexical of the physical presence of the king's body and the bodies of his family at court.

Spending much of his time away from Whitehall both at his other palaces in London and farther afield and at the estates of the aristocracy, this image— both as a representation and an object itself—epitomizes the way that well-placed portraits of the monarch could literally "embody" the concept of the two bodies of the king. Literally a physical stand-in for the royal family, the worldly body of the king is present; it also functioned as a signifier of his taste and status and, as such, embodied his metaphysical persona as "King." The bodies of the royal family, at near life-size, form the core of the image, representing both the corporeality and the "essence" of their place on this earth.

Van Dyck's Great Piece was without question formulated and understood (by patron and painter) as part of a long tradition of dynastic family portraits. The most famous and immediately recognizable of these by 1632 would have been Hans Holbein's earlier dynastic portrait of Henry VII, Elizabeth Tudor, Henry VIII, and Jane Seymour, which the artist painted on a wall of the Whitehall Privy Chamber and which burned in the fire at Whitehall in 1695 (Fig. 13.2). A visitor to or inhabitant of Whitehall would have undertaken a physical progression as he viewed these images; this journey in which the viewing of the paintings occurred in different spaces itself metaphorically reflected and captured an implied and considered progression of styles: the hieratic, static vision of the Tudor royal family (comprised only of adults) would be in this physical and political progression supplanted by the seemingly more informal Stuart royal family (in which children were included), a family "at ease" showing itself in what Oliver Millar has termed "the understated but unquestioned authority of [this] ruler."[9]

As if to reinforce the essential but easy nature of Charles I's kingship, Van Dyck—in what would become one of his trademarks—de-emphasizes the material

---

[8]   Millar, *Van Dyck in England* (exh. cat.: National Portrait Gallery, London, 1982), 46, and Millar 2004, 459.

[9]   Millar 2004, 420.

Fig. 13.2   Remigius van Leemput after Hans Holbein, *Mural of Henry VIII and his successor* (original mural dating to 1537, copy to c. 1660). Source: The Yorck Project, http://commons.wikimedia.org/wiki/ Commons:10,000_paintings_from_Directmedia.

trappings of Majesty; the great swaths of rich fabric, the crown, scepter, and orb of state are, in this composition, mere asides. In fact, Charles and the family wear no actual trappings of royalty: the children wear typical infant attire; the queen's gown, while beautiful, is not a formal court dress that would have had a stiff lace collar; and the king's attire is elegant but not in any way a robe of state.[10] The ornaments the king wears were those worn by all Knights of the Order of the Garter (the sky-blue ribbon and lesser George at his neck and the Star of the Garter on his cape—in fact, the blue garter that was the only insignia that all Knights of the Order were legally bound to wear at all times may indeed be missing), and while these garter insignia are markers of his status as head of the order, they do not demarcate him as king.[11] Van Dyck's sitters are first and foremost a family, and only sparingly identified by iconographic convention as the Royal Family.

It is precisely the "ease" of the Great Piece, rather than its formality, that startles even the most assiduous viewer of family portraits. Van Dyck has imbued his portrait with particularly touching and characteristically childish details, each of which creates an imposing sense of immediacy and naturalism (foremost among them, for instance, the "imitative" hand gesture of the two-year-old Charles and the realistic way Henrietta Maria steadies young Mary, just a year old, with her right hand). While certainly belonging to the tradition of dynastic portraiture as exemplified by Holbein's Family of Henry VIII, Van Dyck's image is equally infused with the artistic standards of early seventeenth-century family portraiture (see, for example, The Lomellini Family, painted by Van Dyck in Italy seven years earlier, Fig. 13.3). The visual continuities with the standards for dynastic family imagery as practiced in early Baroque Europe could not have escaped the well-traveled and visually erudite court audiences lurking around Whitehall in the 1630s. More surprising, however, is that Van Dyck infused the "Great Piece" with the informality that was then becoming the favored format for artists' own self- and family portraits and for portraits of families with whom artists had friendships or personal attachments (see, for example, Fig. 13.4). Of particular note is the interlocking composition in this family portrait, which Van Dyck mimics (albeit to a lesser degree) in his "Great Piece." As in the nonroyal portraits, the artist has, in this monumental image, created a formal image that carries in it more informal touches that give the picture a more immediate humanity: one can almost hear the imminent movements of two-year-old Charles, baby Mary, the rustling dogs whose paws will inevitably scrape against the yellow silk taffeta of Henrietta Maria's dress that Van Dyck has taken such care to paint.

---

[10]   Aileen Ribeiro, *Fashion and Fiction: Dress in Art and Literature in Stuart England* (New Haven and London: Paul Mellon Centre for Studies in British Art by Yale University Press, 2005), 110 and Chapter 2, note 33.

[11]   I am grateful to Dr. Lisa Ford, Yale Center for British Art, for discussing at length with me the codes, practices, and implications of the wearing of the Order of the Garter in this moment. She is currently preparing a study of the Garter that will trace its political development through visual and textual sources.

Fig. 13.3   Anthony Van Dyck, *The Lomellini Family*, c. 1625–1627. © The National Gallery of Scotland, Edinburgh, Scotland/The Bridgeman Art Library.

Fig. 13.4   Peter Paul Rubens, *The Family of Jan Brueghel the Elder*, c. 1612–
                1613. © Samuel Courtauld Trust, The Courtauld Gallery, London,
                UK/The Bridgeman Art Library.

Kevin Sharpe has aptly observed that "in Van Dyck's paintings of the king and queen with their children, Charles's formality ... [is] suspended; there is a warmth and affection in the subjects that encapsulates all that contemporary observers report and which shows, too ... how Charles's marriage (the fulfillment of his self) became central to his perception of his kingship."[12] This family portrait clearly both documented and promoted this notion of his nature as the ideal father and husband, a notion that the king strove to promote throughout his reign since he, like his own father, held fast to the political ideology that the king was the natural and right "father" of his country.[13] Charles is generally considered a loving father (although, according to custom, he spent little time with his brood).[14] This powerful image of Charles as an easy, if not loving, father, was perhaps especially effective at Whitehall, where his family was not often physically present—and therefore not constantly seen—as a group.

If, as one biographer has stated, "the royal family was obviously central to Charles's sense of self,"[15] the paintings of his children that he commissioned from Van Dyck were also central to the vision of his rule that he literally set before his courtiers eyes. We know from documents and accounts that Charles I played out his family life on the court stage, some of which record charming interactions between father and children: upon one return from his travels to the north in 1633, it was reported that "The princes ... welcomed him home with the prettiest innocent mirth that can be imagined."[16]

Between 1630 and 1644, Charles I and Henrietta Maria had nine children, of whom four survived into adulthood. In 1637, Van Dyck completed a portrait for the King of the five children then living (Fig. 13.5). According to a contemporary inventory, this portrait hung in the King's breakfast chamber at Whitehall, another quasi-public chamber off the Privy Gallery.[17] This portrait, like the Great Piece, belongs squarely within the traditions of dynastic portraiture—perhaps even more so. The seven-year-old Prince of Wales (the future Charles II) stands at the center of the canvas, surrounded by his siblings: from left to right, Princess Mary (b.1631), Prince James (b.1633), Princess Elizabeth (b.1635), Princess Anne (b.1637). Van Dyck here again pays clever homage to the great dynastic images of Holbein (see again, for instance, the Holbein Mural that was then still *in situ* in the Privy Chamber; Fig. 13.2). Van Dyck's image, however, deliberately highlights the clear paradox of the children's "adult" comportment and their state of being "as children." Just as the artist's portraits often depict the sitters as posing "in the guise of" gods/goddesses and/or mythological figures, so here the royal children pose in the guise of adults. He calls our attention to their diminutive stature by

---

[12]   Sharpe, 171.

[13]   On this concept, see Sharpe and Carlton.

[14]   Carlton, 122–34; Sharpe, 184–8.

[15]   Sharpe, 183.

[16]   Sharpe, 183.

[17]   Millar 2004, 479.

Fig. 13.5   Anthony Van Dyck, *The Five eldest children of Charles I*, 1637. The Royal Collection. © 2011 Her Majesty Queen Elizabeth II/The Bridgeman Art Library.

placing the group in a full-sized setting which literally dwarfs them: table, chair, ewer & platter, large pan-pan or citron. The mastiff and the small spaniel (of a type that would later be particularly associated with Charles II in his later life, gaining the name "King Charles Spaniel") serve not only as size markers for the group but also as stand-ins for the people of the English realm who will be governed, apparently with ease as just as he controls the dog without any seeming effort, by the benevolent hand of the Prince of Wales. In fact, Van Dyck carefully demarcates the individual destinies of the eldest three children by positioning them as discreet, independent, yet proximate beings; the more intimate and binding ties that the youngest royal children were inevitably allowed to foster is also clearly mirrored in the division of the composition into three groups, the young girls on the right, whose roles at court were less clear-cut than those of their older siblings, becoming part of the beautiful staffage of court life. Like the Great Piece this work mimics the stiffness and rules of "appropriate" depiction required of the regal state portrait while undermining the rules of pictorial stasis: it seethes with potential—nearly imminent—movement. While the wriggling of the baby Anne at right is the only real point of action-in-suspense in the painting, the painting's realism—indeed the sheer virtuosity of Van Dyck's brush that licks the surface to create surface and shadows in the paint that are full of movement—captures the transient nature of the compositional calm: with any subsequent—inevitable—movement of the baby, the dogs at its feet will shift and precipitate a flow of action across the plane of vision. Indeed, a subtle hint of instability from the opposite corner comes from young James's line of vision out past Charles beyond the picture plane: one can almost hear his nursemaid or governor saying in a firm voice "keep still."

That Charles hung this work literally above his head in his breakfast chamber (hardly the private space its name implies) and that Van Dyck put his full powers to the test in the painting's facture attests to the importance of the commission and to the power that this image was considered to have. Just as with the Great Piece, this work was to serve as a visual stand-in for the children and their role as the dynastic tools of the Stuart monarchy both at the moments when they might have been present and certainly always in their more frequent absence. Through his composition that both emphasizes the "childish" nature of the young sitters and strictly confines that "childishness," Van Dyck's image controls and corrects the viewer's perceptions of the royal brood. More than the portraits of Charles I, who was notoriously "controlled" in his person and thus not so different from his image, this painting demonstrates and affirms the statement that for Charles I "the arts were not a mere adornment of life ... but their real function was to bring order and truth to the confusion and experience and actuality, to elicit its meaning, which must if correctly interpreted be nothing other than the will of God."[18]

Taken together—along with the other portraits of the king's children that are not the subject of this essay—all Van Dyck's group portraits of Charles I's children

---

[18]   Richard Ollard, *The Image of a King: Charles I and Charles II* (London: Hodder & Stoughton Ltd., 1979; reprint London: Pimlico, 1993), 39.

are markers of the king's understanding of how portraits of regal children had been traditionally used as agents in the propagation of dynasty. When considered in association with other biographical, anecdotal, and political material, these works could enlighten us even further about how royal children acted and were perceived in the political, social, and cultural context—were we only to know more about the practices of daily life for royal children.

Historians of childhood have had little to say about the precise nature of royal childhood in this period.[19] Indeed, more attention has been paid to the practices of aristocratic childrearing than to those pertaining to royal children. There exists, however, a crucial distinction between aristocratic children and royal children, a distinction that should define the way in which we as historians of childhood must proceed: royal and aristocratic children were not the same. Royalty held itself to its own set of practices, often allowing more leeway in the realms of personal etiquette but stressing, especially for princes but also for princesses, a broader education always carried out at court rather than at schools. Much more archival research must be done to uncover not only the practices pertaining to the royal children from 1600 to 1700 but also to the perceptions surrounding their place and roles at court. This research will greatly augment the ways in which we can understand the full import and multiple "meanings" of the portraits I reproduce and discuss in the context of this essay.

Those social historians who have paid attention to the theoretical underpinnings of "childhood," foremost among them Philippe Ariès and Lawrence Stone, have located the shift in the idea of childhood to the moment immediately following the Reformation, a moment in which differing ideas about education, the nature of man's relationship to God and King, and what Ariès calls the changing demands of sociability interfaced with the recognition of the "growing awareness of the special nature of childhood."[20] In sixteenth- and seventeenth-century England specifically, Stone further asserts that the shaping of the idea of "childhood" occurred within the social, philosophical, and political culture of a rising "individualism," which he carefully defines as "a growing introspection and interest in the individual personality; and secondly, a demand for personal autonomy and a corresponding respect for the individual's right to privacy, to self-expression, and to the free exercise of his will within limits set by the need

---

[19]   Primarily due to the circumstances of Civil War that dominated the adolescence and youth of these little royals, historians have paid little attention to the daily routines of Charles I's children at the court during the "personal reign" of the 1630s.

[20]   Philippe Ariès, *Centuries of Childhood: A Social History of Family Life*, translated from French by Robert Baldick (first published in French by Plon, Paris, 1960; English translation New York: Vintage Books, 1962), 389; Stone articulates this most succinctly as "the identification of children as a special status group, distinct from adults ..." in Lawrence Stone, *The Family, Sex, and Marriage in England 1500–1800* (London: Weidenfeld and Nicolson, 1977), 221.

for social cohesion." Stone goes on to claim that "the interest in the self sprang from the urgent need to discipline the self."[21]

While perhaps audacious to apply this to Charles I himself, Stone's "individual" is clearly in accordance with how even the most divergent biographers present this monarch during his "personal rule": he was a king with a rigid sense of personal and (sometimes) political control, a disciplined public life set up as a contrast to an increasingly visible private one, and a great confidence in his own self-expression, be that as a politic or a patron. Somewhat paradoxically, then, by himself embodying a heightened "individualism," Charles I provided the example to his courtiers that would further foster "individuality" in his courtiers that necessarily altered the ways in which they considered themselves in relationship to themselves, their families, the court, and society as a larger body.[22]

In this climate of burgeoning "individuality," there was also an increasing recognition that children were physically and emotionally different from adults, an idea that would ultimately lead to the articulation of John Locke's view of innate human nature at the end of the seventeenth century. Such ideas about privacy, "self," and social development began to affect the interaction of families and how adults viewed children and youth as potential "individuals" who had to learn to negotiate the "self" within the boundaries of the strict court hierarchies of duty, personal allegiance, and obligation.

When considered then within the specific context of an ever-shifting understanding of the nature and meaning of the elite individual, family, and child between 1600 and 1650, the portraits I have briefly examined here must be seen as reflections of—and agents in—the transformation of notions of family and childhood in Caroline England. The combination of Van Dyck's virtuosity at creating spectacular compositions with sheer painterly force and the specificity of the moment in which they were viewed served to transform these paintings from mere pretty objects into watersheds in the history of art, culture, and childhood. Inter- and cross-disciplinary study of childhood can only enhance our understanding of the ways in which children figured and were figured—in all senses—in the early modern world.

---

[21]   Stone, 224. While there has been a backlash (largely unpublished but vehement nonetheless) against Stone's theories as expressed in *Family, Sex, and Marriage*, his voice remains useful when thinking about the definitions of royal self and the royal child.

[22]   Stone, 222.

Chapter 14
"Second Childishness" and the Shakespearean Vision of Ideal Parenting

Gregory M. Colón Semenza

Although Jaques's "Seven Ages of Man" usually are characterized in teleological terms, the cynical lord outlines a "strange eventful history" (*AYL* 2.7.164) whose ending is the same as its beginning.[1] There may be seven ages, but there are only six states of being, because childishness is said to mark both the beginning and end of the human journey. Jaques's generic man falls backwards from maturity through his own puberty ("his big manly voice,/ Turning again toward childish treble" [2.7.161–2]), into "second childishness" (2.7.165), and finally into a second infancy characterized as "mere oblivion,/ Sans teeth, sans eyes, sans taste, sans every thing" (2.7.165–6). Hardly an improvement over a first infancy of "Mewling and puking in the nurse's arms" (2.7.144), the final stage evokes an image of the very old as utterly dependent, even grotesque beings.

While scholars have noted that the "seven ages" schema was commonplace, none has discussed the relative originality of Shakespeare's imposition of the proverbial idea that "old men are twice children."[2] It seems to have been central to Shakespeare's thinking about extreme old age, however. In *The Rape of Lucrece*, for example, Lucrece laments that "Time's glory is …/ To make the child a man, the man a child" (939–54). Hamlet and Rosencrantz joke that Polonius "is not yet out of his swaddling-clouts": "they say an old man is twice a child" (2.2.383, 385). The notion is central in *King Lear*, as we shall see, and it figures in other plays as well.[3] It is most pervasive when metaphorical and literal parent-child relationships directly influence either the plot or the various psychological and moral crises experienced by the protagonists.

What concerns me is not merely the question of what it means to be childish in Shakespeare's view but, rather, what we might learn about Renaissance ideals of parenting from his plays about very old "children." An important characteristic

---

[1]   All quotations of Shakespeare are from *The Riverside Shakespeare*, 2nd ed., G. Blakemore Evans, ed. (Boston: Houghton Mifflin, 1997).

[2]   Aristophanes's declaration that "old men are boys twice over" (*The Clouds*) is probably the seed of this tradition. Morris Palmer Tilley records the maxim in *A Dictionary of the Proverbs in England in the Sixteenth and Seventeenth Centuries* (Ann Arbor: University of Michigan Press, 1950), 438.

[3]   See, for example, *The Winter's Tale*, 4.4.407–12; *2 Henry IV*, 1.2.173–92; *Henry V*, 2.3.10–12.

shared by most of these characters is that they fail spectacularly as fathers. Shakespeare's old children, this fact reveals, are always men. The typically "absent mothers" of Shakespearean drama may explain the focus on fathers instead of old women or mothers. Hanna Scolnicov, in "Ages of Man, Ages of Woman," shows that discussions of the "ages of woman" did occur in the period.[4] Interestingly, though, second childishness is not discussed in relation to old women, either in the examples Scolnicov surveys or in the Shakespearean examples discussed in these pages. Such a fact suggests the possibility that second childishness was regarded as a specifically masculine experience.[5]

Shakespeare's old men who become babes are themselves notably unsuccessful nurturers, and their descent into childishness is marked by an increased dependence on their own embittered or alienated children. By suggesting that childishness and maturity are as much states of mind or modes of behavior as biological phases of the life cycle, Shakespeare frees his characters to exchange positions as parents and children; what we see repeatedly is a paradoxical dynamic by which "second children" are nurtured to maturity by their more "parental" children.

* * *

In recent years critics of medieval and Renaissance England have sought to correct numerous myths about premodern parenting. Philippe Ariès famously argued in 1960 that "in medieval society the idea of childhood did not exist,"[6] and the English social historian Lawrence Stone went further, arguing that early modern parents lacked even a basic sense of love for their children: "One reason for this was the very high infant and child mortality rates, which made it folly to invest too much emotional capital in such ephemeral beings. As a result, in the sixteenth and early seventeenth century very many fathers seem to have looked on their infant children with much the same degree of affection which men today bestow on domestic pets."[7] The rise in the eighteenth century of what Stone calls "affective individualism" would lead to improved parent-child relations and more enlightened child-rearing practices.[8]

---

[4]   Scolnicov, "Ages of Man, Ages of Woman," *Cahiers Elisabethains* 57 (2000): 61–78.

[5]   We are left to speculate why this should be the case. Perhaps the English language convention of the universal masculine pronoun misleads us in cases where authors did envision a woman's second childhood. Or perhaps period assumptions about adult women's proclivity for nurturing roles swayed the predominantly male writers from considering the "unnatural" alternatives.

[6]   Ariès, *Centuries of Childhood: A Social History of Family Life*, trans. Robert Baldick (New York: Vintage, 1965), 128.

[7]   Stone, *The Family, Sex, and Marriage in England: 1500–1800* (New York: Harper, 1979), 82.

[8]   Stone, 22.

I will not rehearse in this short chapter the objections so many historians have voiced; few if any serious contemporary scholars of premodern Europe share the views of Ariès or Stone. For medieval and Renaissance England alone, excellent work by Nicholas Orme, Keith Wrightson, and especially Linda A. Pollock has cast light on the problematic materials and methodologies of Ariès and Stone.[9] In short, it is clear that medieval and Renaissance children were loved by their parents and recognized as different, physically and emotionally, from the adults who raised them. As J.A. Sharpe remarks, "The overwhelming impression ... is that parents of all social strata were concerned with the welfare of their children, loved them and ... did their best for them."[10]

In fact, contemporary parenting manuals proposed ideals similar to those propounded in the twenty-first century. They reveal that children were perceived as blessings to their parents and as beings with their own unique characteristics and needs. John Dod and Robert Cleaver remarked in 1598, for example, that parents must always "consider how noble a thing a childe is, whom God himselfe hath shaped and formed in his mothers wombe,"[11] and Daniel Burgess encouraged them to pay careful attention to each child's individual needs: "Be as kind as you can with good Conscience. Never provoke 'em, or by unnecessary hard looks, words, or acts, discourage them ... . Observe carefully each Childs peculiar temper."[12]

Such statements were not exceptional. Most Renaissance parenting manuals asserted that the first duty of parents is to love and nurture their children. Edward Wolley stressed there was nothing "formal" about the type of love parents should bestow: "Tender *love* and dear affection towards the children is a *blessing* of the Parents."[13] Parents who failed to show affection for their children typically were regarded as "unnatural" or "beastly." William Gouge, for instance, stated that "The *Fountaine* of parents duties is *Love* ... . Herein appeareth the wise providence of God, who by nature hath so fast fixed love in the hearts of parents, as if there be any in whom it aboundeth not, he is counted unnaturall."[14] An anonymous author similarly declared that "naturally, the affections of children are ... inclinable to love their parents, as well as Parents toward their children. In so much as we account them unnaturall and cruel, which be otherwise minded."[15]

---

[9]   See Orme, *Medieval Children* (New Haven and London: Yale University Press, 2001); Wrightson, *English Society 1580–1680* (New Brunswick, NJ: Rutgers University Press, 1982); and Pollock, *Forgotten Children: Parent-child Relations from 1500–1900* (Cambridge: Cambridge University Press, 1983).

[10]   Sharpe, *Early Modern England: A Social History 1550–1760* (New York: Oxford University, Press, 1997), 74.

[11]   Dod and Cleaver, *A Godly Form of Householde Governement* (London, 1598), 247.

[12]   Burgess, *Advice to Parents and Children* (London, 1690), 21, 37.

[13]   Wolley, *ΕΙΛΟΓΙΑ: The Parentes Blessing their Children: and The Children Begging their Parents Blessings* (London, 1661), 8–9.

[14]   Gouge, *Of Domesticall Duties: Eight Treatises* (London, 1622), 498, 499.

[15]   Anon., *The Office of Christian Parents* (Cambridge, 1616), 224.

Conversely, a "true" father will "love his child with all his heart, and be ready to bestow his life for them."[16]

According to the authors, the two most serious crimes committed by parents were "cockering" (being overly tender or excessively indulgent), which is telling, and being overly harsh. Condemnations of the latter reveal again just how liberal parenting ideals were in the period. In 1535, Thomas Eliot argued, "I wyll not that the parentes shuld be to sharpe or harde to theyr childrē, but some tyme to remytte and forgyve their offences passed," and later manuals appropriated the sentiment.[17] The *Christian Mans Closet* (1581) was most explicit:

> We must not deale with youth by threatnings & stripes ... . [N]ot manie and strict lawes or rules, but good instruction, and honest discipline doe correct the faultes of youth ... . But nowe a days we see and knowe among Fathers of Families, not a fewe which too filthily and shamefully doe abuse their power and authoritie: and are in correcting their children, so ireful, fierce, and cruel, that they seeme to use a tyrannical power, rather than that a man would think they have anye naturall and fatherly affection towardes them.[18]

He goes on to say that physical abuse is the resort of fools. Stefano Guazzo's *Court of Good Counsell* (1607) likewise implored cruel parents to leave their "butchery beating" and "consider rather that for lacke of yeares, their children cannot have perfect understanding and experience in thinges, whereby they are to be borne withal when they doe amisse."[19]

As even these few samples demonstrate, Renaissance minds hardly conceived of children as pets. Instead, "love" and "affection" were consistently praised as the proper foundation of parent-child relationships, and those parents who failed to demonstrate either adequately revealed their inhumanity. In what follows, I hope to demonstrate Shakespeare's significant interest in and idealization of the subject of parenting and what it further reveals about contemporary views of children and parents. Perhaps because of the technical difficulties of staging infancy or (first) childhood, his most poignant engagements of the subject occur where he employs centrally the *senex bis puer* metaphor. Jaques's "seven ages" speech is, of course, the most famous and perhaps the most useful example, and it deserves deeper analysis.

In the nineteenth and twentieth centuries, a major objective of Shakespeare critics was to locate the source for Jaques's speech. The candidates have included Lucretius, Pedro Mexia, Censorinus, Thomas Lodge, and Sir Walter Raleigh,

---

[16]   William Lowth, trans. *The Christian Mans Closet wherein is Conteined a Large Discourse of the Godly Training up of Childen*, by Bartholomew Barry (London, 1581), d3ᵛ.

[17]   Eliot, trans. *The Education or Bringinge up of Children Translated oute of Plutarche* (London, 1535), f3ᵛ.

[18]   Lowth, *Christian Mans Closet*, b3ʳ, f3ʳ.

[19]   Guazzo, *The Court of Good Counsel* (London 1607), g3ᵛ.

among others.[20] While source studies have been useful, teaching us much about the rich traditions of theory on the human lifecycle that inspired Shakespeare, they also have obscured the fact that Shakespeare was as much an innovator as a borrower of ideas.

Jaques's speech is marked by four departures from standard writings on the seven ages. First, it is contextualized within the *theatrum mundi* metaphor with which it begins: "All the world's a stage." Second, Jaques oscillates between describing stages of life and roles that men play (infancy and adolescence versus schoolboy and lover). Third, he excludes the age of the sun altogether, which, Alan Taylor Bradford argues, explains Jaques's Saturnine or cynical view of life.[21] Finally, he imposes on the final age of life the proverbial *senex bis puer* theme that is the focus of this essay; despite the commonness of the seven-ages schema, the metaphor was employed in it by only one writer before Shakespeare: Pedro Mexia.[22]

As several commentators have noted, premodern writers discussed different models for organizing the stages of life, ranging from three-, four-, seven-, and ten-age schemes.[23] The seven-age model is better known to us today because we happen to have been born after Shakespeare. According to the standard version, men lucky enough to live a full life must play the parts of the *infans* (infant), *puer* (boy), *adolescens* (adolescent), *juvenis* (young man), *senior* (elder), *senex* (old man), and *decrepitus* (infirm old man). Later writers correlate each of these roles with one of the seven planets and their related humoral dispositions, so that infancy is allotted to the moon's "milde and moist dominion," boyhood to Mercury, which inclines us "to *sportfulnesse*," and so on.[24] Jaques not only excludes *juvenis* but also exchanges several ages with professions or types: the lover, the soldier, and the justice. Jaques's inexact terminology raises questions regarding Shakespeare's view of the relationship of old age and "childishness." By using the term, child,

---

[20] See the comprehensive survey of criticism in Richard Knowles, ed. *A New Variorum Edition of Shakespeare*: As You Like It (New York: MLA, 1977), 131–2; and Rodney Stenning Edgecombe, "Lucretius and the Seven Ages of Man," *The Shakespeare Newsletter* 48 (1998): 47.

[21] Bradford, "Jaques' Distortion of the Seven Ages Paradigm," *Shakespeare Quarterly* 27 (1976): 171–6.

[22] Though Don Cameron Allen noted the link between Mexia and Shakespeare, he tried to argue that Shakespeare saw the manuscript of Milles's translation of Mexia, which wasn't published until 1613 ("Jacques 'Seven Ages' and Pedro Mexia," *MLN* 56 [1941]: 601–3). I have a simpler solution, which is that Shakespeare read Thomas Fortescue's 1571 translation of Mexia's *The Foreste*. In Fortescue, Shakespeare would have discovered that "if any emonge us passe nowe this last Age … the same then returneth to the state, in manner of Infancie" (Mexia, *The Foreste* [London, 1571], 46ʳ). For this reason, I believe Fortescue is *the* primary source.

[23] See J.A. Burrow, *The Ages of Man: A Study of Medieval Writing and Thought* (Oxford: Clarendon Press, 1986); and Samuel C. Chew, "This Strange Eventful History," *John Quincy Adams Memorial Studies* (1948): 162–7.

[24] From Sir Walter Raleigh, *The History of the World* (London, 1614), 31.

in describing *decrepitus*, Jaques actually compares an old man to a boy, not an infant, though the description clearly is meant to evoke the beginnings of life and, eventually, the idea of a return to dust. The collapse of the first and second ages (infancy and boyhood)—compounded by the fact that the old man turns "again toward childish treble" (i.e., adolescence)—suggests that Jaques's "man" falls down the same rungs he has used to climb up.

By introducing the *senex bis puer* concept in the context of *theatrum mundi*, Jaques transforms ages such as adolescence from archetypal phases into behavioral roles that can be performed—voluntarily or involuntarily—throughout one's lifetime. According to such a conception of age, children would be able to play adults just as old men can play babies. We see the combination of the *senex bis puer* and *theatrum mundi* themes several times in Shakespeare and not infrequently in the context of problematic father-child relationships. The most memorable example is *Henry IV*, where the child-father Falstaff reverses roles with Hal (2.4.433–4). The resulting performance frees both characters to become what they long to be: the immature old man, "inclining to threescore" years old (2.4.425), is permitted for a short while to be the rebellious child he has helped to rear and the rebellious childlike spirit whom those around him seek to reform. Later in his interactions with the old Chief Justice, Falstaff acknowledges this longing:

Fal.	You that are old consider not the capacities of us that are young …
Ch. Just.	Do you set down your name in the scroll of youth, that are written down old with all the characters of age? / … / Is not your voice broken, your wind short, your chin double, your wit single, and every part of you blasted with antiquity?
Fal.	My lord, I was born about three of the clock in the afternoon, with a white head and something a round belly. For my voice, I have lost it with hallowing and singing of anthems. To approve my youth further, I will not. (*2 Henry IV* 1.2.173–92)

Falstaff insists that age has nothing to do with one's natural behavioral impulses and that its irrepressible outward features can be easily manipulated. Hal, the immature son, also grows through role-playing. Playing his real father means assuming a sober perspective long enough to confirm that Falstaff is a "misleader of youth" who must be banished (2.4.462–3). The play-acting scene is temporarily liberating for both characters, but *Henry IV* also highlights the impossibility of sustaining certain age-related fantasies in societies that rigidly define age-related roles. One must always keep growing up, Hal knows too well, but growing young again can only be regarded as regressive. When the newly crowned Henry finally rejects his old friend, he seemingly notices the inappropriateness of Falstaff's "age" as if for the first time: "How ill white hairs becomes a fool and jester!" (*2 Henry IV* 5.5.48).

Shakespeare repeatedly highlights the degree to which the ages of the lifecycle are linked to behavioral roles, as opposed to arbitrarily appointed numbers of years or physical characteristics. In other words, he suggests that age is largely a behavioral mode, which is liberating insofar as characters are free to deny or escape their age to become who they most desire to be; one's refusal to play the part assigned to him usually causes confusion and disorder, however. The Shakespearean drama of senescence, we might say, is the drama of learning how to *"act* one's age" even against one's own natural impulses.

Free from the cynicism that informs and limits Jaques's intelligence, Falstaff shares the melancholy lord's belief that the ages of man are roles people play on life's great stage, though he uses this wisdom to be happy. Having been branded "old" by his former son, though, Falstaff dies as helpless as an ill newborn: "'A made a finer end, and went away and it had been any christom child" (*Henry V* 2.3.10–12). Here the image of the newly christened baby—far from the mewling puker of Jaques's vision—evokes a sense of peacefulness; the Hostess employs the metaphor in arguing that Falstaff cannot possibly be going to hell: "he's in Arthur's [sic] bosom," she insists, personifying heaven (i.e., Abraham's bosom) as a comforting parent, opposite the indifferent nurse of Jaques's narrative. Like Jaques, she figures the old man's end as a sort of second childhood, but for her there is more after death than dust.

Jaques's words should not be mistaken as Shakespeare's words, of course. Despite their eloquence, they fail even to characterize accurately the world of the play in which they are uttered. Famously, Jaques's speech is punctuated by the entrance of "Orlando with Adam." Although Adam resembles Jaques's *decrepitus* in his physical features (he is fourscore years old [2.3.74]), needing to be carried in on the back of Orlando, he is hardly the image of the drooling, senseless child. Adam, named after the father of humankind, maintains and defines the role of the nurturing father even as he becomes dependent on his adoptive child, Orlando. His entrance at the moment Jaques stops talking undermines the great speech even as it confirms some of its more objective claims. In essence, the entrance of Orlando with Adam establishes an alternative vision of the ages of man, one in which dedicated children, having absorbed the lessons of their loving parents, volunteer to take care of them in their old age.

Nonetheless, to the degree that Adam represents an ideal father figure, and to the degree that Orlando successfully takes over this role as Adam declines, the pair stand in stark contrast to the numerous failed father figures of *As You Like It*. Their relationship, reciprocally parental, indicts the beastly parenting of Oliver and Frederick. When Orlando is banished from his home, destitute, Adam expresses his willingness to exchange one sort of comfort in old age for another:

> I have five hundred crowns.
> [...]
> Which I did store to be my foster-nurse,
> When service should in my old limbs lie lame,

And unregarded age in corners thrown.
Take that, and …
[…]
Be comfort to my age! (2.3.38–45)

Adam emerges as the model for a new society, defiantly opposing Jaques's vision of old age even as his body begins to fail him. Unlike others who "sweat" only for "promotion" (2.3.60), Adam is selfless, and his charity teaches Orlando that if happiness ever is a possibility in such a corrupt world, it is only to be found in love: "[W]e'll go along together,/ And ere we have thy youthful wages spent,/ We'll light upon some settled low content" (2.3.66–8). After receiving Adam's gift, Orlando assumes the roles of the loyal son and foster-nurse. Arden awaits these ideal fathers and sons.

Shakespeare's most systematic employment of the "second childishness" metaphor occurs in *King Lear*, whose subject is the burden and blessing of familial love. The opening scene calls immediately into question the parenting of Lear and Gloucester. The first lines—"I thought the King had more affected the Duke of Albany than Cornwall" (1.1.1–2)—about which future son-in-law Lear likes more, establishes the theme of paternal favoritism extended moments later when Gloucester compares his legitimate and illegitimate sons. In his exchange with Kent, Gloucester's feelings about Edmund are difficult to discern. Although he humiliates his son by exposing his bastardy in front of a noble stranger, he claims to love Edmund as much as he does Edgar:

> But I have a son, sir, by order of law, some year elder than this, who yet is no dearer in my account. Though this knave came something saucily to the world before he was sent for, yet was his mother fair, there was good sport at his making, and the whoreson must be acknowledg'd. (1.1.19–24)

How is one to understand the idea that Edmund is loved as much as Edgar because his mother was fair and sex with her was good? How does one reconcile the affection pervasive in "no dearer in my account" and the reluctance in "the whoreson must be acknowledg'd"? In any case, Gloucester violates certain rules of parenting by drawing lines between his children, failing to heed warnings common enough in the period, as exemplified by Guazzo's assertion that "those fathers are greatly to be blamed who … will use one child as ligetimate, the other unlawfull: whereof it followeth, that he which is so meanely accounted of, doth not onely fayle in affection to his kindred, but beginneth to fall to secret warre, with his owne brothers."[25] The passage reads like a psychoanalysis of Edmund the bastard.

In the Lear plot, similar problems result from paternal favoritism. France claims that Cordelia was Lear's favorite (1.1.216)—which is known by Lear's older daughters: "He always lov'd our sister most" (1.1.200). Indeed, Lear concedes the

---

25   Guazzo, *Court of Good Counsell*, g3ᴿ–g4ᵛ.

point after disclaiming paternal care of Cordelia (1.1.123). Surely Cordelia is a child loved appropriately, but how are we to understand Lear's relationships with Goneril and Regan? The older daughters' responses to Lear reveal a formality, a rhetoric of filial obligation, so cold as to preclude even the slightest hints of affection. Yet, this is what Lear seeks from his daughters, a rhetoric of affection that his daughters clearly have learned from him. More questions are raised by Cordelia's stunning refusal to heave her heart into her mouth. Is it enough to love a father "According to my bond, no more nor less" (1.1.93)?

The strangeness of the opening scene raises questions that won't be easily resolved. What is clear, though, is that despite the seeming futility of moral growth in so apocalyptic a world, there is growth, and it hinges on the betterment of relations between parents and their children. The importance of such growth is difficult to overstate, especially in light of Gloucester's contention that the chaotic events of the play are symbolized by the image of children divided from their fathers (1.2.106–12). In their parallel marches to Dover, Lear and Gloucester gradually learn the value of their parental bonds, but only after involuntarily assuming positions of childlike dependency.

As soon as they inherit the kingdom, Goneril and Regan assume the role of the inconvenienced guardians, citing "the infirmity of his age" (1.1.288), ("fourscore and upward" [4.7.60]), as the reason for Lear's erratic behavior. Two scenes later, Goneril introduces the theme that dominates the remainder of the play:

> Idle old man,
> That still would manage those authorities
> That he hath given away! Now by my life
> Old fools are babes again, and must be us'd
> With checks as flatteries, when they are seen abus'd. (1.3.16–19)

The metaphor of second infancy redefines the roles of parents and children in the play, suggesting in this particular case that Lear must be disciplined by Goneril so that his abuses can be curbed. But Goneril's anger also speaks to what she perceives as the literal backwardness of Lear's crawl toward death. Rather than acting his age ("As you are old and reverend, should be wise" [1.4.240]), Lear keeps about him disorderly men who treat the court like a tavern. Goneril and Regan implore him to dismiss them and keep only those that better "besort your age" (1.4.251). In doing so, they impart advice quite standard in conduct manuals for old men.[26] As in *Henry IV*, one should never attempt to be young again.

The Fool relentlessly critiques Lear's decision to reverse roles with his children. Like Goneril, he uses the second childishness metaphor: "thou mad'st / thy daughters thy mothers, for when thou gav'st them / the rod, [thou] ... put'st down thine own breeches" (1.4.171–4). Shakespeare draws here on contemporary wisdom that fathers should never give away their possessions or authority while

---

[26] Most important is Cicero's "On Old Age" in *On Old Age and Friendship*, trans. Frank O. Copley (Ann Arbor: University of Michigan Press, 1967), 40–41.

still alive. Gouge condemned their "folly who put themselves in their childrens power, and let goe all their authority over them,"[27] and Guazzo commanded fathers to "Give no authoritie over thee ... and give not away thy living to another, while thou art alive ... ."[28] The Fool also chastises Lear for failing to act wisely, as old men should: "Thou shouldst not have been old till thou hadst been wise" (1.5.45). Despite Lear's initial denials that he is old, he gradually assumes the role of the *decrepitus*. Shut out in the storm, he finally acknowledges his age, shouting to the winds, "Here I stand your slave,/ A poor, infirm, weak, and despis'd old man" (3.2.19–20), calling attention to his white head for the third time in two scenes.

Gloucester is the other old man of the play, and he too becomes dependent on a loving child. When the two fathers finally meet near the end of Act 4, Lear compares Gloucester's weeping to a baby's crying, conceding that the wheel has, indeed, come full circle:

> Thou must be patient; we came crying hither.
> Thou know'st, the first time that we smell the air
> We wawl and cry ... .
> [...]
> When we are born, we cry that we are come
> To this great stage of fools. (4.6.178–83)

Lear is oddly stoic about the fact that he and Gloucester have entered their second infancy, perhaps because it means they soon will be at rest. Though Lear appropriates the *theatrum mundi* metaphor, "actors" are not free to alter their age-related roles in *King Lear*. The primal suffering of Lear and Gloucester will be relieved only temporarily by the nurturing of their parent-children, Cordelia and Edgar.

The key to these relationships may be Edgar's speech ending with the famously cryptic line, "He childed as I fathered" (3.6.110):

> When we our betters see bearing our woes,
> We scarcely think our miseries our foes.
> Who alone suffers, suffers most i' th' mind,
> Leaving free things and happy shows behind,
> But then the mind much sufferance doth o'erskip,
> When grief hath mates, and bearing fellowship.
> How light and portable my pain seems now
> When that which makes me bend makes the King bow. (3.6.102–9)

Traditionally the line is understood to mean that just as Lear's ungrateful daughters have caused Lear to suffer, so has Edgar's ungrateful father done the same to him. Harold Bloom claims it is perhaps the center of the play:

---

[27] Gouge, *Of Domesticall Duties*, 548.

[28] Guazzo, *Court of Good Counsell*, h1ᵛ.

"He childed as I fathered" has in it no reference whatsoever to Goneril and Regan, but only to the parallel between Lear-Cordelia and Edgar-Gloucester. There is love, and only love, among those four.[29]

I would suggest that the line not be taken out of its immediate context. Although Bloom is partly right, its meaning is simpler. Edgar begins the syllogism by referring to the oddness of witnessing the suffering of so great a man as Lear, which stems from the reversal of roles more proper to their respective positions; that is, as the inferior, Edgar should suffer more than Lear. The subsequent line "He childed as I fathered" is followed by an exclamation point and precedes "Tom, away!", which suggests that it represents a conclusion. As such, it should be understood to comment on the impropriety of their role reversal—"*He* reduced to a child and *I* placed in the position of a father. How unnatural!"—not necessarily as a commentary on the entire play. The line expands the metaphor of the second-child into the metaphor of the child-parent. Unlike Lear and Gloucester, though, Edgar assumes the role of father knowing that "fellowship"—that is love and care—is the antidote to human suffering. And since the line foreshadows Edgar's care of his own father, it might also be said to foreshadow Cordelia's care of Lear. Bloom is correct that from this moment forward there is only love among these four.

In the play's final moments, the bottomless love of Cordelia and Edgar serves to correct the flawed parenting of Lear and Gloucester. In the first scene of the play, devastated by Cordelia's refusal to play the formal game of filial duty, Lear disowns her, disclaiming "all paternal care,/ Propinquity and property of blood" (1.1.113–14). This, despite the fact that as Kent says, Lear has no cause. After he awakens from his nightmare-sleep, he expects that Cordelia will kill him. Despite his gradual recognition that some things do indeed come from nothing—his recognition of the importance of charity, that is—he still is incapable of understanding a world in which humans might actually be charitable to one another. "You have some cause" to poison me, he says (4.7.72). When his daughter repeats the words "No cause" (4.7.73), she betrays a love so unconditional as to seem maternal, and the position of the caring, forgiving woman by the bedside of the ill man sustains the role-reversal at work since the first act.

Cordelia's unconditional love is paralleled by the miracle Edgar grants his father at Dover. Like Lear, Gloucester had disowned his own flesh and blood ("I never got him" [2.1.79]) after having been misled. Also like Lear, he comes to the awful realization that he had no cause to do so (3.7.91). But Edgar, like Cordelia, denies that he has cause for revenge and dedicates himself to reviving his father by granting him the gift of hope: "Thy life's a miracle/ ... Bear free and patient thoughts" (4.6.55, 80).

In their heroic displays of unconditional love, Cordelia and Edgar by no means embody a new model of "parenting." In depicting these ideal children,

---

[29]   Bloom, *Shakespeare and the Invention of the Human* (New York: Riverhead Books, 1998), 485.

Shakespeare adheres rather closely to the advice given in contemporary books on parenting. The majority of such books also featured comprehensive advice about how children should behave toward their parents, the dominant theme of which was "requital" or "recompense"—that is, the idea that children should seek to repay the sacrifices made by their parents, especially in their waning years. William Averell in 1584, for instance, requested that "all children … honour theyr parents, and … cherish them in theyr latter yeeres":

> The wise man saith, My Sonne, make much of thy Father in his age … . As the Storkes that succour theyr parents in theyr aged time, … administering to theyr noriture and necessitie.[30]

The wise man to whom Averell refers is most likely Batholemew Barry, who advised,

> My sonne make much of thy father in his age, & greeve him not as long as hee liveth. And if his under standing faile, have patience with him, and despise him not in thy strength, for the good deed that thou shewest unto thy father, shall not be forgotten.[31]

Robert Cleaver and John Dod argued that one of the five duties of children is "that they doo relieve, maintaine, and nourish their parents, in case they shall fall into povertie or decay," repeating the soon-to-be proverbial idea that "children should "imitate & expresse towards them the nature of the Storke,"[32] which calls to mind the different nature of those "pelican daughters," Goneril and Regan (3.4.75). Gouge described the "inward" and "outward" infirmities of aged parents and says that the "dutie of children is both to *beare with them*, and also to *cover them*."[33] And in a passage even more relevant to *Lear*, Wolley argued that "if the Parent be blind, the Son … is to be the Fathers *Eye*."[34]

In both plots, then, loving children surpass their parents as parents, reinforcing those lessons that their second-children have learned about empathy and distribution by confirming that love is the only solace in a world of limitless suffering. Lear absorbs the lesson, responding to Cordelia's desire for revenge against her sisters by reminding her what she has taught him: "No, no, no, no! Come, let's away to prison:/ We two alone will sing like birds i' th' cage" (5.2.8–9). Lear's beautiful vision of parental love transforms the prison into a paradise, suggesting that love is enough and allowing him to re-assume—however briefly—his paternal authority and dignity. Of course, love will not be enough to protect children in

---

[30] Averell, *A Dyall for Dainty Darlings Rockt in the Cradle of Securitie* (London, 1584), d3ᵛ, d4ᵛ.

[31] Lowth, *Christian Mans Closet*, q1ʳ.

[32] Dod and Cleaver, *A Godly Forme*, 360.

[33] Gouge, *Of Domesticall Duties*, 470.

[34] Wolley, *The Parentes Blessing*, 14.

King Lear, and the final haunting image of Lear holding his dead daughter, pietà-like (paternal love idealized as maternal), dominates our impression of the play. The pain Shakespeare forces us to experience, however, may also be his greatest contribution to the literature of parenting.

There is nothing particularly ambiguous about Shakespeare's vision of ideal parent-child relationships. Throughout the plays, especially where he employs the second-childishness metaphor, different models of parenting are systematically juxtaposed. In nearly all of them, relationships characterized by affection, mutual respect, and love are celebrated, and those characterized by coldness, formality, or disloyalty are condemned. This is not to say that we witness in Shakespeare the invention of the human parent. Rather, Shakespeare's explorations of ideal parenting lend greater eloquence to ideas and ideals pervasive in early modern thought.

Select Bibliography

Primary Sources

Anon., *The Office of Christian Parents*. Cambridge, 1616.

Averell, William. *A Dyall for Dainty Darlings Rockt in the Cradle of Securitie*. London, 1584.

B., Ste. *Counsel to the husband: To the wife instruction*. London: Felix Kyngston for Richard Boyle, 1608.

Barbaro, Francesco. *On Wifely Duties*. Ed. and trans. Benjamin G. Kohl and Ronald G. Witt, with Elizabeth B. Welles. In *The Earthly Republic: Italian Humanists on Government and Society*. Philadelphia: University of Pennsylvania Press, 1978.

Burgess, Daniell. *Advice to Parents and Children*. London, 1690.

Dod, John, and Robert Cleaver. *A codly [sic] form of householde governement: for the ordering of private families according to the direction of Gods word*. London: Thomas Creede for Thomas Man, 1598.

Du Plessis Mornay, Philipe. *Advis sur l'institution d'un enfant que l'on veult nourrir aulx lettres, envoyé à madame la princesse d'Orange, à son instance sur le sujet de son fils. Mémoires et correspondance*, tome V. Genève: Slatkine, 1969, réimpr. de l'édition de Paris, 1824–1825, 65–71.

Duval, Jacques. *Des hermaphrodits Accouchemens des Femmes, et Traitement qui est requis pour les relever en santé, & bien élever leurs enfans*. Rouen: David Gevffroy, 1612.

Eliot, Thomas, trans. *The Education or Bringinge up of Children Translated oute of Plutarche*. London, 1535.

Erasmus, Desiderius, "A Declamation on the Subject of Early Liberal Education for Children" (*De pueris statim ac liberaliter instituendis declamatio*). In J.K. Sowards, ed., *Collected Works of Erasmus: Literary and Educational Writings*, vol. 4, trans. Beert C. Verstraete. Toronto: University of Toronto Press, 1985.

———. "On Good Manners for Boys" (*De civilitate morum puerilium*). In J.K. Sowards, ed., *Collected Works of Erasmus: Literary and Educational Writings*, vol. 3, trans. Brian McGregor. Toronto: University of Toronto Press, 1985.

Gataker, Thomas. *Marriage duties briefly couched together* (sic). London: William Jones, 1624.

———. *A Marriage Praier, or Succinct Meditations: Delivered in a Sermon on the Praier of Eleazer the Servant of Abraham*. London: John Haviland, 1624.

Gouge, William. *Of Domesticall Duties: Eight Treatises*. London, 1622.

Guillemeau, Jacques. *The Nursing of Children. Wherein is Set downe, the ordering and goverment of them, from their birth. Together: with the means to helpe and free them, from all such diseases as may happen unto them. Written in French by James Guillimeau the French Kings Chirurgion in Ordinary*. London: A. Hatfield, 1612.

Lowth, William, trans. *The Christian Mans Closet wherein is Conteined a Large Discourse of the Godly Training up of Childen*, by Bartholomew Barry. London, 1581.

Montaigne, Michel de. "Of a Monstrous Child." *Michel de Montaigne's essays*. Ed. Harold Bloom. New York: Chelsea House, 1987.

Mulcaster, Richard. *Positions wherin those primitive circumstances be examined, which are necessarie for the training up of children, either for skill in their booke, or health in their bodie*. London: 1581.

Paré, Ambroise. *The Workes of that famous Chirurgion Ambrose Parey Translated out of Latine and compared with the French by Th. Johnson*. London: Th. Cotes and R. Young, 1634.

Pritchard, Thomas. *The school of honest and vertuous lyfe: Profitable and necessary for all estates and degrees, to be trayned in: but (cheefly) for the pettie schollers, the yonger sorte, of both kindes, bee they men or women*. London: 1579.

Ward, William. *The Most Excellent Profitable, and pleasaunt Booke of the famous Doctor and expert Astrologian Arcandam, or Aleandrin, to finde the Fatall destiny, constellation, complexion & naturall inclination of every man and childe, by his birth Wyth an addition of Phisiognomy, very pleasa[n]t to read. Now newly tourned out of french into our vulgar tongue, by William Warde*. London: Thomas Marshe, 1578.

Wolley, Edward. *ΕΥΛΟΓΙΑ: The Parentes Blessing their Children: and The Children Begging their Parents Blessings*. London, 1661.

Secondary Sources

Anderson, Ellen. "Playing at Moslem and Christian: The Construction of Gender and the Representation of Faith in Cervantes's Captivity Plays." *Cervantes* 13 (1993): 37–59.

Archer, John Michael, ed. *Enclosure Acts: Sexuality, Property and Culture in Early Modern England*. Ithaca: Cornell University Press, 1994.

Ariès, Philippe. *Centuries of Childhood*. Trans. Robert Baldick. New York: Random House, 1962.

Ariès, Philippe and Jean-Claude Margolin, eds. *Les jeux à la Renaissance*. Paris: Librairie Philosophique, 1982.

Armon, Shifra. *Picking Wedlock: Women and the Courtship Novel in Spain*. Lanham, MD: Rowman and Littlefield, 2002.

Aughterson, Kate, ed. *Renaissance Woman: A Sourcebook*. London: Routledge, 1995.

Avery, Gillian and Julia Briggs, eds. *Children and Their Books: A Celebration of the Work of Iona and Peter Opie*. Oxford: Clarendon Press, 1989.

Avery, Gillian, Julia Briggs, and Kimberly Reynolds, eds. *Representation of Childhood Death*. London: Macmillan, 2000.

Bemporad, Doria Liscia, ed. *Il costume nel 'età del Rinascimento*. Florence: Edifir, 1988.

Ben-Amos, Ilana Krausman. *Adolescence and Youth in Early Modern England*. New Haven: Yale University Press, 1994.

Berriot-Salvadore, Évelyne. *Les femmes dans la société française de la Renaissance*. Genève: Droz, 1990.

Berriot-Salvadore, Évelyne and Isabelle Pébay-Clottes, eds. *Autour de l'enfance*. Biarritz: Atlantica, 1999, 279–94.

Bidon, Alexandre and Didier Lett. *Children in the Middle Ages, 5th–15th Centuries*. Trans. Jody Gladding. Notre Dame, IN: University of Notre Dame, 1999.

Boswell, John. *The Kindness of Strangers: the abandonment of children in Western Europe from late antiquity to the Renaissance*. New York: Pantheon Books, 1988.

Brooke, Xanthe, and Peter Cherry. *Murillo: Scenes of Childhood*. London: Merrell, 2001.

Brown, Pamela Allen and Peter Parolin, eds. *Women Players in England, 1500–1660*. Aldershot: Ashgate, 2005.

Bunge, Marcia J., ed. *The Child in Christian Thought (Religion, Marriage, Family)*. Grand Rapids, Michigan and Cambridge, England: Eerdmann's Publishing, 2001.

Casey, James, Francisco Chacón, Enrique Gacto, Isabel Moll, Primitivo J. Pla, Antoni Simón, Bernard Vincent. *La familia en la españa mediterránea (siglos XV–XIX)*. Barcelona: Editorial Crítica, 1987.

Chedgzoy, Kate, Susanne Greenhalgh, and Robert Shaughnessy, eds. *Shakespeare and Childhood*. Cambridge: Cambridge University Press, 2007.

Comensoli, Viviana and Anne Russell, eds. *Enacting Gender on the Renaissance Stage*. Chicago: University of Illinois Press, 1999.

Cook, Susan C. and Judy S. Tsou. *Cecilia reclaimed: feminist perspectives on gender and music*. Ed. Susan C. Cook and Judy S. Tsou. Champaign: University of Illinois Press, 1994.

Couchman, Jane and Ann Crabb, eds. *Women's Letters across Europe 1400–1700: Form and Persuasion*. Burlington, VT, and Aldershot, UK: Ashgate, 2005.

Crawford, Sally. *Childhood in Anglo-Saxon England*. Gloucestershire: Sutton Publishing Ltd., 1999.

Cressy, David. *Birth, Marriage and Death: Ritual, Religion and the Life-Cycle in Tudor and Stuart England*. Oxford: Oxford University Press, 1997.

DeJulio, Rosemary A. "Women's Ways of Knowing and Learning: The Response of Mary Ward and Madeleine Sophie Barat to the *Ratio Studiorum*." In *The Jesuit Ratio Studiorum: 400th Anniversary Perspectives*. Ed. J. Vincent, S.J. Dumenico. New York: Fordham University Press, 2000, 107–26.

Dolven, Jeff. *Scenes of Instruction in Renaissance Romance*. Chicago: University of Chicago Press, 2007.

Driscoll, Catherine. *Girls: Feminine Adolescence in Popular Culture and Cultural Theory*. New York: Columbia University Press, 2002.

El Saffar, Ruth. *Beyond Fiction: The Recovery of the Feminine in the Novels of Cervantes*. Berkeley: University of California Press, 1984.

Esdaile, Katharine. *English Monumental Sculpture since the Renaissance*. New York and Toronto: MacMillan Co., 1927.

Findlay, Alison and Stephanie Hodgson Wright, eds. *Women and Dramatic Production, 1550–1700*. London: Longman, 2000.

Finucane, R.C. *The Rescue of the Innocents. Endangered Children in Medieval Miracles*. New York: St. Martin's Press, 1997.

Finucci, Valeria. *The Manly Masquerade: Masculinity, Paternity, and Castration in the Italian Renaissance*. Durham, NC: Duke University Press, 2003.

Fisher, Will. *Materializing Gender in Early Modern English Literature and Culture*. Cambridge: Cambridge University Press, 2006.

Fletcher, Anthony and Stephen Hussey. *Childhood in Question: Children, Parents, and the State*. Manchester: Manchester University Press, 1999.

Foisil, Madeleine. "Louis XIII: L'enfance et l'adolescence d'après le Journal de Jean Héroard." *Journal de Jean Héroard*. Ed. Madeleine Foisil. Librarie Arthème Fayard, 1989.

Foster, David William and Roberto Reis. *Bodies and Biases: Sexualities in Hispanic Cultures and Literature*. Minneapolis: University of Minnesota Press, 1996.

Frick, Carole Collier. *Dressing Renaissance Florence. Families, Fortunes and Fine Clothing*. Baltimore: Johns Hopkins University Press, 2002.

Frye, Susan and Karen Robertson, eds. *Maids and Mistresses, Cousins and Queens: Women's Alliances in Early Modern England*. Oxford: Oxford University Press, 1999.

Gavitt, Philip. *Charity and Children in Renaissance Florence*. Ann Arbor: University of Michigan Press, 1990.

Gomme, Alice Bertha. *The Traditional Games of England, Scotland, and Ireland*. 2 vols. London: David Nutt, 1894.

Grancsay, Stephen V. "The Interrelationships of Costume and Armor." *The Metropolitan Museum of Art Bulletin*, new series, vol. 8, no. 6 (Feb., 1950), 184, 186–8.

Grendler, Paul F. *Schooling in Renaissance Italy. Literacy and Learning, 1300–1600*. Baltimore: Johns Hopkins University Press, 1989.

Griffiths, Paul, *Youth and Authority: Formative Experiences in England 1560–1640*. Oxford: Clarendon Press, 1996.

Haas, Louis. *The Renaissance Man and His Children: Childbirth and Early Childhood in Florence, 1300–1600*. New York: St. Martin's Press, 1998.

Hanawalt, Barbara. "Medievalists and the Study of Childhood." *Speculum* 77, no. 2 (2002): 440–60.

———. *The Ties That Bound: Peasant Families in Medieval England*. New York and Oxford: Oxford University Press, 1986.

Herlihy, David. *Medieval Households*. Cambridge: Harvard University Press, 1985.

Higginbotham, Jennifer. *Fair Maids and Golden Girls: Early Modern Girlhood and the Production of Femininity*. PhD Diss., University of Pennsylvania, 2007.

Hillman, David and Carlo Mazzio. *The Body in Parts: Fantasies of Corporeality in Early Modern Europe*. New York and London: Routledge, 1997.

Hufton, Olwen. "Le travail et la famille: La maternité." *XVIe–XVIIIe siècle: Histoire des femmes en occident*. Ed. Natalie Zemon Davis and Arlette Farge. Paris: Plon, 1991, 50–63.

Huizinga, Johan. *Homo Ludens: A Study of the Play-Element in Culture*. Boston: Beacon Press, 1950.

Hull, Susanne W., *Chaste, Silent and Obedient: English Books for Women 1475–1640*. San Marino: Huntington Library, 1982.

———. *Women according to Men: The World of Tudor-Stuart Women*. Walnut Creek, CA: AltaMira Press, 1996.

Hunt, David. *Parents and Children in History: The Psychology of Family Life in Early Modern France*. New York: Basic Books, Inc., 1970.

Hurtig, Judith W. "Death in Childbirth: Seventeenth Century English Tombs and their Place in Contemporary Thought." *Art Bulletin* 65:4 (December 1983): 603–15.

Jiwani, Yasmin, Candis Steenbergen, and Claudia Mitchell. *Girlhood: Redefining the Limits*. Black Rose Books, 2006.

Johnson, Geraldine A. and Sara F. Matthews Grieco, eds. *Picturing Women in Renaissance and Baroque Italy*. Cambridge and New York: Cambridge University Press, 1997.

Jordan, Mark D. *The Invention of Sodomy in Christian Theology*. Chicago, 1997.

———. "Saint Pelagius, Ephebe and Martyr." *Queer Iberia: Sexualities, Cultures, and Crossings from the Middle Ages to the Renaissance*. Ed. Josiah Blackmore and Gregory Hutcheson. Durham and London: Duke University Press, 1999. 23–47.

Kertzer, David I. and Marzio Barbagli. *Family Life in Early Modern Times, 1500–1789*. New Haven: Yale University Press, 2001.

Killerby, Catherine Kovesi. *Sumptuary Law in Italy 1200–1500*. Oxford: Clarendon Press, 2002.

King, Margaret L. "Concepts of Childhood: What We Know and Where We Might Go." *Renaissance Quarterly* 40, no. 2 (2007), 371–407.

———. *The Death of the Child Valerio Marcello*. Chicago: University of Chicago Press, 1994.

Klapisch-Zuber, Christiane. *Women, Family and Ritual in Renaissance Italy*. Trans. Lydia Cochrane. Chicago: University of Chicago Press, 1985.

Koops, William and Michael Zuckerman, eds. *Beyond the Century of the Child: Cultural History and Developmental Psychology*. Philadelphia: University of Pennsylvania Press, 2003.

Kuperty-Tsur, Nadine. "Rhétorique parentale et religieuse: les voies de la transmission des valeurs de la réforme aux enfants." *Les deux réformes chrétiennes: Propagation et diffusion*. Ed. Myriam Yardeni and Illana Zinguer. Leiden: Brill, 2004, 153–71.

Landini, Roberta Orsi. "L'abbigliamento infantile fra Cinque e Seicento," in *Il vestito e la sua immagine*. Ed. Jeanine Guérin dalla Mese. *Atti del convegno in omaggio a Cesare Vecellio nel quarto centenario della morte*. Belluno 20–22 settembre 2001.

Lanham, Sarah Cooper, ed. *The Ties That Bind: Questioning Family Dynamics and Family Discourse in Hispanic Literature*. Maryland: University Press of America, 2004.

Lux-Sterritt, Laurence. *Redefining Female Religious Life: French Ursulines and English Ladies in Seventeenth-Century Catholicism*. Aldershot: Ashgate, 2005.

McManus, Clare, ed. *Women and Culture at the Courts of the Stuart Queens*. New York: Palgrave, 2003.

———. *Women on the Renaissance Stage: Anna of Denmark and Female Masquing in the Stuart Court 1690–1619*. Manchester: Manchester University Press, 2002.

Mehl, Jean-Michel, *Les jeux au royaume de France du XIIIe au début du XVIe siècle*. Paris: Fayard, 1990.

Mendelson, Sara and Patricia Crawford. *Women in Early Modern England, 1550–1720*. Oxford: Clarendon Press, 1998.

Miles, Margaret. "The Virgin's One Bare Breast: Female Nudity and Religious Meaning in Tuscan Early Renaissance Culture." In *The Female Body in Western* Culture. Ed. Susan Suleiman. Cambridge: Harvard University Press, 1985, 193–208.

Miller, Naomi J. and Naomi Yavneh, eds. *Maternal Measures: Figuring caregiving in the early modern period*. Aldershot: Ashgate Press, 2000.

Morant, Isabel, ed. *Historia de las mujeres en España y América Latina*. 2 vols. Madrid: Cátedra, 2005.

Musacchio, Jacqueline Marie. *The Art and ritual of childbirth in Renaissance Italy*. New Haven: Yale University Press, 1999.

Norman, Sister Marion. "A Woman for All Seasons: Mary Ward (1585–1645), Renaissance Pioneer of Women's Education," *Paedagogica Historica* 23 (1983): 125–43.

O'Connor, Mary. "Interpreting Early Modern Woman Abuse: The Case of Anne Dormer," in *Quidditas* 23 (2002), 51–67.

O'Connor, Thomas A. *Love in the "Corral": Conjugal Spirituality and Anti-Theatrical Polemic in Early Modern Spain*. New York: Peter Lang, 2000.

O'Day, Rosemary. *The Family and Family Relationships, 1500–1900: England, France and the United States of America*. New York: St. Martin's Press, 1999.

Ong, Walter. "Latin Language Study as a Renaissance Puberty Rite." *Studies in Philology*, 56, 1959, 103–24.

Opie, Iona and Peter Opie. *Children's Games in Street and Playground*. Oxford: Oxford University Press, 1984.

Orgel, Stephen. *Impersonation: the Performance of Gender in Shakespeare's England*. Cambridge: Cambridge University Press, 1996.

Orlin, Lena Cowen. "Rewriting Stone's Renaissance." *The Huntington Library Quarterly*, vol. 64, no. 12 (2001), 189–230.

Orme, Nicholas. *Medieval Children*. New Haven and London: Yale University Press, 2001.

Ozment, Stephen. *Ancestors: The Loving Family in Old Europe*. Cambridge: Harvard University Press, 2001.

Paster, Gail Kern, Katherine Rowe, and Mary Floyd-Wilson, eds. *Reading the Early Modern Passions: Essays in the Cultural History of Emotion*. Philadelphia: University of Pennsylvania Press, 2004.

Phillippy, Patricia. *Women, Death and Literature in Post-Reformation England*. Cambridge: Cambridge University Press, 2002.

Pollock, Linda. *Forgotten Children: Parent-Child Relations from 1500 to 1900*. Cambridge: Cambridge University Press, 1983.

Pullan, Brian. *Rich and Poor in Renaissance Venice: The Social Institutions of a Catholic State, to 1620*. Cambridge: Harvard University Press, 1971.

Purkiss, Diane. *Literature, Gender and Politics during the English Civil War*. Cambridge: Cambridge University Press, 2005.

———. *The Witch in History*. London: Routledge, 1996.

Rapley, Elizabeth. *The Dévotes: Women and Church in Seventeenth-Century France*. Montreal: McGill-Queen's University Press, 1990.

Redondo, Augustin, ed. *Autour des parentés en Espagne aux XVIᵉ et XVIIᵉ Siècles: Histoire, Mythe et Littérature*. Paris: Sorbonne, 1987.

———. *Figures de l'enfance*. Paris: Sorbonne, 1997.

———. *La formation de l'enfant en Espagne aux XVIᵉ et XVIIᵉ Siècles*. Paris: Sorbonne, 1996.

Riché, Pierre and Danièle Alexandre-Bidon. *L'enfance au Moyen Age*. Paris: Editions du Seuil. Bibliothèque nationale de France, 1994.

Robson, Catherine. *Men in Wonderland: The Lost Girlhood of the Victorian Gentleman*. Princeton: Princeton University Press, 2001.

Roelker, Nancy L. "The appeal of Calvinism to French noblewomen in the sixteenth century." *Journal of Interdisciplinary History*, 1972, 391–407.

Rutter, Carol Chillington. *Shakespeare and Child's Play: Performing Lost Boys on Stage and Screen*. London and New York: Routledge, 2007.

Schleiner, Louise. *Tudor and Stuart Women Writers*. Bloomington: Indiana University Press, 1994.

Shahar, Shulamith. *Childhood in the Middle Ages*. New York: Routledge, 1990.

Silver, Victoria. "The Obscure Script of Regicide: Ambivalence and Little Girls in Marvell's Pastorals." *ELH* 68, no. 1 (Spring 2001): 29–55.

Stallybrass, Peter. "Patriarchal Territories: The Body Enclosed." In *Rewriting the Renaissance*. Ed. Margaret Ferguson et al. Chicago: University of Chicago Press, 1986.

Steinberg, Leo. *The Sexuality of Christ in Renaissance Art and Modern Oblivion*. New York: Pantheon, 1983.

Stone, Lawrence. *The Family, Sex and Marriage in England 1500–1800*. New York: Harper and Row, 1979.

Strother, Darci L. *Family Matters: A Study of On- and Off-Stage Marriage and Family Relations in Seventeenth-Century Spain*. New York: Peter Lang, 1999.

Terpstra, Nicholas. *Abandoned Children of the Italian Renaissance: Orphan Care in Florence and Bologna*. Baltimore: Johns Hopkins University Press, 2005.

Tomlinson, Sophie. *Women on Stage in Stuart Drama*. Cambridge: Cambridge University Press, 2005.

Vollendorf, Lisa. *The Lives of Women: A New History of Inquisitorial Spain*. Nashville, TN: Vanderbilt University Press, 2005.

Wall, Wendy. *Staging Domesticity: Household Work and English Identity in Early Modern Drama*. Cambridge University Press, 2004.

Watt, Jeffrey R. "Calvinism, childhood, and education: the evidence from the Genevan Consistory." *Sixteenth Century Journal* 2002, XXXIII/2, 439–56.

Wilcox, Helen, ed. *Women and Literature in Britain, 1500–1700*. Cambridge: Cambridge University Press, 1996. 9–29.

Wilson, Dudley. *Signs and Portents: Monstrous births from the Middle Ages to the Enlightenment*. London: Routledge, 1993.

Wilson, Jean. "Holy Innocents: Some Aspects of the Iconography of Children on English Renaissance Tombs." *Church Monuments* 5 (1990).

Zerari, María. "L'enfant en question: autour de la nouvelle, de Miguel de Cervantès à Luis de Guevara." In Redondo, ed. *Figures de l'enfance*. 149–66.

Index